Chicken Soup for the Soul®

The Power of Yes!

Chicken Soup for the Soul: The Power of Yes!
101 Stories about Adventure, Change and Positive Thinking
Amy Newmark

Published by Chicken Soup for the Soul, LLC www.chickensoup.com
Copyright ©2018 by Chicken Soup for the Soul, LLC. All Rights Reserved.

The publisher gratefully acknowledges the many publishers and individuals who granted Chicken Soup for the Soul permission to reprint the cited material.

Front cover artwork of word "Yes" courtesy of iStockphoto.com/kchungtw (©kchungtw)
Front cover photo of jumping woman courtesy of iStockphoto.com/wickedpix
(©wickedpix), photo of grassy field courtesy of iStockphoto.com/mycola (©mycola)
Back cover and Interior photo of gallery courtesy of iStockphoto.com/LordRunar)
(©LordRunar) Yes burst artwork courtesy of iStockphoto.com/wissanu99(©wissanu99)
Photo of Amy Newmark courtesy of Susan Morrow at SwickPix

Cover and Interior by Daniel Zaccari

Distributed to the booktrade by Simon & Schuster. SAN: 200-2442

Publisher's Cataloging-In-Publication Data
(Prepared by The Donohue Group, Inc.)

Names: Newmark, Amy, compiler.
Title: Chicken soup for the soul : the power of yes! : 101 stories about
     adventure, change and positive thinking / [compiled by] Amy Newmark.
Other Titles: Power of yes! : 101 stories about adventure, change and
     positive thinking
Description: [Cos Cob, Connecticut] : Chicken Soup for the Soul, LLC,
     [2018]
Identifiers: ISBN 9781611599787 (print) | ISBN 9781611592788 (ebook)
Subjects: LCSH: Risk-taking (Psychology)--Literary collections. | Risk-
     taking (Psychology)--Anecdotes. | Courage--Literary collections. |
     Courage--Anecdotes. | Change (Psychology)--Literary collections. |
     Change (Psychology)--Anecdotes. | LCGFT: Anecdotes.
Classification: LCC BF637.R57 C452 2018 (print) | LCC BF637.R57 (ebook) |
     DDC 158.1--dc23

Library of Congress Control Number 2018935475

PRINTED IN THE UNITED STATES OF AMERICA
on acid∞free paper

25 24 23 22 21 20 19 18   01 02 03 04 05 06 07 08 09 10 11

Chicken Soup for the Soul.

The Power of Yes!

101 Stories about Adventure, Change and Positive Thinking

Amy Newmark

CSS

Chicken Soup for the Soul, LLC
Cos Cob, CT

Changing your life one story at a time ®
www.chickensoup.com

Table of Contents

❸

~Put Yourself Out There~

❹

~Fake It Till You Make It~

❺

~Do It Afraid~

❻

~Believe in Yourself~

❼

~Be Daring~

8

~Find the New You~

9

~Give of Yourself~

10

~Go for Adventure~

⓫

~Let Yourself Trust~

Introduction

Saying yes means you will do something new,
meet someone new and make a difference in your
life, and likely in others' lives as well... Yes is a tiny
word that can do big things. Say it often.
~Eric Schmidt, former executive chairman Google

C hicken Soup for the Soul is celebrating its 25th anniversary this year. That's pretty old for a book series, but the beauty of our model — crowdsourcing our stories from the public — is that it allows us to remain fresh and relevant every year. And what's fresh and relevant right now? Saying "yes" to new things. And stepping outside our comfort zones.

We were inundated with fabulous stories on this topic, so much so that we made two books — *Chicken Soup for the Soul: Step Outside Your Comfort Zone* in fall 2017, and now, *Chicken Soup for the Soul: The Power of Yes!* In this collection, our contributors report on the many ways they challenged themselves to face their fears and try new things. They report how that changed them for the better, and led to *more* new things, and a broader, more meaningful life.

I've been so inspired by these writers, and their powerful stories have motivated me to continue stretching myself — whether it's something as insignificant as trying a new food or something as momentous as paragliding off a 1,000-foot cliff. Every time I try something new, I feel empowered and more in tune with the broad world out there.

Whether you're looking for love, or a new career; overcoming shyness, or a phobia; spicing up your life with a new sport, or reaching out to make new friends; planning to travel alone, or going on that scary roller coaster, you'll find kindred souls in these pages. Just look at these chapter titles, with their positive messages and excellent advice, and you'll get a sense of the journey you are about to undertake:

1. Try New Things
2. Embrace Change
3. Put Yourself Out There
4. Fake It Till You Make It
5. Do It Afraid
6. Believe in Yourself
7. Be Daring
8. Find the New You
9. Give of Yourself
10. Go for Adventure
11. Let Yourself Trust

In chapter 1, about trying new things, you'll meet Victoria Otto Franzese, who was turning fifty and wanted to reclaim the excitement of her youth. So she resolved to do something new every single day, for 365 days. It wasn't always easy, and sometimes she'd be wracking her brain at 11:45 p.m. to find her new thing for the day. But she did it, trying activities as small as doing a sudoku puzzle, and as big as going dog sledding. She even participated in a Guinness world record event, joining a crowd of people jumping on mini trampolines. Victoria says, "At fifty, my life was lush and full of promise. I could continue to grow, stretch my wings, and learn more every day."

Sometimes, we resist change because we're afraid of being better, stronger, more famous, or more *whatever*. In Chapter 2, about embracing change, Sara Etgen-Baker describes the antique "secretary desk" where she did all her writing. It was so small that when she needed to refer to files and books, they had to be scattered on the floor around her. When she and her husband moved into a larger home, he suggested she get a new, larger desk. He thought her little desk was holding her back in her writing career. Sara resisted, until she finally realized that he was right. She had been afraid to go for it — to expand her writing. She ordered the new desk, saying that a "bigger desk symbolized bigger projects, bigger possibilities, more challenging contests, stepping out on faith, and leaving my comfort zone."

Sometimes you have to put yourself out there, and dare to make those human connections, as Kate Lemery tells us in Chapter 3. With three kids under age five, and a new home in a new community, she was a busy stay-at-home mom. But she was lonely. So Kate decided to become a room parent in her oldest child's kindergarten class. She also signed him up for soccer. But she still wasn't making any friends in her new town. Then an old friend suggested she throw a party for all those moms she didn't know. Kate was hesitant, but she sent out the invitations, and now she has hosted several of these "mommy mixers" and finds herself the "glue" that brings the mothers in her community together.

In Chapter 8, we talk about finding the new you, and I loved Doug Sletten's story about doing just that. Doug had a family and a good job as a teacher. He had paid off his student loans and he and his wife had bought their first house. But he'd always wanted to be a lawyer. Finally, he talked to his normally staid, conservative father about his secret dream, and said that he would be well into his thirties by the time he finished law school. His father simply said, "How old would you be in four years if you *didn't* follow your dream?" That was it. Doug's wife agreed and he went on to spend what he called "three of the most grueling years of my life." He says, "I practiced law for twenty-five years, and I was always grateful that my father and my family supported my decision to uproot our lives and try something completely different."

That's what this is all about, trying new things even if we're pretty much terrified. Chapter 5 is all about "doing it afraid" and that's where I put a very relatable story by Linda Holland Rathkopf. Her saga starts as a long line of people is building up behind her on a zip-lining platform. The attendant has just explained that she needs to complete eight more platform-to-platform runs of the zip-lining adventure. That's the only way to return to her starting point. Linda's asking for a "rescue" to be arranged. Finally, she relents, and she discovers that with each subsequent run her anxiety lessens and she is able to keep her eyes open and enjoy the beautiful flora and fauna of the Costa Rican rainforest. She says, "I had stepped out of my comfort zone and into a wonderland." And she admits that she ended her adventure "exhilarated."

I put a wonderful quote from Eric Schmidt at the beginning of this introduction. It makes the point that "yes" is a tiny word, but boy does it carry power. I hope this new collection of stories that we have selected for you will give you some great ideas. You'll probably find yourself making a list of at least ten new things to try before you've even finished reading it! Let me know how you've used the power of yes by e-mailing amy@chickensoupforthesoul.com. And thank you for being one of our readers.

~Amy Newmark

Chapter 1

The Power of Yes!

Try New Things

If you are never scared, embarrassed or hurt,
it means you never take chances.
~Julia Soul

A Year of New Things

Happiness is achieved when you stop waiting
for your life to begin and start making
the most of the moment you are in.
~Germany Kent

T he year I turned fifty, I resolved to do something new every day. When I tell people this, they always want to know what my favorite "new thing" was. They assume that I did something really different and amazing, like moving my family to an exotic place or learning to fly a helicopter. And they are inevitably disappointed when I say that my favorite thing was doing something new. Every. Single. Day. For a year.

Balancing 365 new things with work and family, while still managing to do the laundry and get dinner on the table every night, was not always easy. In the early weeks of the project, I often found myself at 11:45 p.m. wracking my brain for something new that I could actually accomplish in fifteen minutes. Thankfully, it turned out there were lots of things I had never done before that I could complete in a short period of time. I finished my first sudoku puzzle. I signed up for an online class to learn Italian. I smoked a cigar. I curled my eyelashes.

As time went by, I found it was easier to just keep my eyes open to the possibilities that surrounded me. It turns out there were new things everywhere, and all I had to do was make a little effort to enjoy them. And so, on a bitterly cold Saturday when I would normally have stayed home curled up with a book, I bundled up and set off to attend an Ice Festival. I got up crazy early one weekday morning to see a Blood Moon. I celebrated National Dog Day with my pup.

It wasn't long before my friends learned that I was open to almost anything I could consider a new thing, and the invitations began pouring in — not just from friends, but friends of friends. As a result, I went dog sledding, enjoyed stargazing on New York City's High Line, had lunch with Antonia Lofaso, who has appeared on *Top Chef*, attended a Fashion Week fashion show, and met Pulitzer Prize-winning author Gilbert King. I went to numerous lectures on all kinds of topics that I never would have previously considered useful or interesting and found something to appreciate in every single one.

Whenever I learned about something that seemed remarkable,

> *Instead of "Why?"*
> *I began to ask*
> *"Why not?" I*
> *made my default*
> *response "Yes."*

I compelled myself to pursue it. Instead of "Why?" I began to ask "Why not?" I made my default response "Yes." When I learned about a local group trying to get into the *Guinness Book of World Records* by having the most people jumping on mini trampolines at once, I signed up immediately. The designated morning was cold and rainy. None of my friends or family members wanted to join me on my quest, but when I got to the field where the event was being held I found hundreds of like-minded folks. Together, we jumped for more than an hour, exhilarated by the exercise and the joy of accomplishing something slightly weird but totally wonderful.

A fair amount of my new things involved food. I tried wild boar. I ate nettles. I sampled gooseberries. I drank Limoncello. I made home-made pesto and hummus for the first time. I made pizza from scratch. I discovered that Thai eggplants don't look like any other eggplant I've ever seen; they are green and round, but the flesh cooks up soft like a regular oblong aubergine. I found out that I don't like radishes roasted any more than I like them raw, but that I love passionfruit in all forms.

As I look back on the year, it doesn't matter to me that many of my "new things" weren't exactly meaningful. What mattered is that I discovered there is an endless number of new things for me to try. It seemed to me an obvious sign that at fifty, my life was lush and full of promise. I could continue to grow, stretch my wings, and learn more every day for the rest of my life. I enjoyed the idea of changing my mindset, making a mental stretch, and getting out of my comfort zone. If nothing else, it gave me a reason to welcome each day as an opportunity to experience the world a little differently, to counteract all that's easy, predictable, or monotonous.

I can't fly a helicopter yet. But I *am* in a *Guinness World Records* book!

~Victoria Otto Franzese

Extreme Cuisine

*Challenges make you discover things about
yourself that you never really knew.*
~Cicely Tyson

For the first half of my life, trying new foods went only as far as drizzling a different brand of dressing over my dinner salad. I had been eating (and cooking) typical Midwest meals for years. And I admit, there wasn't much variety at dinner — casseroles, roasted chicken and meatloaf dominated the menu.

Shortly after I married, my husband informed me that it was time to break out of my comfort-food comfort zone. That was probably a nice way of telling me that he was getting tired of my cooking.

When he offered to take me to dinner at a nearby restaurant that boasted a grand buffet, I accepted happily. I figured I couldn't go wrong, and envisioned yards and yards of yummy, carb-laden comfort foods.

We gave the server our drink order and then joined the mass of hungry people browsing the buffet. I veered left, and he went right. I piled my plate with salad, topped with my usual dressing, of course, and returned to our table. I was gobbling a dinner roll when my husband joined me, carrying a plate heaped with crab legs.

Now, I'd seen crab legs before. On crabs. In pictures. And on the Discovery Channel. However, I was not prepared for the tangled, spindly mess that sat before me.

This was not *comfort* food. This was *uncomfortable* food — mostly because *I* was uncomfortable.

My husband picked up a pair of small, funny-looking pliers and clicked them at me. "Dig in," he said.

I stared at him and shook my head.

"Come on. Just have a taste. It'll be good for you to try something new."

I lifted a cluster of crab from the plate, and then dropped it. I whined, "It smells funny. And it looks like a big spider."

I glanced around, hoping a fellow diner would rescue me, but no one noticed. They were too busy cracking their own piles of crab legs.

Minutes earlier, I had been surrounded by what I thought were decent, refined individuals. Now? A roomful of Neanderthals, crushing shells and ripping at crab flesh with tiny forks.

> *This was not comfort food. This was uncomfortable food.*

The floor was peppered with bits of white crabmeat. Butter not only glistened in the dish on our table, but dripped from my neighbor's chin. The attractive woman next to him picked up a leg and gave it a quick "snap." Aside from shopping on Black Friday, it was the most uncivilized thing I had ever witnessed.

But I was not above trying new things, and I told myself that as freaky as the crab legs looked, they must have been delicious. As far as I could tell, everyone in the room was experiencing some sort of culinary nirvana.

My husband smiled approvingly and reminded me that trying something new was a good thing. He showed me how to use the funny pliers, and demonstrated how to bend and crack the shell, and then reach inside with the tiny fork to retrieve the crabmeat.

I managed to crush the shell, eat bits of shell, and cut my finger on the shell. I finally ended up using the tip of my steak knife to dig bits of meat out of the shell. My plate was covered in tiny shreds of crabmeat — nearly enough to fill a soupspoon.

I'd never had to work so hard for a meal. I was certain that if I were ever stranded on a desert island and the only food available was crab, I would starve to death.

Surprisingly, it tasted amazing. I enjoyed the rich, sweet flavor. If only I could get more crab out of its package and onto my fork!

As I struggled to dip my crab shreds into the butter, my husband moseyed back to the buffet. At this rate, he'd be finished with his meal and well into dessert before I was able to retrieve enough crabmeat to constitute a second bite.

He returned with a dish of what appeared to be large, ugly insects. I felt my stomach flop as he reached for one of the creatures.

"Are you insane?" I squeaked. "You can't eat those."

"What? They're crawfish, and they're much easier to eat. See, you just twist the head off, pinch the tail and suck out the meat. It's good."

I looked around the room, hoping to see a camera. Was I being punked? Or secretly filmed for an episode of *Fear Factor*?

Pointing at him, I whispered, "Please, put that down." He obliged, and I spread my napkin over the plate — a death shroud for crawfish bugs. Just then, our server stopped at the table and asked, "Can I take this plate for you?" I resisted the urge to hug her and simply nodded.

It's been some time since my first seafood experience, where I sat horrified and starving. Since then, I've mastered the art of cracking crab. Oh, the satisfaction of bending, snapping and opening a shell to retrieve a fully intact, succulent piece of crabmeat. I get hungry just thinking about it.

As far as the crawfish are concerned, I still can't do it. So, if you're a fan, and you think they're delicious, I believe you. Really. I'll take your word for it.

I'm happy to report that, over the years, I've had a lot of fun trying new foods, and recently, it seems the tables have turned.

Last week, I cooked a meal that included a side of herbed quinoa. My husband looked down at his plate and back up at me before picking up his fork and poking at the food on his plate. "What is this stuff? It looks like birdseed."

I smiled across the table at him. "Just eat it," I said. "It will be good for you to try something new."

~Ann Morrow

Chicken Soup for the Soul

I Wanna Rock
and Roll All Nite

Music is feeling. You can try to verbalize it.
It really just hits you or it doesn't.
~Gene Simmons

What was he thinking? My husband had just bought tickets to the KISS concert. Never mind that we're close to retirement age.

Maybe it was a nostalgia thing. We both graduated from high school in the 1970s. That's when the band KISS first burst onto the music scene. Not that they were my cup of tea, mind you. I was a classically trained pianist, and my taste in music ran from classical to soft rock. Beethoven to Barry Manilow. Not KISS. They were more heavy metal. That was more my little brother's style. In fact, the only time I ever listened to this kind of music was if it leaked under his closed bedroom door. I was Miss Goody-Two Shoes. I didn't listen to that kind of music — the kind of music KISS played. And I'd heard about some of the shenanigans that occurred during concerts. Like Gene Simmons spitting out blood. Yuck. Very disturbing.

Still, I must admit, there was something about the rock group that intrigued me. Their Kabuki make-up, Harlequin black-and-white costumes, and perilously high heels definitely captured my attention. KISS was so popular during the 70s that some students dressed like the band and performed at my school's annual talent show. They lip-synced to one of KISS's hit songs. With strobe lights pulsating and a very active imagination, you would almost swear you were watching KISS. Except for the very crude pyrotechnics, which consisted of a guy spitting lighter fluid out of his mouth and lighting it with a BIC Lighter. Impressive — until the stage curtain caught on fire. That's probably why they only came in third place.

So, some forty years later, I found myself going to my first KISS concert. Crazy. The closer it got to the date of the concert, the more anxious I felt. What on earth was I, a relatively conservative middle-aged woman, doing? Still, I decided to go with the best attitude I could muster, and set about picking out the coolest black-and-white outfit I could find in my closet.

It was the night of the concert, and I had no idea what to expect. Our seats were close. As I looked around the concert hall, I was pleasantly surprised to see a lot of people who appeared to be close to my age. It made me feel a little more comfortable about the whole experience. As the time for the concert neared, the room filled. To my right, there was a group of men, I'd say in their thirties, except for the guy one seat over from me. Trying to make small talk before the show began, I asked his name and age. Turned out, he was my son's age. This was his first KISS concert, too. At least we had something in common.

Just before KISS took the stage, a tiny woman appeared at the end of our aisle, weaving her way around people's knees toward the only seat left in the row. It happened to be the seat between me and the young man. Wearing a faded KISS T-shirt, jeans, and tennis shoes, this dear lady sat down. She seemed so out of place. I feared the young guys would poke fun at her. As soon as she sat down, however, one of the them yelled out, "Cool, we've got a Rockin' Grandma sitting next to us."

I had to find out what her story was. Turns out, she was seventy-six years old, close to my mom's age. And not only was she a Rockin' Grandma, but she was a Rockin' Great-Grandma. And, amazingly, she was a huge KISS fan. In fact, she'd been attending KISS concerts since the 1970s. She showed me a ticket stub to prove it. Sure enough, the ticket was for a KISS concert, and only cost $12. Wow, those were the days. This gal was not just a fan, but a mega-fan of the group. She attended all their concerts that came to town. Impressive. Plus, this Rockin' Grandma had come to the concert solo, since her husband was not so much of a fan. This lady was clearly comfortable in her skin and right at home in this environment.

Once the concert started, the crowd jumped to their feet, including Granny. In fact, she stood on her feet during the entire concert. Not only was she standing, but her tiny, wrinkled fist was pumping the air for the entire hour and a half. Tennis shoes were definitely the way to go. Of course, Granny knew that, being the experienced concertgoer that she was. Positively amazing. She put me to shame.

Before the concert, I'd done a little research on KISS, and the rock group's average age was sixty — an even more amazing fact after I saw the height of their heels, especially Gene Simmons', complete with shark-like teeth. They were at least six inches tall, maybe more. And Paul Stanley even looked good in a costume that showed off his belly. He's still got abs. Visible abs. I've never had abs — well, I'm sure they're in there somewhere, but they have yet to show themselves. I would certainly not wear a sparkly crop top showing off my belly.

> I forgot all about the arthritis in my hips and knees, and stood up for most of the concert.

For a little while, at least during the concert, I forgot all about the arthritis in my hips and knees, and stood up for most of the concert — partly because the guy seated directly in front of me could have played center for the NBA, but mainly because I was having such a great time. I couldn't wipe the smile off my face. It appeared at the start of the show and stayed through the entire concert, right up until the final song. And, speaking of the final song, of course, they saved the best for last. Rockin' Grandma had mentioned earlier that she had some leftover confetti in her bag. Suddenly, two towering platforms rose on the stage carrying a couple of band members up with them. Simultaneously, huge confetti machines began shooting tons of multi-colored paper strips into the air as KISS sang their iconic tune, "Rock and Roll All Nite."

After the concert, as I was picking confetti out of my hair, it hit me. I'd loved this concert. And I got why Rockin' Grandma was such a major KISS fan. The concert was an absolute blast. Now, I'm a big fan, too.

~Tamara Moran-Smith

From Opera to Hockey

*The most important thing to remember is this:
to be ready at any moment to give up what
you are for what you might become.*
~W. E. B. Du Bois

called my husband, Larry, at work. "I have good news, and I have bad." I said. "Which do you want to hear first?"

He played along like a good husband. "Give me the good news first."

"You can go to sleep early tonight."

"Okay. What's the bad?" he inquired.

"We're going to the opera!"

The joke was, the last time I made him go, he fell asleep. Even I had to admit it was a boring production. But when someone gave us tickets to the all-time favorite *Carmen*, I really thought he might enjoy it. When he nodded off again, I let him sleep. I only woke him when his snoring became louder than the performance.

Larry and I have always had our basic values in common, but our interests are as far apart as, well, opera and hockey. I love the arts, and he's a huge sports fan. His big passion is NHL hockey. He's shared season tickets with his buddies for years. I must admit there have been times I've been tempted to sell my ticket online or to a scalper. Tempted, but I'd never do that to my husband. Instead, if he wanted to go, we went. I griped and complained, "Oh, not again!" but I went.

We attended the games with other couples. The rest of our group was enthusiastic about the game, even the women. They knew all the players and how to pronounce their four-syllable names.

We'd have a quick bite at the tavern next to the arena, after which I might half-jokingly blurt out, "Can we go home now?"

Our friends would give me a look as if I were from another planet.

I enjoyed participating in the National Anthem, but aside from the meal, that was the only thing I enjoyed about our hockey nights. Instead of appreciating the good seats we had, I'd complain: "It's cold in here!" My husband would offer me his jacket, but I wouldn't take it.

> *Would I actually like this sport if I gave it a chance?*

"I'll just sit here and suffer," I would say. When the game started, my phone would be on my lap. Most of the time, I'd be texting or daydreaming. Sometimes, my texting would be interrupted when the home team scored. I knew they scored because everyone jumped up and exchanged high-fives and fist bumps.

What was so exciting about a bunch of grown men on ice hitting something called a puck with a stick? It was beyond me. When the team scored again, one of the women in our group turned to me and exclaimed enthusiastically, "Isn't this great?"

I shouldn't have said it, but I responded sarcastically, "Oh, yes! I'm thrilled!" Almost immediately, I regretted the snide remark.

I started to wonder. Why was I the only one NOT enjoying myself? Would I actually like this sport if I gave it a chance? What if I tried to change my attitude?

As I looked around at thousands of people cheering and getting increasingly excited, I decided to at least give it a try — for my husband's sake, if not for my own.

It took a few games, but soon I learned who the goalie was, who our latest player was, who had been traded and from where. When the other team scored, I eventually felt a jolt of disappointment with the rest of my crowd.

Soon I was asking, "What is icing?" "What's a hat trick?" and so on. I searched the program to see which part of the globe our players had come from.

My husband was surprised to see me getting involved. I was astonished myself! The cold no longer bothered me. I didn't keep glancing at the clock, counting the minutes until we got out. Time flew. The game was over before I knew it.

When our team won, I jumped up and down in a frenzy of my own. Leaving the arena on winning nights, I cheered with the rest of them.

"Are you coming to next week's game?" someone asked.

I turned to my husband. "Honey, can we? Can we?"

We did go to the next game and continued going often. I soon learned all the terms and expertly discussed all the game's particulars with my husband. Today, one would never guess I hadn't grown up with hockey.

Our friends couldn't believe their eyes when they first saw me sporting my team's really cool green jersey. "What happened to your designer jackets?" they teased.

Larry was so pleased. For our anniversary, he told me he wanted to reward me for being such a good sport, and he wanted just the two of us to do something special. I was delighted.

"I'm taking you to the opera," he announced, beaming.

A tiny twinge of regret went through me. I was hoping we'd go to hockey that night. But I didn't let him see my disappointment. I hugged and kissed him warmly.

The opera was enjoyable. Larry even stayed awake. But I must admit I couldn't resist a peek at my phone to check the hockey score. After all, we were in the playoffs.

Nowadays, it's so much more fun having the same things in common with my husband. Who knows? Maybe I'll even take up golf.

In the meantime, I can't wait 'til we win the Stanley Cup.

~Eva Carter

5

13.1 Is My Lucky Number

*Running is nothing more than a series of arguments
between the part of your brain that wants to stop and
the part that wants to keep going.*
~Author Unknown

Here's what I'd learned after sixty-four trips around the sun: Snap, crackle, pop wasn't just a breakfast cereal; it was me getting out of bed. Afternoon naps were not a luxury; they were a necessity. And chasing after my grandchildren was all the exercise I could manage.

So why was I spending a Saturday morning with my wife in a shoe store that caters to people who sign up for 5Ks, 10Ks, marathons, triathlons and century runs? The place was packed with young, lean, annoyingly healthy-looking men and women trying on athletic footwear of every sort. My wife motioned to an employee. "Pardon me, miss?"

"Yes, may I help you?" responded the young woman, smiling broadly. She was decked head-to-toe in shiny blue Spandex and had the body fat of a sparrow.

"We were told that this is *the* place to come for running shoes. My husband and I are registered for the LA Marathon."

Wait. What did she say? Omigosh! Now I remembered! It was all coming back to me. The guest speaker we had at church a month ago who talked about running for clean water in Africa. Sure, it's a good cause, and I was all for helping out. I'd just cut a check and leave the running to someone else, right? Wrong. "Actually," my wife continued, "we're each running a half-marathon. It's a charity relay."

"That's awesome!" exclaimed Spandex Woman with an even broader smile.

She had us step onto a computerized treadmill that analyzed both stride and foot strike, the results of which would help her select the perfect running shoes for our less-than-perfect feet. Apparently, I'm a pronator. It sounds like some vaguely illicit activity you might hear mentioned on *America's Most Wanted*—*Mark Mason is a sixty-four-year-old retiree who is fond of afternoon naps and is a known pronator.*

Soon, she was ringing up our purchase. "Your total is $297."

"Wow! What a deal!" I joked. "Were these on sale?"

"Actually, yes!" she responded cheerfully. "This is your lucky day!"

But if I thought my bank account hitting the wall was painful, it's because I had no idea of what was to come. Until then, "marathon" meant binge-watching back-to-back seasons of my favorite TV shows while consuming copious amounts of packaged snacks. But here I was, staring down the barrel of an eighteen-week training regimen that, according to our charity, was designed with the sedentary lifestyle of a typical sixty-five-year-old in mind. Yeah, right. A sixty-five-year-old former Olympian is more like it.

We began with a six-week segment of base training consisting of timed walk/runs that became longer each week. I was surprised at how doable it was. By the end of the sixth week, I was actually thinking that I would be able to cover 13.1 miles and cross the finish line without the aid of a stretcher.

But then, things changed. We started distance training. As the name implies, progress was now measured in terms of miles, not minutes. Training days were laughingly divided into three categories: Easy, Hard, and Long. Over the next twelve weeks, I added another category called, "You've got to be kidding." Something else had changed as well. Muscle groups I never knew I had began to make themselves known in the most painful of ways. On runs over three miles, my knees began popping like castanets. My hips cried out for mercy. Even my leg cramps had cramps.

The solution to my dilemma, as it turned out, was embarrassingly simple. In my younger days, I never gave much weight to stretching before running. It was now my religion. As a true convert, I had compiled a repertoire of exercises designed to reduce, if not eliminate, muscle strains, sprains, pulls and worse. Self-educated in myriad runner's ailments, I can now speak with authority on the cause/treatment of everything from plantar fasciitis to patellofemoral pain syndrome. One more thing: Alternating heat and cold after a run works wonders. I wish to thank the inventor of the ice pack. Next to my wife, it has become my constant companion. I named mine Freon.

With two weeks until the marathon, we were facing our longest run yet: nine miles! At this point, my wife was doing better than me. She completed the run, averaging 13:15 minutes per mile. However, I was unable to run it. For two weeks, I'd been plagued by an assortment of new problems that seriously curtailed my running. With race day looming, I chose to work on speed walking in hopes that I would start my half-marathon injury-free.

But then, just one week before the big day, my wife's ankle became too painful for her to walk on, much less run. After all this time, it was beginning to look like we would have to forfeit. A visit to the doctor and one X-ray later, we were told that it was a simple overuse injury, and she would be able to compete if she stayed off her feet for the remaining seven days.

The morning of the marathon, we awoke at 3:00 a.m. with only a few hours of fitful sleep. By 3:40, we were driving to Los Angeles. I parked at a lot in Santa Monica a few blocks from the finish line. It was dark and foggy, but the place was abuzz with activity. We boarded buses to our respective starting points: Dodger Stadium for her and Hollywood for me.

It had been three hours since the marathon started. I huddled with other second-leggers at the relay point on Sunset Boulevard, scanning the constant flow of runners for anyone wearing the signature shirt of our charity. I squinted my eyes and detected a sliver of bright orange moving in a familiar way. Another few seconds, and I saw my wife! I cheered as she ran into the hand-off area with a time of three hours and nineteen minutes. I was so proud!

> *Despite snap, crackle, pop, this body is still able to do things I never thought it could.*

We embraced, posed for a quick photo, and then I began my part of the relay. Three hours and forty minutes later, I crossed the finish line moving like a Clydesdale with bursitis. But it was over! My wife ran up and threw her arms around me. We examined our relay medals—hers with a skyline of L.A. and mine with a beach scene.

Finishing the marathon was great, but it was only part of it. Thanks to the generosity of our friends and family, we were able to raise $1,200 to help provide clean water for Africa. So, here's what I learned. Despite snap, crackle, pop, this body is still able to do things I never thought it could. Afternoon naps are fine, but they aren't as satisfying as running fifteen miles in a week. And as for chasing after my grandchildren, now Grandpa wears *them* out!

Well, I need to wrap this up. It's time to drive my wife to the track at the local high school where she is training for this year's marathon.

And if you ask me why I'm not running, I will look at you with a broad smile and respond politely, "What're you, nuts?"

~Mark Mason

6

Finding the Sweet Spot

Go wide, explore and learn new things. Something
will surely have a kick for you.
~Mustafa Saifuddin

When I first entered college, instead of gaining the "Freshman 15," I gained the "Freshman 20." This is the only time in my life when I can honestly say that I was an overachiever.

Between a full class load, a part-time job, and a steady relationship, I had zero time for exercise. On top of that, my lifestyle as a starving college student lent itself to many a fast-food run. Needless to say, underneath my scholastic "uniform" of matching sweatshirt and sweatpants, I was positively paunchy.

It seems that I had majored in rotundness, with a minor in extra body fat.

After graduation, I decided to take the gym a little more seriously. Accompanied by a friend, I began a regular routine of walking on the treadmill or climbing the stair machine. I was very content with our routine, being the kind of person who did not venture out much. I did not travel; I ate the same foods; I did the same things. Clearly, I liked my routines. My friend, however, became bored.

One day, he suggested that we take up a sport.

Me? Sports? No way.

I had spent my entire life as an uncoordinated person with no trace of athletic ability. I vehemently vetoed his idea. I was not athletic, and no one was going to convince me otherwise. Plus, I was perfectly happy with the gym.

Nevertheless, after a few weeks he convinced me to reluctantly step onto an outdoor racquetball court. As I stood there holding my racquet, I felt ridiculous. I am pretty sure I shot him some looks that could kill before we started our "game." The first few "games" were quite comical. I slammed the ball, sending it flying in every direction except for the direction that I had intended.

Still, somehow, I managed to learn to play at a decent skill level. But just as I was beginning to feel comfortable, my friend decided to pull the rug out from underneath me again.

> **I began to try new things willingly, with a sense of excitement.**

"We're not getting enough exercise. We should play tennis instead." Those were probably the words that came out of his mouth, but what I heard instead was: "I hate you, and I want you to suffer. Again."

Tennis? I can't play tennis! That involves real skills! What part of "I am not athletic" don't you understand? I adamantly resisted his new attempt at ruining my life.

Nevertheless, weeks later, I found myself standing on a tennis court, wondering why he was intent on humiliating me. Awkwardly, I ran after every ball that he served to me, completely missing about ninety percent of them, and hitting the rest into the bushes, the other court, and over the fence. Each time we played, I managed to lose at least one or two balls.

The first few months were quite painful. But one fateful day, as the ball came flying toward me, my racket and the ball finally met in what tennis players refer to as the "sweet spot." I watched in astonishment as my return landed powerfully on the other side of the court, almost exactly where I had aimed. I had finally learned how to play tennis properly!

Tennis would eventually become one of my favorite hobbies. I played it enthusiastically for several happy years, only stopping because of a knee injury.

I learned an extremely valuable lesson during my journey toward mastering racquetball and tennis: I can do whatever I set my mind to. I just need to put in the work, and the results will follow. Had I not stepped outside of my comfort zone, I would have never discovered how much I enjoyed tennis. I began to try new things willingly, with a sense of excitement.

Once I ventured outside my narrow life, my sense of fulfillment grew exponentially. Eventually, I tried new foods, met interesting people, tried unique hobbies, and traveled to beautiful lands. I opened doors that let so many new joys into my world.

When I found the sweet spot in my tennis racket, I found the sweet spot in my life.

~Kristen Mai Pham

Stretching Out in Retirement

*It is not because things are difficult that
we do not dare; it is because we do
not dare that they are difficult.*

~Seneca

A t age sixty, my husband decided he wanted to live his next forty years breathing easier. So he retired after decades of a high-stress, challenging career at a university mental-health clinic.

We've been happily married for thirty-five years and raised three children, but I have to admit that my husband's transition to retirement was one of the bigger challenges in our life together. It was clear from the start that housecleaning, tennis with his buddies, casseroles, home improvement projects, puppy care, and reading weren't going to fill the emptiness from the loss of his creative and stimulating job. For the first time in decades, he felt lost. How would he now find purpose and earn a living that allowed for a healthier, more balanced lifestyle?

The previous Christmas, I'd bought him one free yoga class. I'd found the magic of yoga a few years earlier and wanted to share the wealth. He was kind and appreciative, but the gift card remained buried in his wallet. "I don't know, lovey. You know I've never liked large groups of people working out together." But one evening over dinner, after he'd completed every project possible, including porch repair, rail painting, window cleaning, furniture reconstruction, closet organization, garage cleaning and garden planting, he said something surprising. "I think I may use that gift certificate and take a beginning yoga class."

When my kids were adolescents and announced they were going to do something I had encouraged, I never wanted to get too excited for fear it would backfire. So my response was to say calmly, "Oh, that sounds good." I finished my broccoli as my heart joyously skipped a beat. I knew that one yoga class didn't mean he would choose to practice regularly, but it was a beginning.

It wasn't only that I thought yoga would help his physical flexibility and ailing hamstring; I also knew that the alignment we develop on the mat helps us line up with our goals off the mat. The transition from one pose to the next teaches us how to gracefully make transitions in life. My husband is an athlete and has always been competitive, so I had a sense that his earlier reluctance, in addition to being in a group, was due to the fear of not being good enough. He would soon learn that yoga is not about competing, but showing up without judgment. I was hopeful these lessons would ease things for him as he navigated this new stage of life.

> *The transition from one pose to the next teaches us how to gracefully make transitions in life.*

It took a few days for him to actually throw his yoga mat into the back seat of the car and head off to the studio. I did text him eagerly after class for a report. "What did you think?"

Sometimes a man of few words, he wrote, "Good."

Over the next few months, as autumn turned into winter and outdoor tennis in Colorado became less frequent, daily yoga became part of his routine. We often attended class together, and I was impressed by how easily he mastered challenging poses, standing on his head and hands, reminding us that we are all born upside-down. One day after class, as he backed us out of a parking space, he shared, "So I think I'm going to sign up for an intensive yoga teacher training." I had to smile as I reminded myself that this was the man who really didn't like working out in large groups!

Well, times have changed since then. My husband has always been a gentle man, but ever since retirement and his decision to take a yoga class, he is softer around the edges. He breathes easier, and his smile is contagious. And all three of our grown children now throw a yoga mat in their back seat. If Dad and Mom do it, it's worth giving a try. My husband's intensive teacher training requires months of full weekends, creating an opportunity for me to explore solitude as I find the nooks and crannies of independence at sixty, enriching myself and our marriage.

My son's old bedroom is now a sunny yoga room with a beautiful new wood floor, laying the groundwork for continued change and growth in the years ahead. My husband teaches yoga for tennis players in our home studio, spreading the magic to his tennis buddies. One small gift card for one yoga class became a beautifully wrapped present for a husband that even "stretched" to his family, his friends and beyond.

~Priscilla Dann-Courtney

Taking Back My Life

*Nourishing yourself in a way that helps you blossom
in the direction you want to go is attainable,
and you are worth the effort.*
~Deborah Day

"Mom, I don't like you," my two-year-old son said to me one day.

"Okay… is that because you *love* me?" I asked.

"No, you're not cute." *Gee, thanks kid.*

Being a mother of two kids under three has certainly kept me on my toes. My priorities include keeping the children safe, fed, clothed and semi-clean. My expectations for what I can accomplish at home have been lowered. I've learned to "let things go" when it comes to cleaning and cooking. In prioritizing my family's needs, my own needs get put on the back burner.

By the end of the day, when I finally have time to think about doing something for myself, I'm too tired. I reach for a glass of wine and the remote as I let my body sink down into the couch to watch some mindless entertainment. I zone out. I escape. I let myself dream I am somewhere on a beach or that I am someone else.

Sometimes, I am a gladiator working alongside Olivia Pope in the White House on *Scandal*. Other times, I am on the ranch with Ree Drummond on *The Pioneer Woman* cooking dinner for the cowboys.

And sometimes, I am winning the mirror-ball trophy on *Dancing with the Stars*.

In reality, I am sitting in my sweatpants on a couch that has Cheerios crumbs between the cushions.

I tell myself I am doing the best I can. I am surviving. But our routine is the same: kids, work full-time, kids, relax. With each passing day, I lose myself just a little bit more. Long ago, I waved goodbye to the fun-loving person I once was and embraced the saggy version of my new self.

But something changed on the day my son told me I wasn't cute. That night, as I was washing my face, I looked a little longer in the mirror — not because I was hurt by his statement, but because I noticed the light had gone out from my eyes. My kids have magical eyes. They twinkle with wonder, hope, and adventure. In contrast, my eyes are dull, saggy, and sad. I once had light, a bounce in my step, and a journal full of adventures I planned on experiencing.

> **I listed forty new things to try before I turned forty years old.**

That night, instead of pouring myself a glass of wine and turning on the TV, I got out my favorite pen and started writing a list — a list to save myself; a list to pull myself out of the darkness and put some light back into my eyes; a list to show my kids it is important to have dreams and to prioritize those dreams; a list to show myself I deserved to be a priority.

A list to take my life back.

In the past, I had made plenty of lists and seldom accomplished anything on them.

This list had to be different. It needed to be a mixture of goals that were attainable and goals that would require some work. I added places I wanted to travel, which would mean saving money and being disciplined. I added races and events I wanted to participate in, which would mean exercising and eating healthy. I added reading 500 new books to my list, which would mean turning off the TV. I added activities I always wanted to try. I revisited my old hobbies and added them to the list. I also left five spaces blank to fill in.

I listed forty new things to try before I turned forty years old. I had six years to get moving. Making the list was the first step, perhaps the easiest step. I needed to keep the momentum going.

The first goal I wanted to check off my list was participating in a Polar Plunge to raise money for the Special Olympics. I live in Minnesota and for some strange reason jumping into the middle of a frozen lake in January seemed very appealing. It was an adventure, something new. Every year, my co-workers formed a team, but for the past two years, I was pregnant. This would be my year.

On the morning of the Polar Plunge, I changed into my 1980s workout gear of green neon leggings, hot pink leg warmers and a side ponytail. My son took one look at me and beamed ear to ear. "Mom, you look pretty." Maybe, just maybe, there was already a new sparkle in my eyes.

The anticipation was almost crippling as I approached the platform to take the leap into the frozen lake. *Would I completely freeze? Would it be scary? Just how cold was I about to feel? Would my head go under?* I reached for my friend's hand and let go of my fear. I embraced the challenge. We all jumped together, all of our faces forming an "O" as we screamed from excitement and terror.

I felt happy and proud of myself as I emerged from the lake. I kept screaming, "I did it!" But one of the most exciting parts of the day was when I arrived home. I walked in the front door, my husband handed me a pen, and together we stood in front of my list, which was taped on the refrigerator door. I crossed off item number one. And with that pen stroke, I began to take back my life.

Everyone who participated in the Polar Plunge received a blue, long-sleeve T-shirt. Whenever I wear that shirt, my son asks, "Is that your Polar Plunge shirt?" and I answer proudly, "Yes." Several times, he has stated, "I want to do that too, Mommy." It makes me proud that he remembers I jumped into a freezing lake, and he wants to do activities with me.

Slowly, I am returning. With each goal that is crossed off the list, a piece of myself is restored. Not only am I showing my family it is important to dream, I am showing myself that I am worth it. I am excited to continue my quest to do things I have always wanted to do. I reached out to my friends and family, and several will embark on various adventures with me over the next six years. I am rebuilding my community, I am rebuilding my confidence, and, most importantly, I am rebuilding myself.

~Leah Isbell

The Clydesdale

*The word try, means nothing. There's no such thing as
trying to do something. The moment you begin a task,
you're doing it. So just finish what you're doing.*
~La Tisha Honor, Teen Roach

I was never a fast runner. Throughout my childhood, whenever
we were timed or competed in the 50-yard dash, the quarter-
mile, the potato race or any other type of race, I would finish in
the bottom half.

In my late teens, as a member of the 14th Ward American Legion
baseball team, I had the distinction of being the slowest runner on the
team. In the pre-season practices, the coach would have the sixteen
players on the team line up in the end zone of the Taylor Allderdice
High School football field and do 100-yard sprints to the other end
zone. If we finished in the first half, we were done with practice for
the day. But if we finished in the bottom eight, we had to run another
100-yard sprint. So, eight of us ran again. And this time, the top four
got to leave practice. And then four was narrowed to two, and finally
two to one.

I was always the one running by myself at the end.

And so, twenty years later, when I entered my first and only official
running race — the Pittsburgh Mount Oliver Two-Mile Challenge — at
age thirty-eight, I certainly wasn't expecting to win. Or come close
to winning.

I was there because a college friend, Jim Hosek, was the director of the race, and he asked me to run. The race was a fundraiser for Jim's church — St. Joseph of Mount Oliver.

And so I showed up, paid the entrance fee, had a number pinned on my back, and moved over to the starting line, where I waited with about 250 or 300 others for the race to begin.

I wasn't waiting very long when someone with a microphone made an announcement. "Will anyone weighing over 200 pounds please come down to the scale?"

When I heard this announcement, two thoughts went through my mind. *One, what does weight have to do with running? And, two, I think I am over 200 pounds.*

> **I was always the one running by myself at the end.**

Eventually, I walked down to the scale. A man told me to get on.

"Two hundred and three," he announced. "You're in the Clydesdale division."

And then he wrote down the race number that was on my back.

I suppose I should have asked the man at the scale what exactly it means to be in the Clydesdale division, but I didn't.

Soon after, the race started.

Most of the runners sprinted out ahead of me. Some passed me on the way. There were, however, at least a dozen people walking the race, so I was assured of not finishing last.

It was not an easy course. Much of it was uphill. On the day of the race — Thursday, August 4, 1988 — the temperature in Pittsburgh reached 91 degrees. And that evening, when the race started, it wasn't much cooler, and it was humid.

Even though it was only a two-mile race, volunteers were holding out cups of water for the runners going by. I didn't take any, too scared that if I did, it might break my momentum, or the water would go down the wrong pipe, or I'd stop running.

I finished the race in 22:21. The winner of the race was Dan Driskell, age thirty-seven, of Mt. Lebanon, who came in at 10:20.

To put this in perspective, Dan Driskell was done running about a minute before I got to the halfway point.

Like I said, I was never a fast runner.

Once I did make it to the finish line, there was free beer for all the participants over the age of twenty-one. Never did a beer taste so good.

As I was drinking my beer, someone at the finish line with a microphone kept repeating an announcement, "Please stay for the awards ceremony, which will take place shortly."

At the awards ceremony, Dan Driskell was officially announced the winner and presented with a trophy. Then came a trophy for the first-place women's finisher and the first-place men's and women's finishers from the Borough of Mount Oliver. There were also trophies for the first-place men's and women's finishers over the age of forty.

Then came a final award: the first-place finisher in the over 200-pound division, the Clydesdale division. And they announced my name.

I was quite surprised, but I didn't lose my composure. I didn't faint or cry or anything like that.

I walked over to the awards ceremony and was handed a trophy. The crowd applauded. My wife, baby daughter, and four-year-old son were there to witness this monumental event.

Five minutes after the awards ceremony, I found my friend Jim.

"Jim, I really appreciate this trophy and everything, but how many people were entered in the Clydesdale division?"

Jim opened a folder and looked through a dozen or so pages of official race entrants and results. Eventually, he found the page with the Clydesdale results.

"Two," he said.

"Two!" I repeated. "You mean I only beat one person?"

"Yeah," Jim said, and he started to laugh. I laughed, too.

I guess if there is a moral to this story, it is that not everybody can be a Clydesdale. And even fewer can be a *champion* Clydesdale.

~Steve Hecht

Chapter

2

The Power of Yes!

Embrace Change

*Continuity gives us roots; change gives us
branches, letting us stretch and grow
and reach new heights.*
~Pauline R. Kezer

A Down Under Fairy Tale

You can learn new things at any time in your life if you're willing to be a beginner. If you actually learn to like being a beginner, the whole world opens up to you.
~Barbara Sher

A man was frantically knocking on my window trying to get my attention. "Are you okay? Are you okay?" My head was spinning, and I was in a bit of a daze, but I came to and rolled down the window.

"Yes. I'm fine," I said. "What happened?"

"You just slammed into my car; that's what happened!" he said, agitated. "You spun out from the left lane and hit the back of my car as you were spinning. Thank God, you're okay!"

"I must have fallen asleep," I said apologetically. I looked at him in a state of bewilderment, still confused and groggy.

"Stay there," he said. "I'll call the police."

My car was stalled on the side of I-95 South just north of Boca Raton, Florida, where I lived. It was 3:00 a.m., and I had been driving home from an emergency in the operating room where a man had a heart attack on the table while undergoing a cardiac catheterization for his severe angina. It's what we anesthesiologists fondly refer to as a "Cath Lab Disaster." After three hours of providing continuous life support for my patient, he successfully made it out of the OR and into

Embrace Change | 53

the Intensive Care Unit. My job was done, and I was drained.

The last thing I remember was driving ninety miles an hour down the highway headed home. I remember passing a vehicle in the far left-hand lane and then... well, that's all I remember. Now, I was sitting in my smashed-up BMW 325i on the side of the road, contemplating my near miss at mortality and my life as it was.

This wasn't the life I had imagined for myself. Less than two years into my career as a Cardiac Anesthesiologist, I was already ready to throw in the towel. For more than seventy hours a week, I worked with an arrogant, unremarkable surgeon with a serious God-complex. My downtime was spent with my alcoholic boyfriend and my two cats. I lived in a beachside apartment with a balcony view of the Intracoastal Waterway in the mini New York City of South Florida, where snowbirds congested the roadways from October to April, and pink buildings were as common as weeds. I was exhausted, stressed, and disenchanted. It was time to re-evaluate; time for a change.

> *It was a simple life, and my heart was no longer racing.*

Within three months, my bags were packed, my cats were re-homed, my personal belongings were in storage, and my repaired BMW was sold. My guitar, laptop, two suitcases and I were headed Down Under in hopes of starting anew.

This would be the farthest from home I'd ever travelled alone, and my heart was racing as I boarded the Qantas jumbo jet to Cairns in Far North Queensland, Australia. Located a thousand miles south of the equator, this beautiful, coastal community adjacent to the Great Barrier Reef would be my home for the next twelve months. I had successfully obtained a contract to work as a Staff Anesthetist at the Cairns Base Hospital in the land of koalas, kangaroos, and the ten most deadly everything, from snakes to spiders to sharks and venomous Irukandji jellyfish! My only prior exposure to the country had been watching the movie *Crocodile Dundee*, and the Crocodile Hunter, Steve Irwin, who shocked the world with his crazy antics and enthusiastically declared "Crikey!" as he wrestled with crocodiles.

I was greeted at the airport by a statuesque, full-bearded man wearing a blue, short-sleeved denim shirt with sweat stains in the armpits, shorts, and flimsy thongs on dirty feet. He had a carefree, boisterous voice that was warm and welcoming, and when he introduced himself as my supervising doctor, I was joyfully surprised. This was not a sight you would see in Boca.

As we drove on the left side of the road along palm tree–lined roadways to my new little apartment across the street from the hospital, we laughed often, trying to decipher each other's accents. I quickly settled into my bed and slept for the next twenty-four hours. All the stress and business left my cluttered brain — the accident, the job, the relationship, the chronic fatigue… I just let it all slip away as I entered a blissful slumber to the sounds of kookaburras and cicadas.

Four months passed, and I was finally feeling calm again. Despite the fears and anxieties about journeying to an unknown land, my feet seemed to be firmly planted. Many of the OR nurses and I had become fast friends, enjoying weekly "cuppas" at the local cafés and weekend "barbies" at their homes with families. I visited the rainforest, trekked up mountains, went scuba diving in the Coral Sea, and wrote songs with other young doctors. Many a weekend day, I chose solitude and silence, walking along the waterfront only steps from my door. A clarity and sense of ease seemed to caress my soul during this time. It was a simple life, and my heart was no longer racing.

One evening, at an after-work gathering at our favorite café, my female friend asked, "So, have you dated any Aussie guys yet?"

They all giggled, and I blushed, but the answer was a definite "no." It wasn't my reason for coming. Still, they encouraged me to have a little fun, so what the heck! I took their advice, and less than three weeks later, I found myself having coffee with a charming, blue-eyed, blond man with the most scrumptious, soft-spoken Aussie accent I'd ever heard. He shared pictures of his home and three-acre property, which supported his nursery of native trees and shrubs. He had an Australian Cattle Dog named Diddles and a creek that flowed through his back yard. He was a self-made man, lived a nature-filled life amongst his plants, and was searching for the love of his life with whom to share it all. Who could resist an invitation like this?

Two days later, we met in a town midway between Cairns and his home of Cardwell. He took me to a secluded, sandy cove and created the most exquisite "barbie on the beach" a girl could ever dream of! Shrimp, steak, onions, potatoes, a few "stubbie" beer cans, and juicy plump oranges for dessert. We watched the blazing sun set and the vibrant moon rise, and spent hours under the stars exploring each other's lives.

It wasn't the plan when I left my homeland on a leap of faith months before, but I willingly succumbed to this idyllic lifestyle and fell in love. Five months later, all my new Aussie friends witnessed a garden wedding ceremony in the mountaintop village of Yungaburra—a fairy-tale dream come true. Two years and two babies later, I felt blessed to have survived the accident that changed my life by prompting me to start over halfway around the world.

~Shari Hall

Warm and Familiar

Pearls don't lie on the seashore. If you
want one, you must dive for it.
~Chinese Proverb

After my mom died, I realized I had broken my two promises to her: One, that she wouldn't die alone, and two, that I would live life to the fullest. I failed miserably with the first promise, and as for the second one — to live life fully — how many of us actually do that? How many of us take risks and dare to color outside the lines?

We all have responsibilities, so when I told my mother that I would live my life to the fullest, deep down a part of me knew it was a lie. In fact, I was numb after she died. I had two small children, and each day I went through the motions of being a normal human being, but I knew I was a shell.

I worked as an assistant in a prison, and every night I came home to my family and little apartment in the city. It wasn't much, but the rent was affordable. And although the sounds and smells of city life rose up from the streets, our home was decorated like a cabin on a faraway beach. Seaside paintings covered our walls, seashells became centerpieces, and we even had a little wooden sign that said, "Beach Life."

I spent my days craving a new life while I kept fulfilling my responsibilities.

Unfortunately, those responsibilities involved a lot of despair. My office was set in the health care wing of the prison. Inmates would come and go for everything from spider bites to withdrawal symptoms. I met one inmate who was handsome in a rough sort of way. He always had an air of sadness about him, even though he said optimistic things. He would tell me of the mistakes he had made and that, above all else, he wanted a fresh start in life. He wanted to live clean. He wanted to see the sun rise again, eat a mango on the beach, and kiss a girl in the back seat of his convertible. Most of the guys there talked about big hopes and dreams, but I usually didn't believe them. This guy, however, seemed like he had a solid plan beyond eating mangoes. And this guy, unlike all the others, seemed to know what he had done wrong and was willing to fix himself.

> *I spent my days craving a new life while I kept fulfilling my responsibilities.*

I was happy for him the day he was released. He had made himself a promise that he was going to make changes, and he swore he would never see me again.

When he left, I felt a pang of something. Sadness? Jealousy? Although I could leave anytime I wanted, I was still drawn back to this haunting place that stayed with me, even when I left. I envied the inmates who would leave and never come back.

I continued however, doing the same thing every day. I went to work, and then returned to my cramped little apartment and dreamed of a different life while sitting among my seashell centerpieces.

One day, I had friends over for dinner. It was no big deal. No birthday festivities. No big party. Just a few friends enjoying each other's company and a bottle of wine. We laughed and joked about plans for the summer.

One of my friends said, "Who cares what we plan? This apartment is as close as Erin will ever get to the beach."

She and the others laughed, and I smiled while I seethed inside — mostly because I knew she was right. I knew that I had given up really living.

I went back to work — to the lockdowns, red suits and cinder-block walls with only tiny windows to let in the light. Would it be so bad just living as I was? I had a steady job and a roof over my head. And even though some nights the traffic would keep us up, we were fine with it. We had gotten used to it.

And then I saw him standing with a few fellow inmates, laughing as they awaited their time to go outside in the yard.

It was *him*, and watching him laugh tore at my heart. Seeing him back inside was devastating.

I stood there for what felt like hours and watched him be carefree despite the fact that he was once again caged. When he noticed me, he smiled and waved, and then he walked over to say "hi," grinning from ear to ear.

"When did you get back in?" I asked.

"A few days now," he said. "Ya miss me?"

"I just thought I'd never see you again."

He shrugged then and leaned in a bit closer to me.

"My life is crap," he said. "Total crap. I'm swimming in crap twenty-four hours a day. But here's the thing: It might be crap, but it's my crap. All of it. And the crazy thing about crap is that even though it stinks, it's warm, isn't it? Warm and familiar."

And that was that, wasn't it? The truth behind why he and everyone else on the planet stay in their ruts and routines. Why we avoid risks and never color outside the lines. Because, even if we're sitting in crap, it's our crap, and it's warm and familiar.

My little talk with him changed me that day. I decided that my mother's death, although gut wrenching, was a powerful reminder of how precious life is, and we shouldn't be wasting even a second of it. I decided it was time to step out of my pile of crap and move on. I quit my job without knowing where I would be going afterward, and I packed up our belongings and moved to the beach.

It was a good step toward living a life I truly wanted. I didn't know what I was doing or where I was going, but at least I was doing it with an ocean view.

~Erin Hazlehurst

Into the Future

Education is not the filling of a pot
but the lighting of a fire.
~W.B. Yeats

Her sister had obsessive-compulsive habits, so Mom went out of her way to be different. From the time they were small kids, her younger sister demanded strict, orderly regimens, while Mom lacked any sort of discipline at all, much to the chagrin of their tidy mother.

But by the time she coasted into her seventies, Mom was different. Gone were the days she experimented with new recipes or drove off to explore new stores. Even when she had a houseful of kids, she had still found time to take cake-decorating classes and learn Japanese needle arts. She had enjoyed traveling and trying exotic foods. But now, she looked forward to her comfortable routine of morning oatmeal with fruit, her daily newspaper, and her evening television programs. Aside from visits from the grandkids, she didn't have a social life at all, and we worried about her sphere becoming smaller and smaller. My sisters and I would share our concerns with one another, but we thought that, perhaps, this withdrawing, this shrinking, was a part of growing old.

The world around my mother, on the other hand, was rapidly expanding and evolving. But because she lived with my sister's family, she didn't need to learn how to "work" new appliances or tools to keep up. "Change the channel for me, please." "Which remote is this?" "Do it for me." Everyone was happy to comply until we realized that she was losing interest in doing things for herself.

My sister got her a cell phone, and since it was just like pressing buttons on a landline phone, she managed easily. She loved being able to talk with us wherever she was, although we could forget about a return call if we left a message. Retrieving her messages took more steps than she cared to learn.

"If someone wants to talk to me that badly, they can call back," she would snap. When we tried to show her how to use the added features of her phone or the different remotes for the DVD player or cable, she balked.

"Forget it! It's too confusing!" She'd turn away from whatever we were holding out for her to see. No amount of coaxing or tempting could convince her to try something new, even when we pointed out that she could watch *Hawaii Life* and see a bit of home if she used the remote for the cable box.

Then, I reminded her about her sister who flatly turned down any offer to help her learn how to use a cell phone, computer or even a new kitchen appliance. Only three years younger than Mom, my aunt had given up on driving decades earlier and let her husband read all the tax paperwork and appliance manuals. They had cable, but she still watched only the same three channels. Auntie might have been healthy in body, but her mind was showing signs of early decline. Maybe it was sibling rivalry or a fear of becoming like her sister, whose controlled schedule absolutely irritated her, but we saw Mom trying a bit harder to make things work. I think she began to see that it was good to push one's brain to learn new things, even if it required some effort or was frustrating.

The day she got her new hearing aids, she listened carefully to the audiologist explain how to replace the batteries. When it was time to switch them out, I fumbled with the tiny pieces, but she exclaimed, "I can do it myself." And she could. I was as surprised as she was proud.

The next thing we knew, Mom asked my son to show her how to use a computer. He co-owns a small IT business and was able to hook her up with any type of technology she wanted. After only a little resistance, she finally sat in front of the keyboard as he patiently taught her how to log on and type in the password he set up for her.

Suddenly, Mom was back in touch with high school friends in Hawaii. They e-mailed back and forth daily and made plans to meet up in Las Vegas, which they did on an annual basis. Her world expanded again as she learned how to access different websites, and she loved all the recipes and news "from back home" that were available at the click of her mouse. The next thing I knew, she was able to download video attachments sent by her out-of-state brother and Google medical information for her latest hypochondriac symptoms.

Every so often, I overheard my son on his cell phone with her, walking her through the login process again or reminding her of her password, even though she had "written it down somewhere." He went on many a service call to reboot the cable connection or hook up a new printer or adjust the screen size so her aging eyes didn't have to strain.

> I think she began to see that it was good to push one's brain to learn new things.

"You need to learn how to use the computer," she scolded her sister. "Boy, you can learn a lot! You can get the *Honolulu Star-Bulletin!*" Her sister, stubborn by nature, refused, and my mother only clucked her tongue. "Too bad," she said. "She doesn't know what she's missing."

It felt so good to know Mom wasn't missing out on anything anymore. I'd like to say it saved her life, but even if it wasn't life saving, it surely was life changing. Life enhancing. It made me reflect on my own life habits. Was I continuing to learn new things? My own life, while more varied than Mom's, still had its subtle routines. Work and home had their routines. My hobbies, though enjoyable, didn't compel me to learn anything new either.

My family and I took stock of our own situations, and we realized that none of us were learning anything new. As I gazed into our back yard, the darkened tips on the avocado leaves troubled me. In the past, I'd phone an arborist who never bothered to return the call, and soon I'd forget to do anything about the plight of the tree. A few Google searches revealed that my tree was probably experiencing some salt burn from my incorrect use of fertilizer. As I shared this with my husband, I realized that instead of hiring "experts," we could become experts ourselves with all the information available "out there." I found an online master gardener certification program from Oregon State University's botany department. The first class was free!

In turn, my husband had wanted to hire someone to put recessed lighting in our kitchen and rewire some walls to hang television screens in different places. "Hey, I can learn how to do it myself," he said. I reminded him that a friend of mine took an electrician class. She also took classes on how to bake artisan breads, and how to change the oil, battery and brakes on her car.

We all thought since we "learned" new factoids from the Internet on a regular basis that we didn't need any concentrated study, but there's a satisfaction in seeking deeper knowledge. We both felt an excitement we hadn't felt in a long time, not unlike how prospective freshmen look forward to their first time on a college campus. It was unmistakable: We felt young again!

We all need to be coaxed along the way sometimes. By finally stepping outside her comfort zone, Mom led the way for us to continue growing.

~Lori Chidori Phillips

Stepping Out of the Boat

*Do you want to be safe and good, or do you want
to take a chance and be great?*
~Jimmy Johnson

"**M**om, high school students don't love their teachers. You won't be happy up there." My daughter was concerned about my decision to move from teaching fourth grade — a position I had loved for eleven years — to high school English. And she wasn't the only one.

"Aren't you old to be making a change like this?" Mary's question over the phone stunned me. I laughed, stammered a reply, and quickly hung up.

Was I making a terrible mistake? Should I call the headmaster and tell him I couldn't do it? Then I thought about the past year and knew this move could not be wrong.

The previous August, I had sat in teacher in-service and listened to a challenge from my principal. "Will you get out of the boat?" she urged. "What would that mean for you?" Mrs. Haley referenced the New Testament story of the apostle Peter, who demonstrated his faith by walking on water. "Peter may have faltered at the end, but he was the only disciple to walk on water. He did that by getting out of the boat. Maybe it's time for you to do something bold this year."

As we left the meeting room, Mrs. Haley handed each of us a little plastic boat to remind us to be bold in our lesson planning and unit studies. But I had a bigger step in mind. For four years, ever since I finished a master's degree in English, parents at our small school had been urging me to move to the high school. The head of the English department asked repeatedly if I would consider moving, but I was happy in fourth grade. I enjoyed weaving together all the different subjects; I treasured reading to my students in the quiet minutes after recess; I liked the ocean unit, the morning math, the map studies. But, mostly, I loved fourth graders!

Still, the prospect of spending my days talking about great literature, watching students develop their writing skills, and having meaningful conversations about complex topics was appealing. I imagined how nice it would be to stand at my door and say goodbye to my students instead of walking them in a line to the lunchroom.

I just couldn't decide. Day after day, as winter turned to spring, I saw that plastic boat and thought about stepping outside my comfort zone. Finally, I took a lesson from Gideon, an Old Testament favorite, and put out a "fleece." If a move to high school were right for me, I would not depend on the opinions of parents or other teachers. I'd wait until an administrator asked me.

In late April, I sat in an elementary faculty meeting. As our principal talked about end-of-the-year activities and field trips, I saw Mr. Turner, the high school principal, beckoning me from the hallway. Puzzled, I slipped out quietly.

Mr. Turner invited me to sit at a table nearby. He didn't beat around the bush. "I've just learned that you have a master's degree in English," he said.

"That's right."

"Would you consider teaching at the high school?"

Wasn't this the sign I had been waiting for? I should have answered with an immediate "yes," but I have never taken to change easily.

"I'll think about it. Give me until after graduation, and I'll let you know."

Mr. Turner was gracious. "We would love to have you join our high school faculty."

As he walked away, I turned to him. "I'm happy in fourth grade. Don't quit looking for someone else."

But now the seed was planted. Even though I was truly happy teaching fourth graders, I couldn't stop thinking about high-school English. I began noticing the older students. I watched them as they left the cafeteria. I enjoyed their easy laughter and their energy. Many of these young people had passed through my classroom years before. I imagined getting to know them all over again. The more I thought about a fresh start, the more excited I became. I would do it!

The day after graduation, I called the headmaster, who made final hiring decisions, to tell him I would take the job. Much to my surprise, he hesitated. "We've offered the position to someone else," he admitted. "Come into my office, and let's talk about it."

As I drove to school, I tried to relax, but my mind was whirling with possibilities. What if there wasn't a place for me after all? Could I return to fourth grade? Would I be really content there now that I'd decided to move?

"Mr. Turner thought you didn't want to move," the headmaster explained. "He said your last words were to look for someone else."

I did say that, I thought, *but I also said to give me until after graduation.* I couldn't help feeling a bit betrayed. Aloud, I said, "That's true. I didn't realize you would find someone so quickly."

"If you move to the high school, that will open a spot in elementary," Mr. Patrick said. "Let me take it to the board and see what they recommend."

Now it was my turn to wait. I took the time to get some much-needed rest and kept myself busy gardening and catching up on household chores neglected during the school year. As I pulled weeds and washed windows, I thought about the months of graduate classes, dreaming in the library about teaching the material I enjoyed so much, preparing for the job before me. It was almost within my grasp. I wanted the opportunity more than ever.

In just a few days, I had a call from Mr. Patrick. I held my breath waiting for him to get to the point. It didn't take long. "We'd like to offer the high school position to you," he announced. The joy I felt immediately suggested I had made a good decision. When my children and friends tried to talk me out of the move, I wavered a bit but stood firm.

Twelve years later, I still love my job. It may be true that high school students don't express their love as enthusiastically as ten-year-olds, but they have their own ways of showing appreciation, and I feel it every day.

> *The joy I felt immediately suggested I had made a good decision.*

The excitement I experience each morning when I climb the steps, greet the seniors waiting outside the library, and unlock my door at the end of the hall is continued assurance that "stepping out of the boat" was a good move. The first bell rings, and the desks in my room begin to fill up. A sense of anticipation fills the air. "What are we doing today?" someone asks, and I know I'm in the right place.

~Sherry Poff

On the Wings of Change

Wings are not only for birds; they are also for minds.
Human potential stops at some point
somewhere beyond infinity.
~Toller Cranston

n 2010, my mother-in-law gave me her rather simple but grace-ful, antique "secretary desk." I was delighted to have it and cherished this nostalgic piece, for it both served and inspired me as I began my writing journey.

The antique desk easily fit into the tiny loft at the top of the stairs. I felt so cozy, secure, and confident when I sat down and began each writing session. Despite the desk's appeal, its limited storage capacity meant that I often scattered file folders and books on the small floor space around me. But I also crave organization and closure. So after each writing session, I painstakingly gathered up the scattered tools of the trade and either placed them on a nearby shelf or in one of the desk's three drawers until the next writing session. And because I'm also a creature of habit and routine, I repeated this process hundreds of times — much like a batter who comes to home plate and repeats a similar process each time he prepares to swing at the first pitch.

I accepted this process as the way that I entered into and exited my writing mode. Subconsciously, I convinced myself that the desk and the rhythm of my routine were my lucky charms, and I needed them to be successful.

A few years into my writing journey, we moved into a bigger home, and I subsequently acquired my own office. My husband, Bill, offered on more than one occasion to buy me a new desk for my office, but I ignored his offers.

One day, we stopped at the local office supply store. Bill escorted me to the back of the showroom where he'd found what he thought was the perfect desk for me. "I want to buy this for you, sweetie. My writer needs a bigger desk." He hugged me. "You know you deserve it. Besides, a bigger desk means bigger possibilities."

"But I don't want a bigger desk!" I squared my shoulders, turned around, and marched away. "I like my little desk."

"I don't understand. Why don't you want a bigger desk?" He scurried to my side. "You must be afraid of something. What is it? You can tell me."

Was Bill right? Was I afraid of something?

"Whatever do you mean? I'm not afraid of anything. What makes you say that?" I folded my arms across my chest and looked him straight in the eyes. "Like I said, I really like my little desk. I'm satisfied with it; it inspires me. Besides, we just moved; I've experienced enough change. Switching to a bigger desk will just mess with my writing mojo. So, don't ask me again!"

He didn't.

A few weeks later, while working in my new office, I looked around at the folders, books, and papers strewn all over my office floor. I searched through several stacks and couldn't find what I needed to meet a contest deadline. My heart raced, and beads of sweat appeared on my forehead. I leaned back in my chair, took a deep breath, and looked around my office. The room literally swallowed the tiny desk, making it look a wee bit insignificant and slightly out of place. Maybe I did need a bigger desk. Was Bill right? Was I afraid of something?

Unable to continue writing, I closed my laptop, stood up, and paced around the room, focusing my attention on the certificates, awards, and copies of checks that I'd framed and hung on the wall. When I began writing, I never imagined the success that now stared back at me. Each memento represented either an exciting moment or a significant step forward in my writing career. I was both thrilled and content with the level of success I'd achieved.

I closed my eyes and relived the vulnerability and fear I sometimes felt as a new writer. Often, when I sat down to write, I didn't know exactly what I was going to write or where I was going on my writing journey. But during those early years, I trained myself to love both the ambiguity and the not knowing.

I smiled, returned to my chair, and retrieved C. JoyBell C.'s book of poetry, *All Things Dance Like Dragonflies*, from the bookshelf. I flipped through its pages, and her words about faith jumped off the page into my heart. She talked about how she had trained herself to love the feeling of not knowing where she was going, and just trusting that as she opened up her wings and flew off in an unknown direction, things would work out.

At that moment, I recognized that a bigger desk symbolized bigger projects, bigger possibilities, more challenging contests, stepping out on faith, and leaving my comfort zone.

Bill was right, of course. I was afraid — afraid to force my complacent writing wings to spread wide and begin a new flight. So when my bigger desk arrived a few days later, I sat down at it, opened my laptop, and unfolded my wings, confident in their ability to take me someplace amazing.

~Sara Etgen-Baker

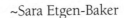

From Rock to Retail

Always walk through life as if you have
something new to learn and you will.
~Vernon Howard

When people learn that I logged thirty years in the music business, their first question is usually, "Did you meet any famous rock stars?"

Of course I did. I also met some infamous rock stars and some not-so-famous rockers, as well as country, hip-hop, alternative, blues, jazz, folk and classical artists, among others.

The music industry was truly a never-ending party — outrageous, loud, hip, cool, fast and, believe it or not, a lot of work. Never mind that we were out late the night before with the newest artist to hit the #1 spot on Billboard's Hot 100. We had to be at our desks the next morning at 8:00 a.m. sharp, ready to analyze sales numbers, write reports, book ads, process orders, implement sales campaigns, communicate with staff and essentially do what most people do when they work in the office of a major corporation.

The story goes that the music biz is all about sex and drugs and rock and roll, but I had to sign a waiver when I was hired that stated sex and drugs with the artists would be a one-way ticket to the unemployment line. I didn't mind signing — I was a single mother of a six-year-old boy when I started working in the industry. For my son's sake and my own, I remained a professional in my dealings with the artists, radio stations, music journalists and retailers throughout my career, which is probably why I lasted so long in the business.

Most importantly, I loved my job. Working in the music industry was a dream come true. I thought I would retire from the industry when the time was right.

Who knew the party would end so abruptly?

In 1999, Internet peer-to-peer file sharing gained a foothold with music fans. Suddenly, music was free. Most of the music retailers closed down for good. As a result, record labels required fewer people in-house and in the field. I was put out to pasture, along with many of my peers.

Unbelievably, I was jobless after thirty fabulous years. I was fifty-eight years old and I had to re-invent myself.

> I was alone in a changing world, with no compass to guide me and no star to follow.

I love to write and had some success as a freelance writer, so I naturally drifted to the local daily newspaper, which ultimately was a terribly uncomfortable fit. The newspaper offered me a job as a sales rep rather than as a writer, but I accepted, hoping to eventually segue to writer. I made enemies the very first day when I arrived in my shiny gold Jaguar. The entire staff became suspicious of my intentions, and the newspaper's sales reps jealously guarded their hard-won territories from the hated "Miss Jaguar." Unfortunately, the situation never improved, so I finally moved on to a publishing company. Once again, I found the landscape so different from what I'd known that I felt out of place and enormously awkward. I left the job several months later.

I had been the fair-haired wonder child of the music industry. Now I was an aging outcast whom nobody liked.

Meanwhile, in the midst of trying to find my new niche, my mother — my greatest advocate and cheerleader — passed away, leaving a huge gap in my soul and filling me with such sorrow that I could barely breathe.

After my mother's death, I was unsure how to move forward. Both my parents were gone, my hair was turning gray, my son was a grown man with a family of his own, and I was alone in a changing world, with no compass to guide me and no star to follow.

And then I found retail.

I should have known I would love retail. When I was a little girl, instead of a dollhouse, I had a Sears store, with little counters brimming with merchandise and tiny plastic shoppers weaving through the aisles.

I finally landed a job with an off-price retailer—women's and men's clothing, kids' stuff, household items, other great stuff. It suited me to a tee and, blessedly, I still work there.

My managers are young enough to be my children, but they like me—and they appreciate my work. I love unpacking the truck. I love organizing displays and what we call "foo-fooing the endcaps." I love unpacking and racking clothes and dishes and pans and faux flowers and candles. I'm very good at helping customers; I truly appreciate their business. I love the hustle, the bustle, the 10,000 steps in each shift, the workout I get folding heavy rugs and lifting gigantic boxes. The whole process, the whole retail thing, makes me happy beyond belief—and being happy at my age is the ultimate goal.

A few weeks ago, a friend asked me if I missed the music industry. I do, and I don't. My industry job was a great job while it lasted; I enjoyed working with the artists and loved helping them all succeed. But that was a long time ago, and we all were very young. Now I believe I'm exactly where I should be—enjoying a new phase in my life, with no regrets and so much to look forward to. The truth is, life doesn't end when the curtain comes down on Act One. Believe this above all else—there's always an Act Two… and more.

~Nancy Johnson

A Blessing in Disguise

*Man cannot discover new oceans unless he has the
courage to lose sight of the shore.*
~André Gide

I ran to answer the phone. I was expecting this call from my husband, a theology student at a college 943 miles away. We knew that we would have to move when he graduated, so I was anxious to hear where his first posting might be.

"So, do you know where we're going?" I blurted out.

Hesitantly and slowly, he replied, "Iqaluit."

"Where?" I asked.

Again, stumbling over the pronunciation, he replied, "Iqaluit."

I had never heard of this place, let alone pronounced it, so I asked him where it was.

"Baffin Island," he said.

"What? Baffin Island? That's way up in the Arctic at the top of the world! A land of ice and snow!" I exclaimed.

Then I thought he must have been teasing me, so I said, "Okay! You've had your fun. Quit teasing me and tell me where we're *really* going."

Again, he replied, "Iqaluit on Baffin Island."

I couldn't believe my ears. Baffin Island was the last place on earth that I would ever want to visit, let alone live! It was very remote, and the only way in or out was via air. I wouldn't be able to see my family or friends for at least a year, as the cost to fly in and out was prohibitive. I had said I would go wherever God sent us… but Iqaluit?

It took me several days to get over the initial shock. I got out the atlas, found the location and then realized that Iqaluit was located in Nunavut Territory — a brand new, two-year-old territory in Canada's far north. At that time, Iqaluit was home to more than 6,000 people, 80 percent of whom were Inuit. For the first time in my life, I would be a minority living amongst a different culture! Did I really want to go?

> *Baffin Island was the last place on earth that I would ever want to visit, let alone live!*

I knew in my heart that I had to follow through with my promise that I would go wherever God sent us. Anyway, the bishop had said we would only have to commit to one year.

I had three months to pack up the house and make all the arrangements for moving. Some days, I was excited at the prospect of seeing and doing something new and different. Other days, I did a lot of talking to myself. After all, I was turning fifty-seven. Shouldn't we be thinking of retirement instead of starting a brand new journey?

In mid-April, my husband returned home from college, and together we looked after the final details of moving. As each day was checked off the calendar, more and more butterflies appeared in my stomach. Was I really doing this?

Our flight was scheduled for June 1st, and our son and his wife drove us to the airport. We boarded with four pieces of luggage containing personal effects, our ten-year-old faithful dog and a nineteen-year-old cat. With a twinge of anxiety, we set off on a new adventure.

Once in the air and on our way, I knew there was no turning back, whether I wanted to or not. Over the course of the flight, my thoughts kept returning to home, and my mind kept replaying the tearful goodbyes we had said to our family and friends. Leaving all of them was one of the most difficult things I have ever had to do.

Three hours later, the plane landed. As I stepped outside into the nippy air and looked at the landscape, I could very well have been landing on the moon. It was all so foreign! The beautiful trees, gardens and lakes that had surrounded me all my life were now replaced by barren tundra. This was June, and there were still snow banks in places.

As we wound our way through town, it felt like we were driving through the last frontier in Canada. Only a few stores dotted the main street, there were no stoplights, and sidewalks were virtually unheard of. Although it was June, people were still wearing parkas. In less than ten minutes, we arrived at our "home away from home"—a 700-square-foot, second-floor apartment. In our thirty-nine years of marriage, we had always lived in a house and had a yard with gardens. Could I get used to this?

Most of the Inuit people spoke Inuktitut. However, English was understood by the younger generation and used in the workplace. I came to appreciate why people want to converse in their mother tongue, as I sure longed to hear English. Everything was so strange.

My husband settled in long before I did. I was very homesick, and many times I questioned what I was doing there. I needed something to do, so I got a job with the territorial government. There, English was the spoken and written language, and I began to settle in.

But still, I had to "work" at feeling like I belonged. I felt like I was caught between home and somewhere else, and I missed my family terribly. Ron often had to fly into other communities, leaving me alone for several days at a time. I was very lonely when he was on those trips, but I could see that his work was important to him.

Once we had lived there for a year, what was once the unknown was becoming the new normal. I was becoming comfortable with the unfamiliar. Being away from everything I knew and loved gave me the opportunity to explore talents and gifts that I didn't know I had. One such venture was opening a small Christian bookstore in our church that was run by volunteers. Two other people and I worked long hours to make this happen. We named the store Blessings.

When the bishop asked us if we'd like to extend our one-year posting, we signed up for another two years. We ended up staying five years in total, and although I never learned to embrace the weather and some other aspects of living in the Arctic, I did come to love the people and the traditions of the far north. I also learned a lot about myself. New experiences allow us to learn and grow, and they open the door for many memories to be made — memories that last a lifetime.

~Carolyn McLean

17

My True Hollywood Story

The biggest rewards in life are found outside your
comfort zone. Live with it. Fear and risk are
prerequisites if you want to enjoy a
life of success and adventure.
~Jack Canfield

When I arrived in Los Angeles in 2005, I had no interest in becoming an actor. First of all, I was much older than most people attempting to begin working in the entertainment industry. Second, I had no training whatsoever in the business and still do not. I assumed that I did not have a look that anyone would be interested in, and I had terrible stage fright. Twenty years earlier, when my wife and I had taped an episode of the *Ricki Lake Show*, I literally froze on camera, and they had to switch the shot to my wife. I looked like a deer caught in the headlights, with my eyes bugging out of my head and my mouth shut tight. Fortunately, my wife loved being the center of attention, so it was not as noticeable as it could have been. From that moment, my mind was made up about having a career in front of the camera — I avoided it like the plague.

Then a strange thing happened: I got a job as an associate producer on a film that received several Academy Award nominations. I had no experience in the industry at all, but the executive producer took a chance on me because I knew how to raise money from investors. *Angels with Angles* had its Hollywood premiere six months later, and I got to walk the red carpet for the first time with two beautiful women who were much younger than me. Although this was not a major motion picture or blockbuster by any means, it did have older star power like Rodney Dangerfield and Frank Gorshin. Since both of them had died before its release, there was very little promotion for the film, but to me as a first-timer, it could not have been bigger. I was bitten by the Tinseltown bug and was going to follow this dream wherever it might lead me — except in front of the camera.

After the premiere, I had to find another job and quickly got one on a movie named *Koreatown*. It was a much smaller film, but had a red-carpet premiere nonetheless, which I got to attend. Again, beautiful people were there, and I loved all the attention I was getting from being a Hollywood producer. Still, I never expected this to turn into a career as an actor. For the next few years, I went from job to job — some in the movie business and others that had no connection with it whatsoever. Once a project was funded, I had to find work, and another movie or show was not always an option at that time.

During the great recession, it was hard sometimes to find anything, so I decided to try working on court TV shows because some of them paid very well, and there was an abundance of them on television. This put me in front of the camera over and over again, and I slowly got used to being filmed and even started to enjoy it. But it was just a fun way to make a living during a hard time. Once the recession ended, I naturally assumed that I would end up behind the camera as a producer once more.

However, by the time the economy was in good shape again, I knew there was no turning back for me. While taking a writing class, the teacher made a post in the students' online forum to me that said, "When you win your Academy Award, please remember me in your acceptance speech." I was shocked by what he wrote because this was my first writing class, and I was over fifty years old. I also completed the class with a score of 100 percent, which was just as shocking as his post. I knew I might have some talent as a writer because the court shows had used my work, but this comment really blew my mind.

Then the last thing that I ever expected to occur happened.

Near my apartment in Hollywood was a grocery store that required I go down the Walk of Fame to get to it. There, numerous people dress up as characters from movies and TV while working for tips from tourists by taking photos with them. Over the years, I got to know several and became friends with them. One day when I was on the way back after shopping at the store, I ran into one of them and a film shoot on Hollywood Boulevard. She knew the producers and asked if I wanted a part in the movie. They needed someone to play the part of a homeless man sitting on the sidewalk, while an attractive girl dropped dollar bills on him. Since I did not have to do anything, I accepted and took my seat on a star on the Walk of Fame in front of Grauman's Chinese Theatre.

> *My acting career in Hollywood began with eighteen seconds in that odd little movie.*

The cameraman took his place, and then the woman walked up to me. She had a handful of dollars and began raining them on me while I stared up at her. The entire shoot lasted less than a minute, and there were no retakes. I got up when it was done and picked up the money. A few months later, I got an e-mail with a link to the short film *Monsanto Limes*. My acting career in Hollywood began with eighteen seconds in that odd little movie. I never did figure out what it meant or even an idea about the plot.

After that, I decided to step out of my comfort zone behind the camera and see if I could book other acting gigs. Little did I know that older actors were in great demand. There were so many young actors available that the competition for gigs was very intense. Most of them had to work other jobs to support their dream, but it was much different for the older ones. There was a much smaller pool of actors and an abundance of gigs for them to work. I have been able to find many different jobs in films, television, commercials, infomercials, and music videos.

I even get to do modeling on a regular basis. Later this month, my twelfth year in Hollywood, I will do a photo shoot for a clothing company and wear their product at my fourth red-carpet premiere. My résumé has nearly 300 productions that I have worked on, and ninety-five percent of them have been filmed in the last three years — all because I decided to say yes and get over my camera fright. I discovered a new career that I love.

~John Davis Walker

18

Who's That Girl?

*A ship in harbor is safe, but that is
not what ships are built for.*
~John A. Shedd

I stopped short when I caught my reflection in the bathroom mirror. The silver hair that shone back at me still threw me a bit off balance. Only a year or so ago, my hair had still borne the deep rich mahogany color of my youth, thanks to that all-too-frequent appointment with the dye bottle. And, truth be told, had I been able to stop the hands of time, I would have remained that striking brunette of my youth. But last year, I had decided that if the change was to come — and clearly it was already here — then I would take control of it and not just survive it… but thrive in it. So, much to my friends' chagrin, I went silver — on purpose. And what a glorious silver it is: thick, long, soft, and shiny. Who knew all that sparkle was waiting there underneath all that pretense?

So here I was just past my fifty-fifth birthday. The world referred to me as a "senior" now. I could get a discount at the grocery store. I was a wife, mother and, yes, grandmother. And still, I was startled by how fast the years had flown by. Why hadn't someone warned me that when we cross a certain birthday barrier, the world begins to think of us differently? Ads for certain medicines began to show up in my newsfeeds. Was this how my mother had felt when she crossed this line? I blinked back tears as once again I felt the pang of missing my mother, who had passed away five years before. As I thought of her, I began to mentally count. When my mother was fifty-five, I had been a mere nineteen years old, newly married and sure I knew everything. My, how time changes things. What was it that Bob Dylan said in his "My Back Pages" song? "I was so much older then. I'm younger than that now."

Lately, my reflection in the mirror seemed to be taunting me, as if it were asking, "Is this it? Is this all you got? Your comfortable life. Your comfortable job. Your comfortable drive to work and back every day. Is this the way you're spending the rest of your life? Nice. Comfortable. And bored out of your mind?"

> *I went silver—on purpose.*

And I was comfortable. I had a good, if somewhat predictable life. A few precious, if predictable, friends. Every day, my husband and I ate dinner at the same time. We watched the same television shows. We shopped at the same grocery store. Life was pleasant, and I felt grateful and blessed.

But somewhere deep inside that fifty-five-year-old exterior, an ember of my younger self still remained. And it was that part that kept telling me that this was not all there was to life. It kept reminding me that I did not have to go quietly into that good night. Maybe there were still things to be learned and new experiences to be had if I dared step out of my comfortable rut. I thought again of my mother. At about this same age, my mother, who had been a housewife all her life, had gotten her driver's license, and gone back to work and school. At the age I was now, my mother had not given up. In fact, it was at this age that my mother had truly started to live.

Did I dare take a back page from her book? Could I finish that second degree I had started? Could I quit that comfortable job and comfortable life and go out there to see what else was waiting? My husband was retired. Our kids were grown. In fact, our sons were constantly asking the two of us to come to the city and live near them. But could I give up everything I knew and remake myself? How would employers react to a silver-tressed woman competing with Millennials for a job?

I wondered what my mother would have said about this crazy

plan. Then I laughed. I knew exactly what my mother would say.

Six weeks later, the boxes were almost packed. The deposit had been paid on the exciting new apartment in the city. I had a new job. My silver hair had not been a deterrent after all. In fact, my new employer had rather liked my self-assured, authentic, experienced self. And, truth be told, I was liking myself more these days, too.

I felt a small pang of sadness as I hugged the girls at work one last time. But then I jumped into my new car with the stick shift that I had just bought a month before. That car was now packed to overflowing with things the movers couldn't fit into the van. As I slipped on my sunglasses and adjusted my rearview mirror, I again caught a glimpse of myself. Only this time, I thought, *Who is that beautiful, confident, excited woman staring back at me? And where is she going?*

As I downshifted and accelerated, leaving behind my old office and old life, I wondered what the next chapter of my life would bring. I didn't know, but I was sure going to find out. And I wasn't afraid.

~Geneva France Coleman

19

Even Jellyfish

True self-discovery begins where
your comfort zone ends.
~Adam Braun

A s a kid, I was particular about what I ate. I hated so many things that my mom gave up trying to pack a school lunch that I'd actually eat, and I found a bag of chips and a juice box in my brown bag. She said it was the only thing she could think of that wouldn't come back untouched.

We lived in the country, in a town with one diner and two fast-food burger joints, so I wasn't exposed to many foods anyway. We didn't even have a pizza place or a Chinese restaurant during my formative years. I remember when our grocery store started selling yogurt — no one could believe that people liked eating sour milk. My hometown was a meat-and-potatoes kind of place and proud of it.

Everything changed when I was eleven and we moved to a bustling suburb of New York City. My mom had remarried, and my stepdad was born in Israel, was a different religion, and had traveled the world having all sorts of amazing adventures. He was nothing like the people from our town, and I loved hearing stories about the places he'd been and the things he'd seen, not to mention the things he'd eaten. In Taiwan, he told me he'd watched someone prepare a meal out of jellyfish.

"But you don't need to travel all the way around the world to try new foods. We have all of that right here if we go to the city!" he told me.

"Even jellyfish?" I asked.

"That and so much more, and we can try anything we want," he told me.

I was hesitant. I couldn't imagine eating a jellyfish. Even thinking about it made me feel sick.

We went to New York City a lot. I loved crossing the enormous bridge over the Hudson, marveling at the lights and tall buildings, walking on the famous avenues I'd seen in movies. I felt like the luckiest girl in the world. My favorite was exploring the cobbled streets of the South Street Seaport, where we'd buy almond-scented soaps at Caswell-Massey. But I also loved Columbus Circle and the all-night gelato shop where I could get a dip each of raspberry and kiwi sorbets in a little plastic cup. My stepdad was excited for Mom and me to try everything. And while I couldn't have been more enthusiastic about visiting new places, I was terrified of some of the new foods he suggested.

The first thing he wanted to introduce me to was the Middle Eastern cuisine he'd grown up with. He took us to Mamoun's, a hole-in-the-wall falafel shop on MacDougal Street, where the line was always out the door. As we waited patiently to place our order, customers filed outside clutching fat, wax-wrapped pitas loaded with baba ghanoush and dripping with tahini. I didn't know what on earth any of it was, despite the fact that Mom assured me repeatedly that I was going to love it. She'd tried it lots of times and, well, it did smell pretty good, but still...

Until that moment, my diet had been a predictable menu of peanut butter, chicken and stars soup, and grilled cheese, punctuated by weekly Sunday dinners of roast beef or chicken and dumplings. My only experience with seasoning was salt and pepper, so I was apprehensive. I remembered that my grandmother had told me that in other countries they ate the same animals we kept as pets, and I was terrified that I'd be tricked into eating frogs or guinea pigs. Falafel? What were those odd, greenish balls made from anyway? What if they were turtle meat?

"I'm scared to eat this. I don't want to eat strange animal parts," I confessed to my stepdad when he handed me my falafel.

He and Mom found this absolutely hysterical.

"I think we need to tell her the truth about scrapple," my stepdad laughed.

"Sweetheart, first of all, falafels are vegetarian, and they're made out of chickpeas, so you're safe. Just eat. Second of all, scrapple… You should be the one to break this to her, honey," he said, looking at Mom, whose mouth was already packed with hummus.

She took a long swig of her Orange Crush.

"You've been eating weird animal parts your whole life," Mom said.

"No, I haven't," I insisted.

But they were right. Scrapple was the most popular breakfast meat in my home state. I'd been eating it probably since I was first introduced to solids, and I loved the flat, greasy rectangles, especially with a slice of buttered toast. But I had no idea what it was, and my worldview was about to be shattered.

> I'd been eating "weird" things my whole life, and I hadn't even known.

"So, yeah. Scrapple is, well, it's scraps. It's all the parts of the pig that no one wants, and they grind it all up and add some spices and cornmeal and shape it into a brick. People fry it in its own grease and eat it," Mom explained.

"Are you serious?" I asked. "How could you let me eat that?"

Mom shrugged. "It tastes good," she said.

"I am never eating scrapple again as long as I live," I declared.

Suddenly, my falafel didn't look half so intimidating. Chickpeas, sesame, a few cucumbers and tomatoes? No problem. I took a bite, then another, and pretty soon I was standing on the sidewalk in the middle of New York City, wolfing down that falafel like I hadn't eaten in my entire life. If only the people from my hometown could see me now. This thing was delicious!

I had a revelation that night. I'd been eating "weird" things my whole life, and I hadn't even known. In fact, I'd liked them, which meant there was nothing to fear. If this falafel was so good, what else had I been missing out on? I realized that I wanted to explore the tastes of the city as much as its sights and sounds. I would try anything, I decided. The worst thing that could happen was that I wouldn't like something, and if that happened, so what? I could try something else instead. No one was going to force me to eat something I didn't enjoy.

In the years since my first falafel, I've kept my promise to try everything, and it has opened me up to a world of fascinating flavors. I'm passionate about food and culture, and I've eaten the national dishes of as many different countries as I could find. It's just part of making sure that I expose myself to as many new and different things as possible. Even jellyfish.

~Victoria Fedden

Chapter 3

The Power of Yes!

Put Yourself Out There

Each friend represents a world in us, a world possibly not born until they arrive, and it is only by this meeting that a new world is born.
~Anaïs Nin

20

When Richard Met Cindy

*When you realize you want to spend the rest of your
life with somebody, you want the rest of your life to
start as soon as possible.*
~From the movie When Harry Met Sally

t was a Saturday like no other. "Dad, I don't know how to tell you this." He took my hand in his, put his other hand on my knee, lifted his little-boy face, looked me square in the eyes and said, "Dad, you need a girlfriend."

Being a single parent had prepared me for just about anything — except this.

"Oh, no, I don't," I replied with a smile. He said nothing and sat rather poised for a child. I continued, "For the sake of discussion, if I did — which I don't — how would you know?"

"Dad, when your nine-year-old son tells you that you need a girlfriend, you need a girlfriend."

"And just what would I do with this so-called girlfriend?" This was risky territory.

"Dad, do I have to tell you everything? You could go to the beach, the movies, dinner... And if you really liked her, you could kiss her!"

"Okay, we've covered this plenty. I'm happy being your dad. That's enough for me."

As we hugged, he said, "If you say so, Dad, but you still need a girlfriend."

Then he added rather speedily, "You're the best dad, and if you find the right person and want to make me a brother or sister, that's okay, too. But I'd rather have a brother first."

This wasn't the first time I was told I needed a girlfriend. Baseball Mom from Little League also told me. I told her, "Not interested." She assured me I was, but I just didn't know it yet.

I love old movies and romance stories. One rainy Sunday, I had the afternoon to myself. I had plenty of time to finally watch *When Harry Met Sally* uninterrupted. I settled in with my favorite blanket, coffee, and bonbons. Halfway into the movie, Baseball Mom called.

"Are you going to bother me about dating?" I asked.

"Only for a minute. I figured you're sitting on the couch with your favorite blanket and coffee, eating bonbons, and watching *When Harry Met Sally*. Why is that one of your favorites?" she asked.

"It's a good movie."

"If you say so, Mr. Blanket and Bonbons. Got to go. Oh, the reason I called: Go online to a Jewish dating website and at least consider it."

"Not my style," I replied.

"Take it from a Catholic Baseball Mom. It'll be good for you."

"I don't think so."

"Okay, Mr. Sensitive. Got to go."

After the movie, I thought about it. Being a parent meant everything to me, but I was also terribly lonely. It took my little boy, *When Harry Met Sally* and Baseball Mom for me to realize I was available.

I wanted a woman of good moral character, as well as someone who was smart, sassy, sensitive and had a sense of humor. A woman like that doesn't just show up at the door and say, "Hi, I'm perfect for you. Let's fall in love, go through hard and great times, grow old together and share a million laughs along the way. Also, without being too forward, Mr. Sensitive, would you like to join me for dinner sometime?" It just doesn't happen that way!

Reluctantly, I signed up for the dating website and proceeded with caution. A month later, I dedicated an entire day to finding the right woman. I read hundreds of profiles, disregarded easy check-off items as well as anything fluffy or overly boastful. Profiles without pictures were more likely to be reviewed. I wanted a relationship where we loved each other heart and soul. Anything less just wouldn't do.

Somewhere around #200, I found her. She lived in a house south of Boston, got her education in a library, liked being home with her children, said that sometimes a party is just the thing to lift her spirits, liked a good cup of coffee, and announced that her annual salary was none of anyone's business. Now that's my type of woman!

We met at the bookstore where a local artist was debuting children's music. At the very least, it would be good coffee. Cindy apparently had a surveillance team. An unusual

> *This wasn't the first time I was told I needed a girlfriend.*

number of fortyish women were strategically browsing aisles while whispering in their cell phones. After the music, we took the kids to eat. She didn't seem to like me, and I didn't know what to make of her.

We had a number of second tries and decided we were better as friends, but we would each try finding someone else for the other.

We met for lunch a few days later, and as we were leaving, I leaned in to kiss her unexpectedly.

"What are you doing? I thought we were going to be friends," she said.

"I think I want to kiss you instead," I replied. I realized I had no intention of finding her a man.

Come to find out, she had no intention of finding me a woman either. It was a rocky beginning, but neither one of us was letting go.

I'd contacted two people on the dating website based solely on their profiles. When profile #2 responded, I replied that I was already talking to another woman, and talking to two women at the same time wasn't appropriate.

A few months later, Cindy was on the phone with her friend Lauri. "He's here right now. Get over here and meet my cyber-date, dream-date."

Lauri was over in a flash. She wasn't in the door ten seconds when she said, "Oh, my god, you're that guy who wouldn't talk to me because you were already talking to another woman."

Cindy piped in, "You two know each other?"

"Cindy, that's the guy I told you about who wouldn't talk to me because he was already talking to another woman. You're the other woman!"

Turns out, Cindy had helped Lauri write her profile and only submitted her own profile because Lauri insisted. Cindy had no intention of responding to anyone. That's why her profile had been down around 200. But she responded to mine, and that's all that mattered.

Cindy and I have had our share of challenges. Through it all, we've managed to build a strong, deeply loving relationship.

Many years ago, my therapist asked how I could be so happy with so many problems. I told her, "It's easy. So many people go through life never getting the right person to share it with, but I got the girl."

I always knew what she'd be like, and with some help, I found her. It took my nine-year-old son, *When Harry Met Sally*, a Baseball Mom, a dating website, and Cindy's friend Lauri to get us together. We've been together more than fourteen years. I definitely got the girl.

~Richard Berg

21

Becoming the Glue

Since there is nothing so well worth having as friends,
never lose a chance to make them.
~Francesco Guicciardini

Our three kids were all under age five, we'd recently moved to the suburbs, and I'd stopped working to be a stay-at-home mom. Most of our friends lived outside our immediate community and didn't have children. This all added up to a nonexistent social life for my husband and me.

I needed to fix this, so I became a room parent in my son's kindergarten class, partly to spend time with him, but also to make more friends within the school community. I also signed my son up for weekend soccer. While those activities gave me the opportunity to socialize with other moms, it was challenging to cultivate friendships. I only saw my fellow room parents a few times a year, usually amid the gleeful chaos of class parties. On the soccer sidelines, I found it impossible to simultaneously watch the game, keep track of my young children, and maintain conversations with other parents.

I craved deeper interactions with the smart, interesting moms I saw around school. But we all led busy lives. How could I make this happen?

"You should throw a party," suggested a friend who happened to be a professional event planner.

"I can't do that. I don't really know these women," I replied quickly. I hardly even had my closest friends over to my house. The thought of hosting an adult party terrified me to my introvert core.

"Just invite a few people that you've talked to and ask them to bring along a friend. You'll meet even more people that way. It will be fun," my event-planner friend said.

I ran this idea by my husband, certain he'd agree it wouldn't work. "Great idea," he said. "I'll stay upstairs with the kids, and the party can take place on the main floor. Can you serve chicken wings?"

Chicken wings were not going to make the menu. However, channeling some of my husband's enthusiasm, I picked a date and set up an electronic invitation, cobbling together a guest list of moms from my son's soccer team, my fellow room moms, and a few other moms I'd started saying "hi" to at school pick-up.

But I didn't hit Send.

I started to talk myself out of it. There were so many reasons this wouldn't work. With five mess-makers in my household, what if I couldn't get my house "party-ready" in time? What if guests noticed the stains on my carpet, or the outdated window treatments that I'd always disliked? What if someone asked to tour my basement, the general dumping ground for every orphaned object my family possessed? What if no one showed up? What if everyone showed up and had an awful time?

"None of that will happen," my event-planner friend assured me. "People will be glad to have a chance to get out and recharge their own batteries."

I wasn't so sure, but I sent out the invitations anyway. Then I waited, checking the online RSVP status approximately 2,000 times a day.

Replies began trickling in. Before long, I was expecting thirty-eight women at my house. Thirty-eight!

I cleaned a lot during the week leading up to the party. This helped distract me from my anxiety. On the designated night, I kissed my husband and kids as they trekked upstairs toward bedtime. I set out an assortment of beverages and tried-and-true appetizers, none of which were chicken wings. I queued up my specially chosen "fun" music program on my iPad. And I nearly bit my nails down to bloody nubs.

But you know what? Everyone showed up. They even seemed

glad to be there, just as my friend had predicted. Soon after the guests arrived, I had to turn up the music because it couldn't be heard over the chatter. Fifteen minutes later, I had to turn it up a second time. Before long, I had the music on maximum volume, and it still couldn't be heard because people were talking and laughing that much. It didn't seem to matter

> **The more I do it, the easier it becomes.**

whether my refreshments or living room were Martha Stewart–approved.

I was euphoric. Throughout the evening, I had a number of great conversations. Several ladies even stayed longer than the suggested end time on the invitation, and we made plans to get together again.

I've hosted more of these "mommy mixers" since then. Guests sometimes bring beverages or appetizers to share, which makes far less work and cost for me. I've stopped biting my fingernails now that I've got my routine in place.

The more I do it, the easier it becomes. My friend network has grown and deepened, and I've met people I wouldn't have otherwise. It feels very good to be in control of having more fun.

One new friend I made through these parties recently said to me, "Every social group needs some sort of glue to keep everyone together. You're that glue!"

~Kate Lemery

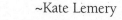

22

A Different Point of View

People who are homeless are not social inadequates.
They are people without homes.
~Sheila McKechnie

During spring break 1987, my church group took a service trip to a homeless shelter in inner-city Chicago. At the time, I had never been to a city that size for more than two days. My roots were planted and nurtured on a farm in eastern Iowa. I also had never been to a homeless shelter or even known anyone who was homeless.

In fact, my politically conservative family believed that handouts like shelters and soup kitchens were a disgrace to our society. We had been taught that if people really wanted a home and food, they would find a way to get it with honest hard work. Even after the recession of the early 1980s, when many such facilities were common, my family members looked down their noses in disgust.

I was in for quite an education.

We drove about four hours on Sunday, to the building in which we would be living and working for the week. It was a former nunnery, and a few nuns remained on staff. The shelter was in the poorest area of the city and surrounded by rundown structures, many of which were condemned. We were instructed not to go out, even in daylight, as it wasn't safe. We settled into our rooms, had orientation and then ate supper. It was the only meal that we didn't help prepare and serve during that week.

Monday morning, after we had cooked breakfast, ate, and cleaned up, I was one of four selected to go on the "Food Run." It turned out to be an eye-opening experience. While we were not completely self-sufficient on our family farm, we butchered our own meat, grew large gardens, and had some fruit trees. We always had fresh fruits and vegetables in season and many home-canned goods the rest of the year.

Gary, a shelter staff member, and we four volunteers climbed into the fourteen-passenger van, only to discover that the back two seats had been removed. *Odd*, I thought.

We made small talk for the next fifteen or twenty minutes, and then Gary pulled in behind a grocery store. One of the employees met us on the dock and started handing over crates, cartons and boxes of vegetables, fruits, meat, dented or rusted canned goods, and day-old bakery items. We went through this same ritual at three other stores, and I finally understood why the back two rows of seats had been removed from the van.

"This is how many stores in the city dispose of food that's still edible but can't be sold to their customers for some reason," Gary explained. "Stores also donate to food banks, churches, or soup kitchens. It's a pretty good deal all around. They aren't throwing it in the landfill, and it cuts down on food costs for us."

The next day, I sat next to Devon at lunch. He was a young man with ash-blond hair that was nicely cut. Unlike many homeless people, his hazel eyes were unafraid and unashamed to meet mine. Curious, I started a conversation with him. He revealed he was nineteen, had grown up nearby and graduated from high school the previous year. He had been unable to find a job since. His parents couldn't help him financially because they had five younger children at home. Having spent part of my working career in the fast-food industry, I asked him if he had considered that option. I explained that if he worked hard, he could eventually enter a management program and make good money. Devon lowered his eyes, and there was an awkward silence. Finally, he admitted that he couldn't read. He couldn't have said anything that would have surprised me more.

"But you have a diploma," I stammered.

"I struggled in school, and they don't have enough resources in the public schools. Too many kids in a class, not enough books. They just kept passing me from one grade to another, whether I had learned what I was supposed to or not."

I was shocked. I couldn't wrap my mind around this. When it finally did, a few circuits blew. If he couldn't read, Devon couldn't fill out a job application. And even if he got around that issue and got hired by, say, McDonald's, he wouldn't be able to tell the difference between a box of French fries and a case of beef patties, or read the menu or the cash register keys. Reading was crucial in our world, and if one couldn't do it...

I came home realizing how lucky I was.

I made an offer, and Devon accepted: Every afternoon for the rest of the week, we found two hours a day to work on his reading skills. I discovered he could read a little. He improved by the end of the week, and we asked one of the staff to continue helping him. I've always wondered where he ended up.

I met Jim and his family of four during supper on Wednesday. He and his wife of twenty-one years, Liz, were in their mid-forties. Their daughters were ten and thirteen. Jim had been employed as a middle manager at a large company for ten years, living an upper middle-class life. Then his company made cutbacks, and Jim was one of the first they let go. Liz had always been a stay-at-home wife and mother. Jim looked for another job immediately, only to discover his company was not the only one eliminating middle management. He was willing to get a lesser job, but no one would hire him for positions for which he was "overqualified."

In two years, they had gone through all of their savings, a good chunk of Jim's retirement fund, and maxed out their credit cards. They lost their home and most of their belongings because they could no longer afford the storage units. They had no family in state, and they were trying to stay in the same school district so the girls would at least have that stability. They were living in their car, but they could no longer afford food. They were trying to hold on until the end of the school year so the girls could finish in their current schools. Then they would have to move to wherever in the country Jim could get a job. Liz would also have to go to work and try to rebuild their lives. They were discouraged, depressed and defeated.

More revelations awaited me that week, as I met person after person, good people who were just down on their luck. I came home realizing how lucky I was. I had a roof over my head, food on the table and jobs that paid my bills. Those people we helped, the ones who my family thought were lazy, now had faces and stories to go with them. I would never see homeless people the same way again.

~Robyn R. Ireland

23

Stepping Into the Comfort Zone

You can't always change your situation, but you can always change your attitude.

~Larry Hargraves

" I don't even want to go on this vacation," I confided to my husband as I heaved the suitcase up onto the bed. "It'll be good for you," Eric said. "I really think so."

"But I'm miserable," I whined, as I tossed random outfits into the suitcase, not even bothering to match tops and bottoms.

"It's been a rough six months, for sure," Eric said. "I know how close you and your mom were, and of course you're still grieving. But sweetie... life goes on."

"I hate when people say that," I moaned. "Maybe everyone else's life has gone on, but mine feels as though it's come to a grinding halt."

"I know, honey, so maybe this trip will be a good change of scenery."

"Yeah, maybe," I said, collapsing into my husband's arms. "It's just that no one gets how much it hurts. No one even talks to me, really. People just shoot me pitiful looks and ignore me."

"I think in awkward situations, oftentimes people clam up," Eric replied.

"Well, I don't get it," I said. "It seems to me that as humans we should prop one another up in times of pain. We should offer advice, comfort, and encouragement."

I took a deep breath and exhaled, feeling my neck for Mom's raindrop-shaped pendant that hung from a delicate, silver chain.

"Can't I just stay home and wallow?" I begged.

"If we didn't have kids, yes, maybe that would be an option. But Christy, our family needs a break. It'll be good to get away. Trust me."

I understood where Eric was coming from, and I did trust him. But I was scared. And sad. And lost. And lonely.

A few days later, our family was sprawled on the beach. The boys built sand castles and played in the waves. I mostly stared into space. *Mom should have been here,* I thought. She often joined our family vacations, and her presence really kicked up the fun factor a notch. I tried focusing on other things, but I couldn't stop thinking about how much I missed her and how much it hurt.

> **You can do this, Christy,** *I told myself.* **Just speak from your heart.**

"Why don't you go shopping?" Eric suggested one evening after dinner.

Out of habit, my ears perked. Oh, how I loved to shop. But almost immediately, my spirits fell. Mom had been my shopping buddy since I was a teenager. The thought of popping in and out of stores without her by my side was almost too much to bear. Still, I knew I had to adjust to my new reality. I needed to learn how to venture out on my own.

"Alright," I said. "I'll be back in an hour."

For the next thirty minutes, I meandered in and out of little souvenir shops, perusing beach towels, mugs, and key chains. I was studying a blinged-out baseball cap when a teenage girl suddenly caught my eye. It was clear she was with her mother. Immediately, my heart sank, forlorn that one-half of my mother-daughter shopping duo was gone.

I couldn't help but watch the girl, who was probably sixteen or seventeen years old, as she sifted through a bin of sandals. When she opened her mouth to address her mom, however, my breath caught in my throat.

"You're only wanting me to get the bigger size so that you can wear them!" she hissed. "Mom, you're such a b----!"

My eyebrows shot up. The mother sighed. The girl rolled her eyes.

It broke my heart to hear a child speak to a parent with such disrespect.

"How much are they?" the mom asked.

"Sixty-seven dollars."

The mother shook her head. "Nope, that's too much."

The girl exhaled sharply and repeated her earlier insult.

Customers watched with gaping mouths as my eyes filled with tears. I felt an urgent need to do something, but what? I was never one to approach a stranger, especially in such an uncomfortable situation.

For the next several moments, I played a game of emotional ping-pong in my head.

Go over there! I thought with one side of my mind.

No way! Who am I to butt into their conversation? the other side argued.

Just go! Say something! the first side insisted.

Like what? I don't know what to say. Just keep quiet! the other side said.

But even as I battled it out in my brain, my feet began walking toward the girl. And though I hadn't a clue what to say, I didn't stop until I was standing directly in front of her.

You can do this, Christy, I told myself. *Just speak from your heart.*

"I'm sorry," I said softly as I reached out and touched the daughter's shoulder, "but I have to tell you…"

A lump formed in the back of my throat as tears trickled down my cheeks.

Mom's raindrop-shaped pendant hung from my neck. I touched it with my trembling index finger to garner strength.

"My mom died six months ago, and I miss shopping with her so much. I miss *her* so much."

The girl got very quiet and looked at me with a befuddled expression that was a mixture of pity and surprise.

"I know your mom loves you," I continued as I tenderly brushed the long bangs out of the girl's eyes as if she were my own daughter.

"In the grand scheme of life, it's a pair of shoes, you know?"

She nodded.

"Be grateful that you have your mom here with you because this time is precious and fleeting."

Instinctively, I leaned in and gave the girl a hug. To my surprise, she hugged me back.

She never said a word to me. And that's okay. I was just glad I found the courage to deliver a message of affection, acceptance, and appreciation.

I exited the store, not making it more than a few feet before a steady stream of tears began flowing from my burning, puffy eyes. But something inside me had changed… shifted.

For the first time in a long while, my heavy heart was full of hope. Reaching out to this young girl offered me a new perspective on why people might have been avoiding me since Mom's death. Perhaps they wanted to say something, but were afraid they would say the wrong something.

It was a life lesson not just for the teenage girl, but also for me. That night, I learned that making a human connection and stepping outside my comfort zone might actually provide, well… comfort.

~Christy Heitger-Ewing

24

From Lonely to Loved

A friend may be waiting behind a stranger's face.
~Maya Angelou, Letter to My Daughter

Shy and lonely. Those are two words I often used to describe myself. I could start a conversation with the cashier at the grocery store, but not with a stranger at a party. Being timid made it difficult to make new friends, and my old friends had disappeared during the years of my troubled marriage.

My life revolved around my daughter. When I wasn't focused on her, I worked a lot of overtime and read a lot of books. These were my escapes to avoid facing reality.

Eventually, I had to make a change. I needed to become a strong, happy woman for my daughter. I filed for divorce, and she and I moved to a wonderful, sunlit apartment in a suburb with a great high school.

Life was going to be awesome. We were two girls making a fairy-tale life in the world.

Boy, was I wrong! Although my daughter was the center of my world, she was a teenager, and her life did not revolve around me. I had a boyfriend I saw occasionally, and I made friends with a cashier at the local gas station. The cashier worked in the evenings, and my boyfriend was busy raising his own kids, so I still spent many nights on my couch watching TV in the dark.

My boyfriend and I were enjoying a picnic lunch one summer afternoon when, in a melancholy moment, I described my loneliness. I wanted friends and a social life. I needed someone I could call "just because." I longed to be a part of a circle of friends, like the groups of women I saw at the restaurant while I was picking up my take-out.

Loneliness sounds like it should be so easy to fix. Just make a friend. That's effortless in kindergarten, when you can strike up a conversation on the playground. If only it were that easy as an adult.

My beau suggested a book club as a possible solution. Book clubs are usually formed by friends who read, rather than by readers who become friends, but I was willing to try anything. I spent that evening at home researching book clubs online, but I could not find one. Instead, I found a social networking site that helps facilitate meeting other people with similar interests. I signed up!

That same evening, there was a knock at my apartment door. I opened it to find a process server. My ex-husband was taking me back to court to renegotiate his visitation schedule with our daughter. I took it as a sign and went back online to that same website, found a divorce support group, and immediately joined. I figured someone in this group would have experienced the same kind of court appearance. Maybe I could get some advice.

My beau was concerned. He envisioned the group as a bunch of people sitting around on metal folding chairs, drinking coffee, and talking about their problems. He was also concerned this might be a hook-up group. I wasn't interested in either of those things. I told him I would try it out and leave if it wasn't what I was seeking.

There were about twenty people signed up to meet at a comedy club in the city, so I decided that would be my first meeting. When I arrived, though, the club was wall-to-wall with people milling about with drinks in hand. I didn't know anyone, and I couldn't find the group I was meeting, so I left. I sat in my car in the parking lot and sobbed from the pain of loneliness.

I don't tolerate self-pity for long, so I wiped my tears, blew my nose, and vowed to try again. I returned home and e-mailed my apologies to the group for being a no-show. I explained I could not locate them, but I promised to try something else.

My next attempt was meeting seven other people for a trivia competition at a pub near our homes. I found this small group with ease.

We did not mope about our divorces. The topic never came up. Instead, we spent a couple hours laughing, talking, and enjoying ourselves. And we won the trivia contest! The very next night, I joined a much larger group for bowling. They were easy to spot because I already knew a couple people from trivia the previous night. I was greeted with hugs from strangers who immediately helped me feel like I belonged.

> *I introduced myself to every new person, and I embraced every new experience.*

I made a commitment to myself to spend a year doing things with this group. I participated in every activity that fit my budget. I introduced myself to every new person, and I embraced every new experience. Jim Carrey's movie, *Yes Man*, was released halfway through my year. His character was doing the same thing, saying "yes" to everything.

It was a year of bowling, trivia, and football parties. It was a year of dining out with large groups and meeting for drinks with small ones. There were picnics and holiday gatherings, dancing and backyard fires. That year of friendship and fun continued well beyond my initial commitment. I met about 200 new people, and I grew my circle of close friends, from one to more than thirty.

The most surprising transformation was the shift in my beau's attitude. When we first began dating, I spent a lot of time waiting for him — waiting for his phone call, waiting until he had time away from his kids, and waiting for the ten minutes he had to meet me on our drives home from work.

I was no longer waiting. I was out making friends, experiencing things, and living life. I had become outgoing and confident, but I continued to choose him. He noticed and began to treat me as a prize he did not want to lose. I asked for one weekly date night, and our Thursday night dinners were set in stone. Instead of fitting me into his life when possible, he deliberately made time for me.

Five years later, that wonderful man asked me to be his wife. We were married eleven months later in a casual ceremony surrounded by more than 200 family members and friends. Six wonderful people stood up in our wedding party. Three of them can be tied directly back to that first trivia night and that first bowling night.

~Aviva Jacobs

25

The Wooden Bench

There is no exercise better for the heart than
reaching down and lifting people up.
~John Holmes

I was sixty-eight years old and retired, and I was sitting on a wooden bench in the county jail, hoping I would be rejected. The gray tile floors echoed the sounds of the officers' shoes as they went from one room to another. People came in from outside, and the scent of greasy take-out food wafted through the facility.

Then they called my name.

A guard took me to the middle room where I was searched and patted down. My nametag was checked, and the officer signaled the tower to open the gate. There was no turning back.

I was still wondering how I got there. Our church had joined a jail ministry group, and the pastor had asked me to think about being a teacher. I had said, "No." Instead, I volunteered for the Angel Tree ministry, taking Christmas gifts to children of the inmates. Then I was invited to go with the jail ministry team to tour the jail and be educated about what was expected of the inmates as well as the teachers. On that tour, the clanging metal doors sent chills through me. I knew I couldn't handle being locked behind those doors, even as a volunteer who knew she was getting out. I did not feel safe, even though we were with the guards.

Then a woman named Margo started talking to me about being

her partner. She was young and full of energy. She had prior experience volunteering in a prison, and she felt she could speak to the women's needs and be a good influence. I enjoyed being around her, and her positive attitude was contagious. The more she shared with me, the more the idea didn't seem so crazy.

I talked about it with my daughter. "Am I too old to begin something like this? I am not comfortable with the idea."

"Mom, you could be like a mother figure or grandmother to those women in jail. They would appreciate you."

When I asked my husband, he suggested I give it a try.

My confidence began to build, and I finally told Margo I would be her "buddy" and volunteer with her. She was so excited.

That was how I found myself sitting on that wooden bench waiting to be approved to go to jail.

After I was approved, Margo and I scheduled our first visit. I was nervous. I pictured the room we would be in, with the metal stools fastened to the floor and a buzzer to push by the door if we needed to summon a guard. I packed my jail bag with the soft-covered Bible, unstapled handouts and my pencil with no eraser. I also put in a little packet of tissues.

> *This ministry I once feared continues to draw me weekly to the jail.*

We arrived at the jail and sat on the now familiar wooden bench after signing in. The guard came in, and I felt my heart race. But then he said, "The women are not coming out tonight as there is a problem in the pod."

Margo was so disappointed. "I can't believe, after we got everything ready, that they can't come out."

"We will try again next week," I said. I tried to sound disappointed too.

We were back on that wooden bench the next week. The guard came out and said the women did not want to come out for the service. Apparently, there was a good television program on. Margo wiped away a tear, and I felt guilty at the relief that I felt.

"I don't think I am supposed to be part of this ministry," I told Margo. "I don't feel your disappointment when they don't come out. Frankly, I am relieved."

"You can't quit now," she pleaded. "Give it another week."

I agreed.

The next week I arrived at the jail first and signed in. I sat on the wooden bench. The phone rang, and the secretary called me to the window and told me Margo had called and said she couldn't come, as her child was ill. I turned to get my bag and head out the door when the guard came out.

"Ready to go," she motioned me forward.

"Alone?"

I was checked and patted down, and then followed the guard through the clanging metal doors. The echo of the door mechanically unlocking made me jump. I was in the room, and soon the women would be filing through the doors. I prayed.

One by one, the women in orange entered the room. I was stunned. I saw daughters, mothers, and grandmothers. They had all made bad decisions for one reason or another, but they wanted a better life. I felt no fear, and suddenly I couldn't wait to share encouraging words with these women. Before I knew it, our session was over and the women were thanking me for coming.

 Fifteen years have passed now. This ministry I once feared continues to draw me weekly to the jail. I have seen thousands of women and heard their voices echo, "Thanks, Granny Bev," as they follow the guard down the hall to their cells, and I go through the clanging doors in the opposite direction.

~Beverly LaHote Schwind

It All Started with an Open Door

*When you meet the one who changes the way your
heart beats, dance with them to that rhythm
for as long as the song lasts.*
~Kirk Diedrich

was fifty-four years old. I had been divorced for ten years after a twenty-five year marriage. I was lonely but I was afraid to try online dating, even though everyone told me I should. I wanted to fall in love again, but I figured it would just happen. I didn't want to deliberately go after it.

And then I was invited to a pig roast by my long-time friend Carol. There I was again, alone in a crowd. Weaving in and out of people, making conversation here and there. On the deck, going into the house, I reached to open the door, but suddenly it was opened for me. I looked up from the arm that was holding open the door, and there he was, a tall man, looking directly at me with his big, brown, beautiful eyes.

He said, "I don't believe we've been introduced."

I told him, "I'm Carol's friend Nancy."

He answered, "I'm Tim, but I suppose you've already heard all the bad things about me."

It took me a moment to realize that he was Carol's ex-brother-in-law. I knew of him, of his character and continued good standing

Put Yourself Out There | 105

with the family, even through the divorce. To my relief, I was able to answer him honestly. "I've only heard good things about you." He smiled, and we parted.

That was the extent of our conversation. Over the next few months, that short conversation and those brown eyes came into my mind a lot. I could recreate the whole thing, frame by frame. A few months later, on Christmas Day, I called Carol. To my surprise, she told me that my name had come up the evening before at a family gathering. Tim was asking Carol about the woman at the pig roast. He was describing me! He said he would like to meet me again sometime.

To my chagrin, nothing came of it at that time. I later learned that Carol felt awkward setting up her sister-in-law's ex-husband with one of her friends. Tim now tells me that he assumed Carol had assessed the situation and found him not good enough for me. Poor guy.

> I'm so grateful that I found the boldness to contact him.

Obviously, our story wasn't done. In May, Carol's mother died. A group e-mail was sent out to family and friends about the service. Reading it, I noticed Tim's name and e-mail address. It was as if it was flashing in bright neon yellow! I saved the e-mail. The next few days I attended viewings, the church service, and the wake. I was filled with anxiety about potentially seeing him, making sure my hair was just right and my clothes just so. I felt guilty about my distracted focus. Carol's mom was a dear woman to me! Here I was at her funeral, hoping to see Tim. How crazy is that?

He did show up to the funeral, and we spoke very briefly at the entrance of the church. He remembered my name!

At that point, it had been eleven months since he opened the door for me at the pig roast. After explaining the whole story to my hairdresser (isn't that why we go there?) she encouraged me to figure out an excuse to send him an e-mail. "You gotta take matters into your own hands." She's a very wise woman.

I happened to know that his daughter was expecting a baby. It took me two days to write one paragraph wishing him well on his future role as a grandpa. I was terrified hitting the Send button and shocked that I actually did it! I was never this forward, and this was totally out of character for me.

The next afternoon, I got a reply. He was surprised. "I didn't even think you knew who I was. We never really had an opportunity to chat. I'm flattered by your letter. Let me know if you would like to meet sometime. If not, I understand."

Well, we did meet, at a local brewery. I found out he had just bought a boat. He found out I loved to fish. I even baited my own hook and took the fish off, too.

How nervous I was. I had not had a "first date" in thirty-nine years.

That brewery date was two years ago. My wish to be in love again is officially checked off my bucket list. I'm sharing all the love in my heart with a man who is sharing his love, too. I feel like a teenager. People tell me I'm a new person and have come out of my shell. I glow and giggle. I'm so grateful that I found the boldness to contact him. It all started with an open door, but I'm so glad I had the courage to walk through it.

~Nancy Beaufait

27

Subway Rules

Let us go singing as far as we go:
the road will be less tedious.
~Virgil

W e were just outside the Toronto subway. I couldn't believe what I was hearing from my stepson. "People are in their own world, and they don't want you interrupting their day. Folks on the subway don't talk."

Josh knew I was friendly wherever I went, and he felt it important to let me know about subway rules. I was raised on the prairies, in a small town called Taber, which is known for its sweet corn. Everyone talked to everyone.

As we climbed on the subway, there was only one seat. My husband nodded at me to take it. I scrunched into the space beside a grey-haired woman, and immediately she muttered in a disgruntled manner, "Oh, yeah, she had to sit here. Make me all uncomfortable. I shoulda known."

"I'm sorry," I told her. "Do you want me to move?"

With a huge sigh, she muttered back, "I suppose you can stay."

The words were okay, but the tone of her voice told me I was not welcome in the seat.

"I'll move if you would like me to. I don't mind, especially if it is bothering you," I told her.

Another sigh. "No, it's okay. You can stay."

Since we were already talking and she had started it, I felt challenged to change her negative perspective. I asked her if she had ever been out to Alberta. She waited all of two seconds, and then responded, "No, but we've been through on the way to Vancouver."

"I love Vancouver," I told her and went on to mention the great weather, friendly people and beautiful plants. "Where are you from originally?" I asked her.

Now here was a topic she wanted to talk about, and soon I heard about her life in the old country. She talked until it was time for her to get off, smiled warmly and bid me goodbye.

I wondered if there might be more people who break the subway rules.

At a station the following day, my husband and son went to buy tickets, and I stood watching people. The ticket taker caught me watching him, and he frowned. I smiled at him, and he glared back at me. I kept on smiling and would not turn away. He strode over to me with a stern look.

"Did you want to sing a song for me?" he asked.

Surprised, yet pleased he was talking, I responded, "I would sing you a song, except my husband is with me, and it would make him feel uncomfortable. If I was alone, I would sing you a song in a minute."

"Did you want me to sing you a song?" he asked. Oh my, he had a twinkle in his eyes, and there was a hint of a smile.

"Yes, please, I'd like that," I told him.

Then he sang "Strangers in the Night." I gasped at his beautiful, deep voice. It was exceptional. I felt I was receiving a special subway gift.

Soon, my husband and son joined me, but I would not take my eyes off the man with the magnificent voice.

When he finished, I said, "Your voice is exquisite. You need to share it."

"I did. I was an opera singer."

"You must continue to share this lovely voice with others," I told him.

"This I can no longer do," he told me. "You see, I am ill and cannot be counted on for bookings. I never know when the illness will flare up."

I thanked him for this special performance. By now, I was wondering what else could happen on the subway. My stepson must also have been puzzling over these two events. I hadn't really believed him — that I couldn't talk to people on the subway. I decided to keep breaking the rules.

That night, returning on yet another subway train, I found a seat next to a couple. I turned to them and said, "I know I'm not supposed to talk to you."

"Why ever not?" the man asked.

"I am told people on the subway do not want anyone to speak with them," I explained, "but have you seen *Crocodile Dundee*?" I paused for them to remember this movie character, and then I stuck out my hand. "Hi, my name is Ellie, and I'm from Alberta." With that, they began to laugh as they took turns shaking my hand.

> I decided to keep breaking the rules.

We chatted like old friends, drawing the attention of a gentleman two seats away.

When the couple stood, they said they were sorry to end the conversation, but their stop was coming up. They turned again as they left, smiling, waving, and bidding goodbye.

As soon as they were gone and the subway train pulled out again, the gentleman who had turned to look at me earlier got up and came over. Apologizing, he said, "I could not help overhearing a bit of your conversation and…" We were soon in conversation.

He stepped off with us as we pulled into our station, speaking in an animated fashion. He said he was thrilled for the opportunity to chat on the ride. Who on earth made up those silly no-talking rules?

As we stood out on the platform, he grinned at us and said, "Thank you. I enjoyed our chat and want to sing a song for you."

It was more of a question, and pleased to have two songs in one day, I responded, "Great!"

Then, with a most pleasant voice, he began to sing, and I gasped at the coincidence for his choice of songs was "Strangers in the Night."

I had the distinct feeling that the universe was trying to tell me something, and I agree: People should chat, even on the subway.

Canadians are friendly in the large cities — so much so that not only do they want to talk to you, but they want to sing for you! And if perchance someone tells you otherwise, for heaven's sake, tune out that person.

~Ellie Braun-Haley

28

Frisbee in the Kalahari

Life begins at the end of your comfort zone.
~Neale Donald Walsch

As I jumped for the imitation Frisbee, I collided with a thorn bush, thrashing my legs and tumbling backward onto the ground. After my earlier spear-throwing debacle, I had hoped to redeem myself with a game from *my* world. But challenge Kalahari Bushmen to a throwing contest, even with an object they've never seen, and chances are they'll have the upper hand.

As the afternoon sun dipped low, I had one of those thoughts that happen when you've journeyed beyond your sphere of reality:

Dude! I'm playing Frisbee… in Botswana… with Kalahari Bushmen! Nobody at home is going to believe this.

Our Land Rover had lurched into the desert at 8:30 that morning. A tribe of San Bushmen, clad in the hides of kudu, a curly-horned antelope species, had been waiting for us at a pre-arranged cluster of shrubs since before sunrise. Pinpointing a more specific time was impossible, our local guide, Neeltjie Bower, had explained, because Bushmen distinguish only three times of day: "before sunrise, when the sun is out, and when the sky is red."

A fifth-generation descendant of immigrant Dutch cattle ranchers, Neeltjie had grown up on a Kalahari farm. As a child, she had played with Bushmen children and learned their language. Now, as manager of the Grassland Safari Lodge near Ghanzi, Botswana, she occasionally took small groups like ours to meet her childhood friends.

In lots of places where I've traveled, I've been herded on tourist junkets, so-called "nomadic experiences," which really are just shows put on for money. This was different. This group really did live in the desert as nomadic hunter-gatherers. They followed a lifestyle that has remained unchanged for millennia — sleeping in huts made of sticks, hunting for food with handmade spears, fashioning clothes from animal hides, and sharing their few possessions communally.

Neeltjie translated as her friends walked us through the desert. They showed us medicinal plants they use to treat everything from headaches to nausea to menstrual cramps. They demonstrated how they dig for water and then rebury it for the dry season in ostrich eggshells. They acted out a kudu hunt. The man playing the role of the kudu made us laugh as another man snared his leg.

> I reached in and selected a warm, barbecued beetle nearly an inch long.

In the afternoon, they took us to the piece of land where they lived. Two gumdrop-shaped shelters of mud and sticks marked the central gathering spot. Around a smoldering fire, they shared a favorite snack: charcoal-grilled beetles.

"You have to try one," Neeltjie goaded me. "Come on! You're the tour guide!"

Technically, she was right. Never mind that it was my first time in southern Africa, and I was feeling more out of my element than ever before. I was co-leading this trip, along with Bill Given, a wildlife biologist. Bill was doing the real guiding, along with local experts. My job was to teach writing classes to our safari group, and to perform other tasks as needed, such as administering first aid to anyone dumb enough to crash into a thorn bush.

Another part of my job was to appear fearless and try everything that was offered. If a trip leader didn't play that role, it would instill doubts in the rest of the group. And so, as a young woman held out a basket of — from her perspective — delicious snack food, I had no choice but to stifle my squeamishness. I reached in and selected a warm, barbecued beetle nearly an inch long.

It crunched like popcorn, yielding a squishy interior. A bit of shell got stuck between my teeth. Nausea hit before I even swallowed, but I talked myself down. If the beetle wasn't in my stomach yet, the insect was not what was making me queasy. My thinking about the insect was having that effect.

The men challenged me to a spear-throwing game. The object was to get a running start, holding a whittled stick behind the shoulder; then, with a snap of the wrist, bounce the stick at a mound of sand, sending it flying as far as possible. They made it look easy. They sent their spears eighty feet or more. On my best attempts, I at least hit the mound, only to watch my spear plunk down inches away.

I was looking inept, but we were having fun. Only… something was worrying me.

While this tribe of Bushmen was still maintaining their ancestral traditions, others, Neeltjie said, were abandoning desert living for sedentary comforts. I wondered: *Was our presence damaging their culture?*

I thought of the film, "The Gods Must Be Crazy." In the 1980 faux-documentary, a pilot tosses a Coke bottle from his airplane as he flies over the Kalahari. Believing it's a gift from the gods, the Bushmen fight over the strange object. It brings strife and confusion.

I didn't want to be like the pilot, oblivious to the harmful effects of my seemingly trivial actions. Neeltjie reassured me, though, that our visit was positive.

"If there's anything that's going to save the Bushmen," she said, "it's tourism. But only if it's done in a sensitive way."

Koba, a woman who appeared to be in her sixties, seemed amused when I asked if encounters like ours might be altering traditional Bushmen life. "What we enjoy is we pick up languages and ways we don't see," she said through Neeltjie's translation. "We pick up things that are different. It works nicely. They teach us. We teach them."

But changing her way of living? She laughed at my suggestion.

"I like to eat other food I don't know, and I give it a go," she said, "but it's always what you're used to that's most tasty."

I got it. At the end of the day, I wasn't trading pizza for charcoal-roasted beetles. And, vice versa, neither was she. To suggest she would abandon her world for mine was condescending.

The group had shared their culture with us all day. I wanted to give something back. I clawed through my bag and found a Frisbee I'd carried for two years on trips through Europe and Asia, on the off chance a game might come in handy someday. It wasn't an actual, brand-name Frisbee. It was thin and floppy, red vinyl stitched around a wire ring one could twist and fold to make pocket-sized.

The Bushmen had never seen such an object. *I will impress them with my prowess,* I thought. But, no, they were instant experts who sent me sprawling as the disk zoomed high above my head. I laughed as I picked myself up and brushed sand from my scrapes.

The winds were picking up. A storm was creeping closer. Our Land Rover's engine grumbled to life. It was time to say goodbye.

Sometimes, when I travel, I connect with people I want to stay in touch with. We exchange e-mail addresses or Facebook info. Here, all I could offer was an imitation Frisbee. I handed my disk to the guy who'd landed me in the thorn bush.

"I'll see you again," I shouted as I climbed into our Land Rover. I really hoped I would.

"Come, come!" Koba called back. "It makes us feel alive!"

~Dave Fox

Chapter 4

The Power of Yes!

Fake It Till You Make It

*Your future is created by what
you do today, not tomorrow.
~Robert Kiyosaki*

29

A Day at the Spa

From caring comes courage.
~Lao Tzu

After weeks of treatment following a stroke, Mom was about to be released from the hospital. Without giving it a second thought, I had taken on the responsibility of being her full-time caregiver. Apparently, I'd completely overlooked a very important duty — giving Mom her bath.

"It's your mother's bath time, so if you ladies would like to come with me, you can observe the proper procedure," the nurse offered rather nonchalantly.

Since my mother had always been an exceptionally modest person, I hadn't seen her without clothing since my toddler days. It was not surprising that I grew up with a similar sense of modesty. To say I was uncomfortable with the nurse's suggestion to observe the bathing would be putting it mildly.

My daughter was employed full-time, so she would rarely be helping me with Mom. But when the nurse asked if Jacqui would also be providing care for her grandmother, I answered before she could open her mouth, "Yes. Yes, she will!"

Jacqui glanced at me somewhat puzzled for a moment, but my glare made her understand. If I was going to have to face up to seeing Mom naked as a jaybird, she was, too! I grabbed her arm, and off we trekked on the heels of the remarkably confident nurse.

I would be lying if I said the venture was easy — it wasn't. Emotionally, it was extremely uncomfortable for me. Although physically and mentally capable of handling the job, I wondered if this was something that would ever become second nature.

> I'd completely overlooked a very important duty—giving Mom her bath.

After several days home from the hospital, I could no longer put off the inevitable. Summoning up all my courage, I suggested to Mom that we give her a bath. She agreed; it must have sounded refreshing to her after spending so much time in the hospital.

Never had it taken me so long to gather bath towels, washcloths, shampoo, and conditioner. Ultimately, after laying out some freshly laundered, comfy clothes, I got Mom undressed and transferred to the bath bench.

We let the soothing, warm water fill the tub so she could soak her tired feet as I gently lathered up her body, meticulously scrubbing the residue that remained from the sticky heart monitors and bandages. After thoroughly rinsing her with the handheld spray nozzle, I vigorously massaged the pleasing herbal-scented shampoo into her wet scalp.

Mom's entire body relaxed; it was as though she exhaled every ounce of tension that had built up throughout the past several weeks. Simultaneously, I was so absorbed in making the bath as relaxing and comfortable as possible for her that I was utterly oblivious of any discomfort on my part. To the contrary, the experience was uniquely gratifying for me.

Once Mom was dried off with the thick, fluffy towel, I rubbed lotion over her arms, legs and feet before getting her dressed. When her hair was finally set with rollers, I gently applied her favorite Oil of Olay moisturizer to her face and neck.

"Mission accomplished. We're all done, Mom."

My tired but contented mother looked up at me with her beautiful smile and whispered her first clear words since the stroke: "Thank you!"

"You're welcome," I beamed. "It was sort of like a day at the spa, wasn't it?"

Those were my sincere feelings. Once I jumped in, everything had fallen into place, and bathing Mom had instantly become almost second nature. It was an incredible blessing for both of us!

~Connie Kaseweter Pullen

Sliding into Fun

You don't stop laughing because you grow older.
You grow older because you stop laughing.
~Maurice Chevalier

"Cheese!" I said under my breath, holding a smile as the camera snapped. My grandchildren Levi and Taylor danced at my feet as I walked over to the counter to collect my theme-park pass.

"Grandma, now you can go on all the rides with us!" they exclaimed. I nodded my head, imagining myself standing next to a merry-go-round horse while making sure a small passenger didn't fall off. This was going to be a fun summer!

Then my daughter Kelly suggested we take them on the helicopter ride. "Sounds great," I said, preparing to stand, watch and wave. However, it turned out to be a ride for all ages. I found myself ducking my head as we climbed in and perched on the tiny bench. Actually, a very small percentage of me "perched." The rest was overhang, which jiggled and bounced while we rode along a narrow rail twenty feet off the ground.

We had barely touched down when we were airborne again, this time on a spinning tower. Up we went, all seated in a fishbowl-type unit, surrounded by windows. We slowly descended, rotating as we went. I peeked down and realized how high up we were. Closing my eyes, I hid my face behind the unfazed three-year-old on my lap.

Next, we were off to the water park area. I was fine with that idea;

I was ready to wade in the baby pool while the children splashed. That's just what I did, too, until Levi noticed the water slide. He pointed at it, and I shook my head. "Oh, no, honey, that's for bigger children and grownups," I pointed out. I was glad to close that case.

I continued my stroll through the twelve inches of water. "Actually," I heard my daughter say, "there's a water slide over there that the kids could go on if we rode with them." I shushed her, but it was too late. Four tiny ears had heard exactly what she said. Two wet little hands grabbed my own, and I was dragged, grumbling and fretting.

Up the stairs we went while I did mental calculations. Could a bottom with a berth of 24 inches fit on an inflatable tube with a circular opening of 18 inches with a bumper area of 10 inches? If I happened to get wedged into the circular opening somehow, how many strong men would it take to pry me out? If the tube had to be deflated to extract me, how many onlookers would record the humiliating process on their phones?

> *I didn't stop shrieking until we landed with a massive splash in open water.*

"I'll take Levi, and you take Taylor," my daughter instructed when we got to the top. I watched as she picked up a tube, placed it on the slide and sat on it. Levi climbed on, and off they went with a hoot and a holler.

I looked down at Taylor, who reached her arms up so I could lift her. "Ready, Grandma?" she asked.

I was most certainly not ready, but the people behind me in line were growing impatient. I plunked down the bright yellow tube and positioned myself on top of it. I turned to the attendant and asked him to kindly pass the child. Taylor was deposited on top of me as I gripped the handles of the tube. I waited. Nothing happened.

I heard the words, "Looks like you need a push," just as we whooshed off at top speed. Apparently, weight makes a tube travel faster. I didn't stop shrieking until we landed with a massive splash in open water. Instinctively, I wrapped Taylor in a bear hug as we spun frantically in a circle. At that moment, I started to laugh — harder than I had in the past twenty years. I could hardly catch my breath.

The theme park had disappeared, and all that existed was the sky, the sun and my joy. I had been reintroduced to the kind of fun I thought could only be found in my memories.

My euphoria was interrupted by the attendant. "Ma'am? Ma'am? You need to get out of the water now." Reality returned, and I attempted to climb out of the tube.

"Please take the child," I warned. "This is not going to be easy." Once they had lifted Taylor off, I again began calculations. *A turtle on its back needs to be rolled to the side. If I roll, will the fact that my bottom is crammed into the circular opening mean that I will then be trapped upside-down underwater? How long can I hold my breath?*

Suddenly, I was hoisted upwards. My derriere popped out of the tube with a loud "thunk" and I climbed out of the water, still giggling. I was handed Taylor, and I carried her over to my daughter and grandson. "Grandma, I've never heard you laugh so hard!" Levi exclaimed with a big smile.

I gave him a squeeze. "I didn't think I still had it in me!"

I had assumed that with advancing age, that type of fun was behind me. But I discovered that it wasn't gone; it was merely lying dormant. It was waiting to be shaken awake and fully enjoyed once again, with a whoop and a holler and a mighty big splash.

~Marianne Fosnow

Imperfect Steps

Better to do something imperfectly than
to do nothing perfectly.
~Reverend Robert H. Schuller

Back in the day, the place to be was CBGB. The gritty and grimy club at 315 Bowery hosted some of the most prolific bands in rock and roll history. Bands such as the Ramones, Blondie, Talking Heads, and The Clash graced the stage in black leather jackets and safety pins.

I was fortunate enough to be part of that scene as a music and theatre student at nearby NYU. CBGB became a second home for me.

The owner, Hilly Krystal, had always been kind to me. He booked my band a few times and even gave me a role on a cable sitcom entitled TV-CBGB. (It ran twice, I'm told.)

After graduating, while taking some classes at Katharine Gibbs School (to learn some marketable skills), I found myself in a new band that rehearsed twice a week in Howard Beach. It was a long train ride, but I felt it was worth it as all the musicians were good players.

I stopped by CBGB one day to say "hi" to Hilly, and to my surprise he offered my new band a gig! It would be on a Friday night, no less. We would be one of four bands appearing that night, but that didn't matter. It was CBGB!

I remember sitting on the A Train to Howard Beach bursting with excitement. I couldn't wait to tell my fellow band members that we had our first gig! It was scheduled three weeks out, so we'd have plenty of time to rehearse.

The announcement, however, caused great confusion as the band explained that we simply were not ready to play in public.

Disappointed, I responded, "We've been practicing for close to a year. Of course, we are ready."

These were very talented musicians, and we were all familiar with each other's style and capabilities. Together, we had at least ten original songs under our belt (which admittedly were not anything to write home about), but we're talking punk rock... not Mozart! CBGB had a respectable reputation, but it wasn't exactly Carnegie Hall.

The reason for declining the offer, they continued, was that the songs needed to be perfected.

Well, I'm all for quality art, and we certainly had a fair amount, but I replied, "We will never, ever be perfect."

I quit the band that night and waited for my boyfriend (now husband) to pick me up. I waited awkwardly in the drummer's living room as he seethed on the sofa while the other band members remained silent.

A few weeks later, I took the stage with my boyfriend on guitar and his friends on bass and drums. The songs were easy to learn. I played my keyboard (which I had tackily attached to a guitar strap) and sang a few originals and some covers.

Although we received no high praise, we were okay. The experience was a true spirit lifter, and we didn't break any eardrums, which was good.

I would never have imagined that by taking a risk that night — and putting myself out there (literally and figuratively) — it would lead to so many open doors.

I met other musicians, who later introduced me to more musicians, and within a year or so I was touring nationally as a keyboard player for various rock bands.

I never felt that I was a great musician, but that's okay. I was good enough and, honestly, it would have taken years to become anywhere near perfect.

Looking back now with clarity and a more refined ear, I realize that the songs we played that night weren't very good. Ironically, it would not have mattered had we played them "perfectly" or not. They would still have been considered just "okay."

I'm reminded every so often — in parenting, working, housekeeping, or even in writing a story — that I'll never be perfect, and waiting for perfection would take a lifetime.

> *I take small but bold, imperfect steps, and those imperfect steps lead to new experiences.*

So, I take small but bold, imperfect steps, and those imperfect steps lead to new experiences.

The writer Anne Lamott says, "Perfectionism is the voice of the oppressor, the enemy of the people." I believe that.

This summer, I'll be playing keyboards for my husband's band at SoulFest, one of the largest Christian music festivals in the country. His band needs a keyboardist on a few songs, and I'm "good enough." I'm over fifty, and I certainly won't be perfect, but I'm doing it because it's a new experience. I've learned over the years that taking steps in imperfection are still steps forward in my life.

~Mary C.M. Phillips

Finding My Inner Superhero

You can have anything you want in
life if you dress for it.
~Edith Head

realized as I stood in a fluorescent-lit dressing room that I had
no idea how to buy a suit, or any business-related professional
clothing for that matter.

For the previous eight years, my business uniform had been
a military-issued flight suit and combat boots. When I had precious
time off, I loved nothing more than the comfort of a T-shirt and shorts
or sweats.

After honorably separating from the military, it was time to assemble
a business wardrobe for the next stage of my life — and I had zero idea
how to do that. I Googled and saved images of outfits to my phone. As
an introvert who hates shopping, I felt clueless and terrified, simply
too embarrassed to ask anyone for help.

So, the first day I went to a giant department store in an equally
giant mall, I became so overwhelmed that I abandoned all the clothes
in the dressing room and left in tears. "I can't do this," I told myself
from the safety of my car in the dim light of a parking garage.

Then my phone chirped with a new e-mail notification. "Could
you come in for an interview on Thursday?" the subject line read. It was
Monday. This should have been great news. A prestigious consulting

firm wanted an in-person interview!

But in my mind, I could only see the empty space in my closet where some form of professional attire should be hanging.

I shook my head as I looked at the screen. Sure, I could come to the interview — in flip-flops and shorts, because that was literally all I had with me after moving from California to Washington, D.C., for my husband's next military assignment.

I shoved my phone back in my purse and fished out my keys. Unfortunately, a chunk of my cheap sunglasses came, too. Part of the frame had looped itself through the key ring and snapped free when I yanked out my keys.

That was the last straw. I screamed at the steering wheel.

I'd loved sunglasses since I was a little kid, but up until that point my sunglasses had always come from the twirly rack at the gas station. You know, the rack right next to the spinning hot dogs.

But not today. Something snapped, and I thought, *Enough!*

Maybe it was seeing other women walk by with giant bags of clothes and pretty dresses wrapped in slick plastic garment bags, their faces lit up with ear-to-ear smiles. Or the fact that I could let something as silly as a shopping mall intimidate me. *It's just a pile of bricks, clothes, and glass*, I told myself.

I strode back into that mall. This time, I didn't head for another clothing store. I headed for one of the boutique sunglass shops. It smelled like leather and window cleaner as I came in.

I picked a gorgeous pair of Ralph Lauren aviators to try on. And I felt like a million bucks looking at my reflection. Then I looked at the price tag. They were over three hundred dollars! This was insane. I gazed again at my reflection with those fancy glasses on and noticed the woman in the mirror looked a lot different than I felt. She looked strong. Confident. Beautiful. And I wanted her to hang around for a long time.

I took a deep breath and handed my card to the cashier. I'm certainly not advocating that people go into soul-crushing debt on a shopping spree, but I realized that day how powerful a "superhero item" can be in one's life. It could be a watch, earrings, or even the perfect coat or scarf — something that makes us feel invincible every time we wear it. For me, it turned out to be a pair of sunglasses.

There was a wonderful ripple effect in my self-esteem that in turn poured confidence into other areas of my life. I had my superhero sunglasses, and I felt I now looked like a million bucks. But, more importantly, I felt something in my soul shift and whisper, "You are worth a million bucks. And more."

Sunglasses proudly tucked in their protective leather case in my purse, I went back to one of the giant stores. I found the suits. And when the saleslady asked me if I needed help, this time I said, "Yes!"

> I realized that day how powerful a "superhero item" can be in one's life.

Three days later, I sashayed down the streets of Washington, D.C., trying to act as if I had already aced my job interview. The words my husband told me that morning echoed in my brain: "No one knows you're nervous unless you tell them. Act as if."

It was pouring rain. By the time I reached the office, my forehead was damp from rain and sweat, and I had already sweated through the armpits of my black pinstriped suit. I elegantly dabbed my face with a tissue as I came in, and the interviewer smiled and greeted me. She thanked me profusely for making the interview on time despite the rough weather. I touched the side of my purse, feeling the hard edge of my sunglasses case — a reminder of the powerful woman I was, or was trying hard to be. I tried my best to feel as if I were the best candidate for this job — or something better.

After the interview, the clouds cleared, and the sun came out. I popped on those fancy sunglasses and sashayed around the city. I had never been alone in a big city by myself.

I went the wrong direction on the metro, realized it five stops down, and had to get off, find the right train, and go back the other way. I decided to go to a Smithsonian museum by myself, and enjoyed it so much that I went to another one before deciding to get lunch.

At lunch I proudly asked for a table for one at a swanky tapas restaurant and asked to sit at the window, which I never would have done before. When I saw delicious descriptions of things on the menu that I wanted, but with labels I couldn't pronounce, I simply swallowed my pride and pointed. To my surprise, instead of making fun of me, the server proudly rolled off the word in Spanish, then repeated it with a smile until I could say it, too. And I sipped wine as I watched strangers scurry by.

My phone pinged again. This time, the subject line said: "OFFER." I floated on air as I put on those three-hundred-dollar sunglasses and waltzed home.

Six years and three moves later, I've resigned from that position, gone to grad school as one of the oldest students in the class, and started my own business. But those glasses are still in my purse.

Nothing gives me more of a boost than putting those fancy sunglasses on when I need a lift. I go for a walk outside — proudly wearing my superhero shades — and my smile returns immediately.

~Kristi Adams

Wrestling with Imposter Syndrome

*Courage doesn't always roar. Sometimes courage is
the quiet voice at the end of the day saying
"I will try again tomorrow."*
~Mary Anne Radmacher

I arrived at my very first writers' conference and workshop, nauseated at the thought that the whole trip might be a huge waste of money and effort. After years of struggle, I had a few good short-story publications to my name, but so far, I'd failed to achieve my biggest goal: selling a novel. I had signed with a literary agent — a major accomplishment — but she hadn't been able to sell my book.

I had worked on a new novel over the past year, and my agent was about to send it on to editors for the first time. If that book didn't sell… well, maybe that was my sign to give up.

I knew there was a name for how I felt: imposter syndrome. The negative chatter in my head said that I wasn't really a writer — that my publications and my signing with an agent were mere flukes. Indicators of dumb luck, not skill, certainly nothing I had earned. So far, I'd continued to write and revise my work, but as my novel's submission time approached, the voice of my imposter syndrome had become awfully loud.

I checked into the conference hotel and then made myself leave the shelter of my room. As I waited for the elevator, battling my self-consciousness, I reminded myself that I was there to make connections and become a better writer. That wouldn't happen if I hid in my room. I didn't want to squander the money I'd spent on airfare and registration, either.

> *I knew there was a name for how I felt: imposter syndrome.*

Workshop staff members were setting up a conference room. Taking a deep breath, I introduced myself. "Can I help?" I asked.

They were happy to put me to work putting paperwork in binders. I began to relax; no one had outed me as a fraud yet. More attendees began to show up, including some writers I knew from groups online. Soon enough, I had an invitation to eat supper with some new friends.

The next day kicked off the full conference. One of the speakers talked about how his first book was rejected by every publishing house, but his next book sold — and he was then able to go back and sell his first book, too. I felt a strange surge of hope.

I sidled up to him during the next break and explained my own predicament. "What do you do when your book won't sell?" I asked. "What if the next one doesn't sell either?"

He looked me in the eye and offered me an understanding smile. "You do the only thing you can do: keep writing."

I walked away, mulling that answer. That was the crux of the matter. If I wasn't writing, I didn't know what I'd do with myself.

But if my new book didn't sell…

My imposter syndrome wouldn't shut up.

That afternoon, attendees split into groups for the workshop portion. We had exchanged stories online several weeks before and already typed up critiques of each story.

Though I had given and received critiques through Internet writing workshops, I had never done anything of the sort in person. Another woman's story was up first, and we each took turns sharing our brutally honest assessments of it. Soon enough, it was time for my story to be eviscerated.

One of the men in the group passed me his notes on how he felt

I could improve my story — and they were two times the length of my actual story! He then elaborated on his criticism in passionate tones. I shrank into my chair and nodded at his points. Inside, I was mortified. The other people in my group provided much milder feedback, but the conclusion was the same: My story was broken.

I returned to my room, numb.

I had submitted that story to the workshop because I knew it needed a little work; it had already had a few nice personal rejections from magazines. But now I knew the story's problems couldn't be fixed. It was junk.

Maybe that same word could describe my entire writing career. If I could even call it a career.

My old novel was unsalable.

My new novel might be a total failure, too.

Why was I even here at this workshop? Getting rejections by e-mail was bad enough. Getting them in person was physically painful, even though the feedback wasn't intended to be cruel. Maybe I was just too thin-skinned to make it as a writer.

I glared at the dog-eared stack of story critiques. I couldn't help but start flipping through the sheets again. A lot of the advice made sense. I could change the starting point. Deepen the relationship between the mother and daughter. Do more research into post-apocalyptic survival.

I started laughing out loud. The story was broken, yes, but I'd fixed broken stories before. I was a writer. I couldn't help but keep on writing. I jotted down notes as I looked for common ground in the feedback.

Satisfied with my sketchy revision plan, I ventured out to join my fellow writers for the evening. They were likewise shell-shocked from the critique sessions, but we soon relaxed as we shared stories about rejections, acceptances, and our everyday lives. My lingering self-consciousness about my flawed story soon dissipated, replaced by a desperate desire to get home and get to work. I had a story to fix.

My need to revise wasn't just about making the work presentable enough to submit to magazines. No, it was about proving that my imposter syndrome was wrong. The writing workshop had affirmed that there was only one way I could do that: by writing.

I returned home, and over the next few weeks I rewrote the story almost entirely from scratch. Only a few sentences remained untouched. While the basic premise had remained the same, the story developed new, raw levels of emotion. I had raised the stakes for my characters, and for myself as well.

Meanwhile, my agent submitted my novel to publishing houses in New York City. Now, all I could do was wait as the manuscript made the rounds. I tried not to think about it, and I let my short-story work absorb my time and energy instead.

When my imposter syndrome flared up, as it inevitably did, I fought back by continuing to write.

After months of revision, more critiques, and more revision, I sent the newly drafted story to a magazine. It was rejected. I gritted my teeth and sent it out again, to gain another rejection. Again. Rejection.

On the fourth try: an acceptance! And to one of my dream publications! I cried as I read the e-mail. This was vindication, proof that all of the work was worthwhile. I was a real writer.

That wasn't the only good news to come my way.

That new book I feared would never sell? It sold, and to one of the biggest publishers in the world.

Even with those successes, I still struggle through awful rough drafts and long strings of rejections and bad reviews. I continue to battle imposter syndrome. But through it all, I keep writing. I'm a writer, and that's what I do.

~Beth Cato

34

The Girly Girls Try Something Different

*There is no comfort in the growth zone
and no growth in the comfort zone.*
~Author Unknown

All the girls in my family are girly girls. My mother, my three daughters, my two granddaughters, and I all enjoy feminine things. I love knitting, crocheting, sewing, cake decorating, jewelry making, teaching kindergarten, and reading magazines about movie stars. My daughters and I love make-up, hairdos, fashion, and anything made out of lace or satin. My daughters and I all participated in ballet lessons, tap dance lessons, baton twirling, and cheerleading. We all love the color pink.

My husband has always been outnumbered by the females in his life. One of his favorite sayings is, "I always wanted to be surrounded by a harem of pretty girls, but being Dad in this family shows God's sense of humor."

Nevertheless, when the girly girls needed to help out their poor, outnumbered man, they came through beautifully. It started when we moved from California to Colorado to be closer to our mothers, who were beginning to need our help.

An expert black belt in kung fu san soo, a Chinese martial art, my husband opened a kung fu san soo studio. I had no interest in it and rarely went to watch his workouts or demonstrations.

After his kung fu school was open for about a week, the girls and I decided to see how it was going. We were profoundly upset to see there wasn't a single student in the school as we drove by. My husband was standing alone in the dojo waiting for customers.

We had to act!

We each got a kung fu uniform called a gi, curled our hair, painted our nails, and decided to be his students until he got some "real" students. We thought it was better to have five people in the school rather than just him if a passerby looked in the window. He started teaching us moves and forms. We found that some of the techniques actually were similar to ballet moves. We learned to block with the left hand, step right, punch with the right hand, leg sweep, and bring down the opponent. It was kind of fun — and challenging, too!

Eventually, we got actual students in our school. There were many macho men and teenage boys, but we attracted lots of other girls and women as well.

We were hooked by then, so we stayed on as students. We learned how to kick, block, punch, do various aikido techniques, grapple, and protect ourselves after being knocked to the ground. We learned to throw men over our shoulders as well as how to be thrown over a man's shoulder. We learned to break boards and use many different weapons, such as Chinese swords, butterfly swords, spears, staffs, and nunchucks. Of course, I favored the fighting fans because they were beautiful yet functional. We learned to fight off attackers with knives and also fight off multiple attackers.

We participated in many demonstrations through the years. My daughters and I all reached the black-belt level. I ended up teaching the women and children with my daughters' help. I also taught self-defense classes to women in the community over the years. We taught at the kung fu school for seventeen years. Eventually, I became one of only a dozen women in the United States to become a master black belt in this extremely physical martial art. Kung fu san soo ended up being a wonderful family bonding activity.

We made the kung fu school attractive and welcoming to anyone who entered. We had a prize display for kids who did well in school and in kung fu. Besides the traditional plastic weapons, Bruce Lee magazines, headbands with yin and yang symbols, and other toys boys enjoyed, we included Barbie dolls and costume jewelry. There was something in that display for everyone. It was quite a hit!

One special student was a frail seven-year-old girl. She was going blind and had other health problems. Her mother brought her into our school one day, and we took it from there. With my daughters' help and encouragement, this little girl got to be a real karate kid. She enjoyed learning to kick and punch and participate in the demonstrations. Although she is now a blind, grown adult, we are happy she learned kung fu with us, and I'm confident she can protect herself if she needs to.

> *I am proud to say my daughters can protect themselves if attacked.*

I am proud to say my daughters can protect themselves if attacked. They are more self-assured in every area of their lives. Of course, my husband used to say when they were teens, "I know they can fight off guys who try to bother them. It's their boyfriends I worry more about!"

This experience taught me to step outside my comfort zone in other ways as well. I have since tried things I never would have considered trying before kung fu. I have parasailed above the ocean, competed in a mechanical bull-riding contest, swum with sharks, and learned Spanish in my fifties, to name a few. I haven't been successful in all of my endeavors, but I'll give almost anything a try!

~Ginny Huff Conahan

35

Stand and Deliver

Never be afraid to try something new because life gets
boring when you stay within the limits of
what you already know.
~Author Unknown

Most days, I'm a minivan-driving, homework-hovering mom. When I'm not thinking about my kids, I'm fretting about work deadlines.

But on this weekend, I was holding a microphone in a whiskey bar in Edinburgh, Scotland, and for the first time — at age forty-eight — performing stand-up comedy! I've always been able to get people to laugh at my stories. But never did I think I could "kill it" in a room full of strangers.

Yet there I was, cracking jokes in a land that was far away — both geographically and experientially — from my regular life.

Each summer, Edinburgh hosts an outrageous Festival Fringe, during which comedy sketches and comedians fill the city. We'd come to Scotland so my husband could attend a serious conference. I was not looking forward to two days on my own. I didn't want to see all the sights without David, and frankly, how many shops could I look in? In desperation, I began reading through the 300-page Festival Fringe catalogue for things to distract me.

And then I spotted the ad: "Learn Comedy in Two Days @ The Edinburgh Fringe."

It sounded like one of those matchbook covers: "Learn to Drive the Big Rigs." Like those come-ons, this ad promised much: In two four-hour workshops, I would learn the basics of comedy while developing a five-minute routine, all for eighty dollars. I figured it would be fun — even if I couldn't imagine having the guts to get up on stage.

The class was located in the Royal Air Force (RAF) building — the Scottish version of a VFW Hall — fragrant with the scent of ancient beer and cigarettes. After walking up some ratty blue-carpeted steps, I entered a long, narrow room with a small stage and microphone. One look at my classmates and I wanted to run. I was simply terrified.

My terror did not subside when our teacher, a professional comedian, asked us to "say hello in a funny voice." The first guy sounded like a pirate; the next woman like Dame Edna. I blurted out something in a lame, New York accent. Oy!

> I was holding a microphone in a whiskey bar in Edinburgh, Scotland.

Among my classmates were an overweight, forty-something Scottish computer analyst; a shaggy-haired, forty-seven-year-old social worker from Edinburgh; a cute eighteen-year-old who looked like a cross between Harry Potter and a young Bob Dylan; two thirty-ish women from England; and a couple of American teens who'd recently moved to Scotland.

Yet, an unexpected thing happened. By the end of the first day, I felt bonded to my fellow funny people and a little more at home in a city where I knew no one. Back at my hotel, I worked on my routine, which I was certain had all the humor of the six o'clock news. The next morning, I trudged back in and found that my new friends were just as unsure about their stuff — but we were all rooting for each other. One by one, we tried out our material. Some of the bits my peers had come up with left me roaring.

When I tried out my own, my classmates helped me make my wry observations funnier. By the end of the day, with my group's help, I actually had a five-minute shtick. I walked from the workshop back to my hotel, practicing my lines in my head. When David told people at the conference what I was doing, they wanted a performance.

So, that night, I took the microphone in the whiskey bar where all the participants had gathered. I riffed on vacationing in Edinburgh and the difference between how men and women travel. I figured on a few chuckles, but people were howling! The five minutes passed as if they were five seconds, and only when it was over did I begin to shake with nervousness.

I'm not likely to change careers, but it was a life changing experience. On this trip, I unpacked a whole lot of fears, and I carried home a new self-confidence and the knowledge that I can successfully step outside my comfort zone, scary as it might be.

~Andrea Atkins

What's the Story?

*If you dare nothing, then when the day is over, nothing
is all you will have gained.*
~Neil Gaiman, The Graveyard Book

"'d like to know why you don't cover more women's
sports." A few faces turned toward me as I stood with
my hands on my hips in the office of *The Silhouette,*
McMaster University's student newspaper.

Indignation had fuelled my journey here to *The Silhouette's* office
in one of the many magnificent, old brick buildings that dotted the
campus. Now that I'd articulated the source of my ire, I felt uneasy.

Who was I to march in and make demands?

I'm not sure what I would have done had I been in the sports
editor's shoes — sorely tempted, perhaps, to put an upstart in her
place. But he took a different approach, regarding me contemplatively
for a moment.

"I'd love to include women's sports stories," he replied in a cheerful
voice. "Problem is, we don't have anyone on staff who's volunteered
to cover them." He paused. "What about you? Are you interested?"

"I — uh — " This was so not going the way I'd expected. "Me?"

I felt a surge of panic. Sure, I'd helped to edit a newsletter in grade
school. But a university newspaper, issued weekly on real newsprint,
operated at a whole different level.

Part of me wanted to turn and run, to retreat into the familiar cocoon
of classes, visits to the library, and the odd night at the campus pub.

Another part of me felt intrigued, and that part said, "Sure. I'll give it a try."

For the remainder of my undergrad years, and on into grad school at Dalhousie University, I attended games and penned stories — even opinion columns. I was often uncomfortable — interviewing coaches for post-game comments, travelling with the players to offsite matches, and sweating with anxiety while I consulted my notes and compiled stories with deadlines looming.

> **Part of me wanted to turn and run.**

And yet, the experience honed skills that I would later apply to a paid job as a sports reporter for a newspaper in Halifax, and beyond that to freelance writing. I even found some new friends among the varsity athletes.

And, of course, there was the buzz I still get to this day whenever I see my byline affixed to a story.

Petrified though I may have felt when the editor made his initial offer, I've never regretted accepting the challenge. It set me on a career path that I might not have otherwise been offered.

~Lisa Timpf

Horse Sense

There's a great deal of power in pretending.
~Suzanne Palmieri, The Witch of Belladonna Bay

M y husband John and I bought two horses six months into our marriage. We wanted to renew a mutual childhood love of riding. My horse was a gentle half-Arabian mare named Se-Se. John, being more of a risk-taker, bought a fiery purebred stallion named Jur-Raja.

"I'm told he's got a fine bloodline," he said.

Not knowing one horse pedigree from another, I said, "That's nice, honey. Just don't ask me to ride him."

What I didn't want John to know was that somewhere between childhood and twenty-something, I had developed a fear of horses. I wondered if city life had stolen my childlike fearlessness.

Our first day at the riding stable, John and I were to join a trail-riding group.

"I can't ride her," I said. "I'm afraid."

"That's ridiculous," John said. "She's the gentlest horse in the county."

"I know you must be right," I said. "I'll work on my courage."

John took the first trail ride without me while I stood in the barn in front of Se-Se's stall, trying to use positive thinking to muster up my courage. Se-Se stuck her head out of the stall and nuzzled my shoulder gently. I jumped.

At the next trail ride, I balked again. I had Se-Se saddled up. I even managed to bridle her myself. But then I couldn't mount up.

"I can't," I said. "I'm too scared."

"Suit yourself," John said as he rode into the woods with the other riders. "See you when we get back." I knew he was applying reverse psychology, knowing I wouldn't move if it wasn't my idea.

This time, I couldn't stand it. I didn't want to be left behind again. Danny, the barn attendant, hoisted me up onto Se-Se's back, and away we went.

"Well, look who's here," John teased. "Miss Scaredy-Cat. Or shall I say, Miss Scaredy-Horse?"

"Ha ha," I said. I ignored him then while Se-Se and I ducked under low-hanging branches and stepped over logs on the path. We made it to the end of that trail ride, and I started breathing again.

"You did okay out there today," John said.

"No thanks to you, Mr. Meany. You could have had a little sympathy for me."

"Sympathy don't make a coward brave," he said in his cowboy drawl, ducking when I smacked him with my hat.

Through the summer, John and I rode the trails near the stables. We even ventured out to other trails in the area. As we rode, I got to know Se-Se better. I had gained trust in her. I was busy patting myself on the back when the bigger test of courage came.

"I have to go to L.A. next week, and I need you to show Raja to a prospective buyer from Tillamook." John had decided to sell Jur-Raja and find a larger horse.

"You are surely kidding," I said. "There is no way."

"All you have to do is put him on a lead line and run him up and down the barn so the man can see his confirmation and gait."

"Gait, my foot. That horse snorts when he runs. You know how he is around those mares in the barn."

"Raja's all flash. You can handle him."

To make matters worse, the horse trainer from Tillamook decided to come in a day early, leaving no time for me to practice showing Raja while John was still there.

The day of reckoning came. My greatest fear was that I would lose control of Raja. He might trample me. He might trample the visiting buyer! The more I imagined trouble, the bigger the disasters grew.

I thought, *Where is Danny? I'll get Danny to do this.* I went to the office and asked for him.

"It's Danny's day off, dear."

"Drats!" I said as I headed for Raja's stall.

The buyer showed up and I was stuck.

"Show me this horse, young lady. I have about fifteen minutes to look him over."

My hand shook as I took down the lead rope and walked to Raja's stall. It had been raining hard, and he had been kept in his stall an extra day. He was, to say the least, raring to go.

> **"Acting is pretending. You can be anyone or anything you want to be."**

I went to the stall and opened it, and Raja tried to push past me. I closed the stall door and pushed my back against it. I noticed the buyer pacing at the entrance to the barn. As I closed my eyes and took a deep breath, I suddenly remembered what my college drama coach used to say to me.

"Acting is pretending. You can be anyone or anything you want to be. Just be someone else."

Something clicked. I loved acting. I could be anyone I wanted to be. Fear had no place.

Okay, I thought. *Apply the rules of acting. You are a professional horse trainer. You've been handling horses all your life. You are the horse whisperer. Horses kneel at your command!*

Just as pretending worked in drama class, pretending began to work for me now. I grabbed that lead line, swung open Jur-Raja's stall door with a sweep, and grabbed his halter. As I snapped on the lead line, I said, "Okay, mister, you're going to prance down this barn aisle like the purebred stallion you are. And you are not going to stop to sniff those mares, or I might have to whip your butt. And don't step on my toes!"

Raja gave me a startled stare and leaned into the lead line. He was prancing now, and I was scared to death. But this was my moment.

I was the horse whisperer, and I was going for an Academy Award.

Raja and I trotted down the aisle, him prancing and me holding on for dear life. He flew right past the mares in the stalls and stopped like a champion in front of the buyer. We sashayed back and forth a few times to show him Raja's fancy gait.

"He's a nice stallion. Good confirmation," he said. "Nice coloring."

After Raja made a couple more turns, the man left, leaving me his card.

"Thank you, young lady. Nice showing."

Raja snorted and looked toward the mares' stalls. I said, "No way, buster. Back in your stall."

When John returned, he told me the man decided not to purchase Jur-Raja, but he had mentioned me, saying, "Who was that lady trainer you had showing him? She did a nice job."

John told him, "That great trainer is my wife and she'd be pleased to hear that. But I need to tell you this: She's not quite ready for prime time."

And I said to John, "Oh, yeah?"

~Kaye Curren

Chapter
5

The Power of Yes!

Do It Afraid

Fight your fears and you'll be in battle forever.
Face your fears and you'll be free forever.
~Lucas Jonkman

A Mountain of Doubt

*Don't fear failure so much that you refuse to try new
things. The saddest summary of a life contains three
descriptions: could have, might have, and should have.*
~Louis E. Boone

The company's social committee planned a two-day ski trip to the Rocky Mountains, just five hours from my hometown of Edmonton, Alberta. My colleague, Michelle, was a skier, and she was excited at the prospect.

"Come with us! We'll have a great time! We'll ski all day and dance all night. It will be the most fun you've ever had," she assured me.

While I agreed that she would no doubt have a blast, skiing was something "sporty" people did, and I was a bookworm. I'd never done anything sporty in my life, and at twenty-five, I reasoned, I was too old to start.

At first, I used money as my excuse not to go. "I just can't afford it," I claimed, confident that that would end the conversation. But I was wrong.

"We'll be travelling in a bus, sleeping four to a room and bringing food from home," she explained. Adding up the total, even I had to admit the cost was reasonable.

I pointed out that I didn't have any ski clothes or equipment, and I wasn't going to invest a thousand dollars on skis for one weekend. Michelle blew aside these arguments, promising she had extra clothes

Do It Afraid | 151

that would fit, and that I could rent boots, skis and poles on the hill for a nominal fee.

"What do you normally spend for a weekend's entertainment?" she asked.

Still, I resisted. I thought back to high school, where we'd had a ski club. The jocks belonged to the ski club, as did the rich kids. Skiing was for the social elite, not for misfits like me.

Having lost the affordability argument, I fell back on my boyfriend as my excuse. "He doesn't want to go, and he doesn't want me to go without him."

Gently, my co-workers helped me to see that this was unreasonable of him, and a very poor reason to stay home.

> I wondered what else I'd been missing out on because of unfounded fear and insecurity.

One by one, they knocked down my arguments, which were based not so much on physical fear, but the deep-rooted belief that skiing was for cool people, and I couldn't be a skier. No one in my family had ever skied, despite the proximity of several of the world's most popular ski resorts. I admitted that the trip sounded like fun, but still I told them to count me out.

They just wouldn't take no for an answer. The clincher came when Don, a co-worker and former ski instructor, announced that he would spend the first morning on the bunny hill with me, teaching me how to ski, how to steer and, most importantly, how to stop. He assured me over and over again that, within three hours, I could learn to ski enough to handle the beginners' slopes.

I had run out of excuses. Like it or not, I was going on a ski trip.

With great trepidation, I got on the bus on Friday night with a borrowed but complete set of appropriate clothing and a bag of homemade cookies to share. My co-workers were happy and excited, and we told jokes and sang songs during the long drive to Sunshine Village in the beautiful Rocky Mountains.

The next morning, I felt a surge of confidence as I donned my borrowed ski pants, turtleneck and heavy, warm socks. As I drew up the zipper of Michelle's bright blue ski jacket, I thought how well the color suited me, and that I would at least look good for the après ski activities.

Don met me at the base of the hill and said, "First, I'm going to teach you how to stop, then how to get on and off the chairlift."

My courage vanished as I looked at the chairlift: small, unenclosed benches hanging from a cable by a metal bar, carrying skiers up into the clouds and out of sight.

Oh, this was a mistake. I can't possibly get on that! What was I thinking? I said to myself as panic set in. I couldn't even hear what Don was saying. I just watched dumbly as he showed me how to turn my feet inward to create a snowplough to slow my speed.

"Keep your knees bent and crouch forward to speed up. Lean back and snowplough to stop," he instructed.

Numbly, I watched small children confidently hop on the chairlift and told him, "Oh, I can't do this! What if someone runs into me and I break my neck? What if I run into someone and knock them out?"

"Just keep your knees bent, and keep your poles down and close to your body. You won't be going fast enough to hurt anyone, I promise. I'll be right beside you all the way."

Finally, after a lot of reassurance and coaxing from Don, I dug my poles into the snow, bent my knees and pushed off toward the chairlift. As I ascended into the sky, I was stunned at the beauty of my surroundings. I realized with crystal clarity that I had almost missed out on a truly fabulous experience, simply because I felt too unworthy to take a chance at something new.

I got off the chairlift, not gracefully but at least without falling. True to his word, Don stayed beside me as I made my first attempt to get down the bunny hill, snowploughing slowly all the way while young children swooshed by me, laughing with delight at their speed.

I can't say I never fell that day, but the snow was soft, and I learned how to use my poles to get back up. A whole new world of joy and beauty opened up to me, and I mastered the easy runs and learned that I loved skiing.

On the long bus ride home, I wondered what else I'd been missing out on because of unfounded fear and insecurity. I vowed right then to keep an open mind as opportunities present themselves in the future.

~Jo-Anne Barton

The Hardest Mile of My Life

You can conquer almost any fear if you will only make up your mind to do so. For remember, fear doesn't exist anywhere except in the mind.
~Dale Carnegie

I was driving back east from Chicago when I saw it: a sign for the Allegheny Mountain Tunnel. I was panic-stricken. "No, no, no. This can't be."

I had almost been crushed by that tunnel just a week earlier. There was no way I could drive through it again.

I can barely say the word "tunnel," much less ride through one. This crippling phobia has been part of my life since my late twenties. Although I had lived for years in big cities before joining the Peace Corps, upon my return I unexpectedly found myself in a full-blown panic attack when my crowded subway car ground to a sudden halt between stations. In that moment, I could not move or breathe. I felt the weight of the entire glass and steel city upon me, crushing my windpipe, burying me alive. My mind screamed at me to get out, to see daylight, to feel the air and heat I had become accustomed to after two years of living under the vast African sky. But, of course, packed in a metal tube in a dark tunnel under a concrete city, I couldn't get out. I could only panic.

I got through that subway incident only because a kind man saw my wild-eyed terror and gave me an encouraging smile. That human contact flipped a mysterious switch in my brain — a switch I was too far gone to reach myself or even know how to find.

Since that moment over twenty years ago, I have diligently (and annoyingly) avoided tunnels whenever possible. In big cities, I take buses or taxis, or simply walk. On road trips, I pore over maps to plot tunnel-free routes. Although some GPS systems include easy clicks to avoid highways or tolls, finding tunnels is a manual process. Locating tunnels underwater is easy because maps show water as blue, but land tunnels are often unmarked.

That's what had happened the previous week. Driving west on the Pennsylvania Turnpike, I had happened upon the Allegheny Mountain Tunnel. I was with my boyfriend, a man as soothing and accepting as I have ever known. It was a lovely summer day, and we were on our first road trip together. I had started a new job. I was calm and happy. My phobia seemed a distant memory. *Surely,* I thought, *I can handle one little tunnel by now.* Traffic was light, and the roads were empty. A few years ago, I had managed a small tunnel near my house with only mild alarm. "I can do it," I told him.

Wrong. I could not do it. Halfway through that mile-long tunnel, I felt the ugly tingling of pre-panic. *Oh, no,* I thought. I started to fight it, but my wayward brain was already racing. It knew we were under tons of rock. It knew both ends of the tunnel would seal, and we would die there like miners in an avalanche. "No!" I screamed as I felt my body begin to swoon.

In a tunnel, there is nowhere to pull over. My boyfriend put his warm hand on my thigh and whispered encouragement. "You can do this, babe," he said. I had to. The only other option was to crash.

I white-knuckled the wheel and pleaded with my careening brain to focus on the road, his hand and voice. I emerged from the tunnel shaken and crestfallen. I pulled over, and we both breathed. Panic attacks are terrifying. My heart felt like it would burst. It felt like dying in slow motion. It took my body and psyche hours to calm down. I understood that I could never drive through another tunnel again for the rest of my life.

On my way back home a week later, I gave the Allegheny Mountain Tunnel a wide berth. Sure, it would add forty-five minutes or so to a long road trip, but I could not handle getting anywhere near another panic attack. Ever.

So imagine my horror when I found myself at the gaping black mouth of that exact same tunnel.

This time, I pulled over immediately. I wasn't going to endanger anyone's life again. I was with my sister this time. We checked the map on my phone. We looked for off-ramps. There were none. We were on a divided highway with no access to the other lane. There was absolutely no way around this. I got out of the car and screamed. I felt swamped by decades of time-consuming workarounds, humiliation, and soul-draining panic. It all caught up to me on the side of that road.

> This phobia had controlled me long enough.

After my scream, I felt better. Then I got mad. This phobia had controlled me long enough. I am a woman who moved to New York City alone at the age of nineteen. I traveled through Morocco solo at twenty. I had climbed mountains. I had joined the Peace Corps. I had finished law school while pregnant and nursing. I had left a bad marriage after almost twenty years and started fresh. In my late forties, I had become a competitive open-water swimmer. I was fearless. I was titanium. I *was* going through *that* tunnel.

I took stock of the tools at hand. My older sister is one of the people I love and trust most in the world. No stranger to mental-health issues, she does not judge mine. Yoga has taught me deep, meditative breathing that focuses my mind and body. I also had a CD of house music. Ever since my teens, music and dance have been places of exultant transcendence for me. In the back seat was a towel I used for swimming — a bubbly blue activity that soothed my mind.

I had a plan. I put the towel over my eyes, breathed its chlorine smell, cranked up my dance music, rolled down the window, and told my sister to drive like heck. I forced my lungs to breathe their familiar sequence: eight counts in, seven count hold, twelve count out.

The wheels of my Mazda peeled gravel. There, surrounded by

love, sport, music, and my own fighter's will—the very things that had sustained me my entire life—my brain and I glided effortlessly through that tunnel.

"We did it!" my sister screamed when she saw the evening twilight at the other end of that endless mile. "We did it!"

And so we had.

Now my phobia—and I—know who I am.

~Joyce Lombardi

The Courage to Sing

He who sings frightens away his ills.
~Miguel de Cervantes

'm an introvert. Growing up, I always dreaded sleepover invitations. Oh, I went — and ended up having great fun — but it never made me more eager the next time the phone rang. It was just so hard to tear myself away from my reading spot on the couch. Youth group, games, dances — which my peers adored — overwhelmed and drained me.

I didn't change as an adult. Church picnics, banquets, business meetings — all were torture. I even had to muster up courage for my own family reunions.

How did I hate them? Let me count the ways.

I hated dressing up. Driving someplace. Walking into a roomful of people who were all talking to each other — or worse, turning and looking at me.

Deep down, I knew it was healthier to interact with people. So I forced myself, especially as I watched my mother slide into dementia, surely accelerated by her own isolation.

My church provided a built-in social outlet, but I tended to avoid the picnics, concerts, dinners, and all activities involving meetings.

This avoidance extended to the choir. I loved singing, but reserved that for Sunday morning in the pew, when I belted out hymns like I was auditioning for Broadway.

One day, the minister told me, "You ought to join the choir. God's given you a gift, and you should be using it."

Though I thanked him and promised to think about it, I didn't think too long or hard. I figured he was just like other people sitting around me, who'd also occasionally told me the same thing. I'd heard his off-key singing and realized he was no judge of musical ability... just loud enthusiasm.

For three years, I listened to the anthems and Easter cantatas. I lip-synched many a beloved song, wishing I could join in. But when it came down to it, I couldn't make myself show up and face a room full of people who'd all been singing together for a long time. And I just couldn't commit to nine months of Wednesday nights and Sunday mornings.

> *Deep down, I knew it was healthier to interact with people.*

But all my excuses just came back to fear. I was afraid I wouldn't fit in with this polished-sounding choir. That they wouldn't want me.

One Sunday, I really leaned into "Blessed Assurance." It was an old, old favorite. When I shut my eyes, I remembered sitting on the hard pew between my mother and grandma. I could hear the wheeze of the organ and smell the altar flowers in that childhood church. I remembered how I'd watched the choir process in their black-and-white robes and anxiously waited to be old enough to join.

Maybe this really was my gift — and my little social group. Maybe it had always been.

That day, an older gentleman who occasionally played the trumpet for services turned around and addressed me: "You should be singing in the choir."

Still, I let Wednesday nights go by, unable to make myself walk in and see those faces turn and look at me. Unable to pick up a piece of music I could barely read, and try to jump in and sing.

One Sunday, it happened again. A woman in front of me turned around. "You have a beautiful voice. You should be singing in the choir."

Flushed with embarrassment, I thanked her. Nancy was a professional singer and voice teacher. And she'd turned around and spoken to me right after the hymn — she hadn't even waited for the end of the service. Maybe I really could do this. Maybe it was a sign.

I decided to go for it. But the night of my first rehearsal, I watched other singers walk into the building while I hid in my car. I still had time to chicken out.

Finally, I got up and went inside. But I froze again. They were already singing! My first rehearsal, and I was already late.

I started fleeing. But the singing had stopped, so I resolved to slip inside the choir room during the lull.

But no sooner had I stepped through the door than the anthem resumed. I'd have slunk back out again if I hadn't been spotted. Again, the singing stopped — because of me.

"Welcome," the director said. "We're glad to have you. What part do you sing?"

My first rehearsal was rocky. Though I love to sing, I read music poorly. In the past, I'd learned my parts through rote repetition. Suddenly, I was thrown into a group that seemed far more musically literate than I was and was zooming through a lot of hard music.

By the time it ended, I escaped with only a sheepish nod to the director, who thanked me for joining them. I dreaded returning. I hoped it would get better once I got used to the pace and got to know the other choir members.

But it didn't — not for what seemed like a very long time. I stressed over my first service — where to walk, and when to stop, turn, stand, and sit. The anthem went surprisingly well, and my small mistakes were pretty well covered, but anxiety left me exhausted. This continued through my second service. And on through the next several weeks.

Over the next few months, the amount of new music only escalated as Christmas approached. I had little opportunity to get to know the other choir members. We smiled and exchanged small talk, but our time was so limited and intense that we never got into a real conversation.

Somehow, I survived Christmas. Then, we were into Easter music. If I'd thought we were cramming a lot of music before, I'd had no idea.

But the music was beautiful, and it nourished me to sing it. I loved knowing it did the same for the congregation. Now, I knew when and where to stand, and which way to turn.

I was also figuring out how to just do my best and not overstress. I began to realize other people made mistakes, too. As our director told us one evening, we were a volunteer choir. Our available rehearsal time was much more limited than many other choirs. "But you really do a good job," he told us. For once, I felt like he was talking to me, too.

I was getting to know the people who sat near me. On Easter, we had a break between services. We sat around and chatted over a light brunch. The woman next to me worked on a knitted collar. We talked about knitting, the daughter-in-law who'd be receiving it, and my new friend's recent surgery. The woman on my other side confessed her worries about her son, and I shared mine.

I left after the second service to bake my casseroles and watch my granddaughter hunt Easter eggs. I was singing one of our anthems as I drove home. It was gloriously warm and sunny. The grass was green, and flowers were blooming.

I was happy, of course, because it was a beautiful Easter — but, even more, because I'd played a small part in making it beautiful for others. I recognized, too, the joy I felt in not allowing myself to be held captive by my anxieties. I was glad I'd finally said yes to all those suggestions and persevered to become a choir member.

~Katie Drew

41

To Jump or Not to Jump

I learned that courage was not the absence of fear, but
the triumph over it. The brave man is not he who does
not feel afraid, but he who conquers that fear.
~Nelson Mandela

The stream ran downhill beside us as we hiked the trail to the top of Seven Sacred Pools on the east coast of the Hawaiian island of Maui, just past the little town of Hana. The two-mile trail ran through a bamboo forest and past a series of small falls. Our group of six friends talked and laughed as we climbed and crisscrossed the stream a few times, thinking how nice it would be when we could slip into the cool water for a dip. We'd brought dry bags with us for keys and wallets, with our swimsuits ready under shorts and T-shirts.

When we arrived at the last waterfall, its height startled me, and I felt an uncomfortable tingling in my legs as we watched some daredevils jump off the top into the pool below. They seemed to hang in the air forever. "You don't expect us to jump off that, do you?" I asked the friend who had organized the trek.

"Don't worry," he said, and led us to a spot about thirty feet above the pool.

Now I was worried. My worry intensified as he pointed to a narrow rock overhang about ten feet below us and said, "We'll jump from there." As the others started climbing down, I hung back, looking around and thinking of escape, but I didn't want to be left alone. Also, I was wearing flip-flops. Tenderfoot that I am, I couldn't imagine hiking back down the hill in the wet-slippery rubber things — or without them over rough twigs and sharp rocks.

One by one, my friends reached the small ledge and jumped off, leaving only my friend Jerry and me. Somehow, he coaxed me down onto the ledge, where I pulled myself to the rough cliff face and clutched it for dear life. When I turned to look down, the drop looked like a hundred feet. I felt paralyzed with fear.

The four in the water were all encouraging me to jump. "It's easy. The water feels great," they chorused. But I still couldn't move.

> *Why was something that seemed so easy to others, so terrifying for me?*

Jerry was getting impatient. "Hurry up," he growled. "The ants are biting me." Ants? I hadn't noticed. I stayed glued to the wall.

"Give me your shoes," Jerry demanded. I obeyed mindlessly. He threw them into the water, saying, "Now you can't go back."

I'm prone to overthinking, and my overthinking mechanism was amped up to high. So many things could go wrong: I could trip and fall headfirst; I could break my legs if I hit an underwater rock; I could panic and drown; I could land on top of someone. The list went on, and it felt agonizing. I was at an impasse. I couldn't go back or move forward. Why was something that seemed so easy to others, so terrifying for me? My friends had jumped, and they were all fine. With all those thoughts, as well as Jerry's impatient voice rattling around in my brain, I felt overwhelmed and exhausted. That's when I gave in and let go.

I turned around and announced, "I don't care if I die." Then I jumped.

The cold water was a shock to my warm body, and it seemed like I was underwater for an eternity. But when I surfaced, I felt elated. I had done it.

My friends were cheering for me, and all my stress had disappeared. One at a time, we slid down the slippery rocks of the first small waterfall into another pool, and then another, swimming, sliding, and pulling ourselves onto large, dry boulders to relax and warm up, and then plunging in again.

It was an idyllic day, and I often think of what I would have missed if I hadn't taken that jump. That memory serves me well whenever I become fearful of something I've never done before. Whether the challenge is physical or mental, I'm more willing now to take a chance on a new experience. I know I can feel the fear — and still, I can jump.

~Jennifer Crites

42

Along for the Ride

> *Ultimately, we know deeply that the other*
> *side of every fear is freedom.*
> ~Mary Ferguson

I sat behind the wheel of my dad's Saturn Ion and tried to fight back my tears. "You've put it off long enough," my dad said, snapping his seatbelt into place.

For years, my dad drove me to and from work without any complaints. He knew I was terrified of driving, so he never pushed me. It seemed as if he actually liked driving me around, probably because he was able to spend uninterrupted time with me. I didn't want to admit it, but I enjoyed our rides just as much.

Now I wondered what had caused this change of heart. Had I done something wrong?

My chest started to feel as if someone was sitting on it, and it was becoming harder to breathe. It was only fifty degrees outside, but I felt like it was over a hundred. "I can't do this," I mumbled.

"Yes, you can." My father put his hand on my shoulder. "You know how to drive. Just take a deep breath and start the car. I'm right here." He smiled and gave me a wink.

I nodded, took a deep breath and started the car. I eased my way out of the parking lot and onto the street.

"See there," he said. "You're driving. It's just like riding a bike. Once you learn, you never forget."

I couldn't believe it. I was actually driving. I hadn't been behind the wheel of a car since my road test in high school. I don't even know why I was scared in the first place — until I saw a speed sign that someone had run over. Visions of horrific car crashes popped in my head. I gripped the wheel tighter and tried to block the images from my mind.

"Remember when you were learning how to ride a bike?" My dad interrupted my momentary panic. "You kept falling off. You even rode right into the hedges." He chuckled.

I definitely remembered that. I still have the scars on my legs.

"You were so determined to learn how to ride that bike. I told you that you could do anything you set your mind to. Next thing I knew, you were flying down the street." He broke into a laugh that turned into a coughing fit.

> *I hadn't been behind the wheel of a car since my road test in high school.*

I glanced quickly over at him while we were stopped at a red light. "You still have that cough?"

He waved me off. "It's just a little tickle in my throat." He popped a peppermint in his mouth, turned up the music and started singing. He had The O'Jays' greatest hits playing. Fridays were always O'Jays day. He knew "Livin' for the Weekend" was my favorite song on Fridays.

Before I knew it, we were home and without loss of life or limb. Unfortunately, I couldn't say the same thing for the hedges. I drove right into them trying to park the car in the driveway.

My dad shook his head. "I don't know what you have against those hedges."

"They just keep jumping out at me, I guess." I smiled. "Hey, Dad?"

"Yep." He eased his way up the porch.

"Why did you make me drive today?"

He sighed as he stepped inside the house. "I didn't want to worry you, but my vision was blurry, and I was seeing double for a minute. I even ran into a sign on the way to pick you up."

I tried not to let the panic show on my face. What if something worse had happened? It would have been all my fault. I would never have forgiven myself.

"I'm fine now." My dad once again interrupted my mini panic attack. "It's probably just my blood pressure again. I'll be back to driving you to work on Monday, at least for the sake of those hedges. Now, come on in here and help me get dinner started."

Sadly, that was the last drive I had with my dad. It wasn't his blood pressure. It was cancer that had spread from his lungs to his brain. I never gave up driving, though, and I will forever be grateful for all those car rides with him. I'm mostly grateful that he made me remember there is nothing I can't do if I set my mind to it, even overcoming a paralyzing fear to drive. Every time I get behind the wheel of my car, I hear him singing the O'Jays and feel his reassuring hand on my shoulder.

~Tammy Nicole Glover

Gliding On

Thinking will not overcome fear, but action will.
~W. Clement Stone

"Lady, you can't go back. You have to continue on," the zip-line worker instructed me.

"What?" I asked incredulously. "I only wanted to zip-line over the Costa Rican rainforest once... one time. I did it. I think I'm going to throw up now."

"I'm sorry," the worker answered, as he ever so slightly distanced himself. "Those are the rules. Besides, the lifts only go in one direction. You have to go all the way to the end in order to get back."

All I really wanted to do was brag to my friends back at the hotel that I had done it. And, of course, to heroically challenge myself to conquer my paralyzing fear of heights and dangling in the air. But I had figured on one and done.

"Lifts? How many more lifts are there in order for me to get back to the beginning?" I asked, my voice quivering as I tried to contain my nausea.

"Only eight," he mumbled casually, as though it were kids' stuff.

"*Only* eight?" My voice was now in an octave it had never reached before. "I barely got through the first time. You don't understand; I'm afraid of heights, really afraid. The halter is too small, way too small, and I'll fall out. The wind is... windy," I wailed as I looked down on the waterfall I had just, miraculously, passed over with my eyes closed tight. That's more than I could say for my mouth, which was repeating,

Do It Afraid | 169

"Oh my God, oh my God, oh my God" all the way over.

"Sorry, lady. Like I said, those are the rules," he repeated.

"I'm changing the rules." I stood firm as I looked at the people behind me, waiting excitedly to mount the zip-line contraption.

"You can't do that," he said, as he, too, began counting the number of people piling up and waiting. "There is no other way to get you back. You must go over the eight other lifts. Didn't you read the instructions at the information desk?"

"What information desk? What instructions?" At that moment, I thought about all my vintage Bakelite bracelets going to strangers because I had yet to sign a will. This would not do.

"Get the manager," I shrilled, as though I was in Macy's arguing over an item.

"I *am* the manager!" he replied, glaring at me.

I heard the shuffling of feet behind me. "Come on," a man yelled impatiently. "Why did you come here if you're not getting on?" Good question. I pondered it while my face reddened and my heart beat faster.

I tried feigning illness, so as not to have to go back over what I considered Dante's Inferno. "I don't feel very well. Would you please call the EMTs, an ambulance, anything to helicopter me out of here?" I moaned.

"You'll feel better when you get to the other side," the manager answered with what I considered a meager amount of sympathy. "Besides, we don't have DMTs or helicons."

> I had stepped out of my comfort zone and into a wonderland.

Defeated, I whispered, "No helicopters?" I acquiesced and got on the contraption again.

This time, I challenged myself to open my eyes. My heart was still racing, and all I wanted to do was scream, "Save me, save me!" But my pride kicked in, and I didn't want to embarrass myself in front of all the other people who were smiling happily on the zip line.

I began to convince myself that it wasn't that high, and the odds were getting better. I had already survived one lift — only eight more to go. I mustered all my courage. Surprisingly, with each lift, I felt my anxiety lessen, and I began to keep my eyes open to actually see the incredible views of the turquoise waterfalls, the emerald jungles, the rainbow of birds, and the unique greenery of the rainforest. I even waved at a toucan gliding by. I had stepped out of my comfort zone and into a wonderland.

By the time I finished the eighth zip line, I was exhilarated and didn't want to get off. I had said "yes" to adventure and experienced the power of confronting my fears. It was a great feeling.

~Linda Holland Rathkopf

44

But You're a Teacher

*The worst speech you'll ever give will be far
better than the one you never give.*
~Fred Miller

I had just presented an oral report on the invention of the X-ray machine. "Very interesting, Miss Nilsen," my tenth-grade English teacher said, "but you gave your entire presentation to that maple tree outside the window." Mortified, I hurried back to my seat and stared hard at my desk.

As a young girl, I was shy. Oh, I could play easily with my siblings and friends, and we'd laugh and talk wildly about anything and everything. But stand in front of a classroom of hyperactive fifteen-year-olds and make a presentation? I'd rather have all of my teeth pulled.

And then I became a teacher. What a strange profession for me to enter. "What on earth are you thinking?" asked family members and friends.

"What on earth *are* you thinking?" I asked myself throughout my college years. It didn't make sense, but I managed to sweat and grimace my way through any oral presentations I had to give and through the classes where I was a student teacher. Those seventh-graders didn't rattle me that much, probably because their minds were usually elsewhere.

However, on the first morning of my job as a "real" teacher, I woke up, silenced the alarm, and decided to call in sick. My husband felt my forehead, shoved a packed lunch into my hand, and pushed me out the door. "Have a great day," he yelled, as I nervously backed out of the driveway and right over the trash barrel sitting by the curb.

High school teens can be fierce critics, but they can also be very forgiving. They stared at me that first day, and I sweated profusely. And that was it. They seemed to accept me after that, and I was able to relax my shoulders and unglue my eyes from the back wall. For some strange reason, over the course of my twenty-five years of teaching, I rarely felt uncomfortable. What did create unease in me, though, was forcing the timid students to make speeches in front of the class. My heart ached for them.

The years passed quickly, and in the final few weeks of my last year of teaching, I was relaxed and ready for my much-anticipated retirement. And then the bomb dropped. From out of nowhere returned the demons from my youth.

As I prepared for my first-period class one morning, a senior student approached me with a wide smile and asked if I would be the guest speaker at the National Honor Society Induction Ceremony. I shuffled a few more papers, mumbled a few incoherent syllables, and managed to croak out an answer.

"I am deeply honored, Susan. I will give it some thought tonight and let you know tomorrow."

That night, my thoughts careened back and forth: "Yes, I will; no, I won't." My husband reasoned that it shouldn't be anything to worry about as I had little trouble teaching my classes. But teaching high school students was different from speaking before parents, teachers, administrators, and town dignitaries. So, I made my decision; I would take the easy way out.

The next day, I gave Susan my answer, but her response wasn't what I expected.

"But you're a teacher," she said, frowning.

"True," I answered, "but I feel I must turn down your request."

"But you make your students give speeches!" she replied.

This was going to be more difficult than I thought. I told Susan I would spend the weekend thinking it over and would give my final answer on Monday. I cried that night because I had no backbone. All night, I tossed and turned until I began to think about the look Susan gave me. It wasn't a look of sadness or anger. It was a look of disappointment. And I knew it was disappointment in me as a teacher — as one who was supposed to teach by example.

John A. Shedd once said, "A ship in harbor is safe, but that is not what ships are built for." I had opted to keep my ship in safe harbor, and now I was disappointed in myself. I contacted Susan on Monday morning and told her I had changed my mind.

The theme of my speech would be courage and how it can be a powerful weapon against our fears. Writing the speech was the easy part; preparing to deliver it was not.

As I waited on stage that night, my knees were trembling and my mouth was dry. With sweating palms, I gripped the edge of the podium. Instead of looking out the window or at the faculty and parents in the back, I looked at the students who sat in the front rows. I thought of my own students, the ones who were terrified of giving a speech but who did it anyway, in my classroom. And I thought of Susan and her comment to me: "But you're a teacher." I couldn't let down those students or Susan. I couldn't let down myself.

> I was demonstrating the very theme of my speech through the action I was taking.

I began by telling them of my fear — a simple but paralyzing fear nevertheless. They would often encounter rough seas on their own journey through life that would be more daunting than having to give a speech. Their faith in themselves would be tested, just as mine was tested. They might make excuses for not taking up the challenge, just as I had, and they might want to take the easy way out by keeping their ship in safe harbor. But it is through courage that we learn that the challenges and obstacles in our lives often exist only in our minds.

I looked down and saw eyes gazing at me intently, along with a few smiles and nods of heads. They had probably never heard a teacher admit to the same insecurities they may have felt.

As I continued to speak, I began to feel an enormous weight lift from my shoulders. I was demonstrating the very theme of my speech through the action I was taking. And I felt no fear. As Eleanor Roosevelt once said, "Courage is more exhilarating than fear and in the long run it is easier. We do not have to become heroes overnight. Just a step at a time, meeting each thing that comes up, seeing it is not as dreadful as it appeared, discovering we have the strength to stare it down."

I'm not certain I allayed any of the students' uncertainties about the future that night, but hopefully I demonstrated that, with courage, we can overcome challenges that we face. The demons from my youth were chased away because a student reminded me that I was a teacher, a role model. Because of her, I was able to look deep within my soul and come to realize that obstacles truly exist only in our minds.

~Gretchen Nilsen Lendrum

45

Coffee for Murderers

He has not learned the lesson of life who
does not every day surmount a fear.
~Ralph Waldo Emerson

On a sunny spring day in May 1983, I started working at the Edna Mahan Correctional Facility for Women in Clinton, New Jersey. I was twenty-two years old. The prison is located on acres of rural land, the epitome of freedom — an insult to those locked inside. Clusters of deer roam about the prison grounds, peering in at the inmates, taunting them with their freedom.

As a new corrections officer, I entered the prison grounds bearing nothing more than a recently acquired criminal-justice degree, an exorbitant amount of make-up, and gigantic man-shoes that felt like they weighed more than I did.

In high school, I was voted "Most Quiet" because my biggest fear was talking to people. I was socially awkward and never fit in. My mother was shocked at my decision to be a corrections officer. I still lived at home, and she knew I was afraid to go down to the basement by myself or to be home alone at night.

The irony was not lost on me that I chose one of the most dangerous jobs there is. I suppose that my determination to make it in the field of criminal justice outweighed everything else, including the fear. Also, at the time, there weren't a lot of career options in this field.

As I started working in the Administration Segregation Unit, I was frightened by the fact that I would be locked into a unit for eight to sixteen hours a day with women who had committed murders. I was virtually trapped in a long, dimly lit hallway that housed twenty inmates. I was numb with the knowledge that my predecessor had been severely assaulted; other officers refused to work in this unit.

The fear of having my braid wrapped around my throat, a repeated warning, was soon superseded by the fear of not being accepted by the inmates as their corrections officer. What if I could not control the unit? I later learned that the other officers had an ongoing bet as to how long I would last in the unit. They took one look at me and said: *Let's see if Barbie Doll makes it to the end of the week.*

The inmates also looked me over in harsh judgment; they instantly disapproved of me. They wanted an old, matronly officer, and I could not give them that. Maybe they resented that my lips were glossy red, and my eyelashes were still thick and lush from my previous night's club-escapades — in sharp contrast to their pale, lifeless faces. They smirked and looked me up and down as if I were some silly girl who had no business working in a prison.

The inmates were really no different from the mean girls in high school, rolling their eyes at me, laughing at me and my big shiny shoes, calling me flat-chested, clown face and Pippi Longstocking. Pippi was a children's storybook character — a little girl with a sloppy braid who possessed superhuman strength and was absolutely fearless. Other than the sloppy braid, we were nothing alike.

The inmates taunted me constantly: *Why does someone so skinny have fat arms? Why does her face look like a clown? What's up with all those freckles?*

Sticks and stones will break your bones, but names can never hurt you. Not true.

At times, the verbal attacks were the hardest part of the job. The job itself was not that different from a flight attendant as I made my way up and down the hall serving three meals a day. As I moved from inmate to inmate, they took the opportunity to throw things at me and make fun of my physical appearance. The inmates could sense my fear. I couldn't hide the flushing of my face, the beads of sweat on my brow, or the shaking of my hands as I poured their morning coffee.

Oddly enough, I soon learned that my ability to connect with the inmates and gain their respect and acceptance hedged on my ability to make good coffee. It did not help matters that I did not drink coffee at this point in my life, and I knew nothing about making it. The inmates repeatedly shook their heads in disapproval, and some spit it right in my face. The complaints varied: too watery, too muddy, too strong, too weak. I continually tried different recipes. I scooped more, I scooped less, and I experimented with the water levels. Each day, I worked diligently to perfect it.

Eventually, they had to admit I had gotten it just right. It was hard won over long months of repeated trials and errors, but the day came when they smiled and gave my coffee a thumbs-up. It wasn't just about the coffee, though. I ultimately learned that being a good officer isn't about being loud and brash. It's about being fair, respectful, and consistent. The inmates came to appreciate this, and they gave me respect in return. When they saw that I wasn't going anywhere, they came to respect me even more. With time, the fear I once had dissipated. I stuck it out. I made it as a corrections officer, and even more, gained the respect of the other officers. I think a lot of officers lost money on that bet.

When I think about my time in this prison all those years ago, random thoughts come back to me: the stale, funky smell of the unit; the sticky, sweltering summers; an old, decrepit floor fan that oscil-

> **Freedom lives in my head, just on the other side of fear.**

lated slowly back and forth, pulling my braid apart repeatedly throughout the day. I recall AC/DC and John Cougar Mellencamp being blasted on radios. I recall the sound of someone coughing and a toilet flushing as the unit awoke to start yet another day. I remember the pungent aroma as I opened a gigantic vat of coffee, the smell hitting me in the face.

I recall the fatigue I felt at the end of a sixteen-hour shift as I'd watch the sun begin to make its way above the trees — daylight breaking — always a sign of hope for a new chance to start over.

I remember leaving the prison at the end of a grueling day, the cool air hitting my steamy face. As I exited the prison grounds, I drove down a road ironically called Freedom Road. Heading in one direction, I moved toward freedom. Heading in the opposite direction, I moved away from freedom. What I have learned is that this is all just an illusion. Freedom lives in my head, just on the other side of fear.

That is what I remember most: how I overcame that fear.

It will always be fear itself that truly prevents us from being free.

~Carolyn McGovern

46

Sunrise on the Mountain

Travel and change of place impart
new vigor to the mind.
~Seneca

When my father was diagnosed, we started making plans. We made a pact that, when he was better, we were going to take a trip somewhere neither of us had ever been before, somewhere spectacular. That wasn't hard for me, but Dad was pretty widely travelled. After much debate, we finally decided on Peru.

We pored over travel guides and paged through glossy magazines as we planned exactly where we'd go and what we'd see. We practiced our admittedly terrible Spanish while he received chemotherapy. Our trip was going to be a celebration, the adventure of a lifetime.

Dad lost his battle that November.

I was devastated. I was furious. I had really thought he'd make it. I'd never let myself consider otherwise. My life careened wildly sideways, and I scrambled to try and cope, to make sense of it. The books and travel magazines were put away and forgotten.

More than a year later, as I was packing to move after graduation, I found all those brochures and guides. It was a surprise. I thought I'd thrown them out. I mentioned my discovery to my mother, and she said, "Go."

It was absurd. The farthest I'd ever travelled was to Disney World with family when I was twelve. And I'd be going completely on my own. Also, I hated to fly.

But I kept thinking about it. I figured, what could it hurt to look into it? I made some calls and talked to some people. And the next thing I knew, I had reservations and flights booked.

> *Getting into the cab to the airport was one of the hardest things I've ever done.*

Getting into the cab to the airport was one of the hardest things I've ever done. I was terrified. I almost cried. Painfully shy and a world-class introvert, I was flying not only to another country, but to another continent where I didn't know a soul. I spent most of the ride trying not to hyperventilate.

Sixteen hours later, I was in Lima.

I didn't follow our planned itinerary exactly, but I did have the adventure of a lifetime. I camped in the Amazon as parrots and monkeys shrieked in the tree canopy. The river was our road, and anywhere we didn't walk, we took a boat as caimans napped on the muddy shore. There were trees so big that twelve of us with our arms outstretched couldn't encircle the trunk, and insects, snakes and frogs so brilliantly coloured that they looked like carved gemstones.

I travelled to Cuzco, which is eleven thousand feet above sea level, and explored monasteries and old catacombs with low ceilings and the weight of old stone above my head. We took a boat out to the Islas Ballestas in the Pacific Ocean, and saw sea lions napping in the sun. I ate ceviche with new friends on the shore and stumbled across an archaeological excavation.

I flew over the geoglyphs of Nazca, sailed to a village of woven islands on Lake Titicaca, and hiked to the Sun Gate along the Inca Trail.

And as I stood on a balcony in Machu Picchu, a city built in the mountains by the Incas half a millennia ago, I looked out at the sunrise and had a revelation. That trip had let me see just how huge and beautiful the world is. It helped me put aside my anger and bitterness that life could end so cruelly, as it did for my father.

I'd been terrified to go, but now I couldn't imagine my life without that experience. I can still close my eyes and taste salt and lime on my tongue, still hear the drumbeat of the music that people somehow convinced me to dance to. And even though a part of me would probably still be scared, I'd go again in a heartbeat. Being afraid is okay, as long as we don't let it stop us from doing the things we want to do.

My life is mine. Tomorrow is a gift, but never a promise. I'm going to go places I've never been, talk to people from the far corners of the world, eat new food, love and live.

~A.L. Tompkins

Chapter
6

The Power of Yes!

Believe in Yourself

Don't let the noise of others' opinions drown
out your own inner voice.
~Steve Jobs

47

The Bon Jovi Challenge

It's a great thing when you realize you still have the
ability to surprise yourself. Makes you wonder what
else you can do that you've forgotten about.
~Alan Ball

Not long after I turned forty, my husband surprised me with tickets for the local leg of Bon Jovi's Have a Nice Day Tour. The band had been a favorite of mine since the 1980s, when I couldn't get enough of "You Give Love a Bad Name," "Wanted Dead or Alive," and "Livin' on a Prayer." I was excited to see the Jersey boys again and enjoy a blast from my past, and possibly hear a hit or two from their more recent musical endeavors.

I headed off to the show ready to revisit those bygone glory days. At the time, I wasn't depressed about hitting middle age, but I had come to believe that all the "big moments" of my life were behind me. I had married a wonderful man, had three beautiful children, written several reference books, published articles in national magazines, and worked on a number of television productions. I viewed my remaining years as a time of a quiet complacency, devoid of any fresh conquests. Sure, there would still be things to look forward to — my children's graduations, their weddings, becoming a grandmother one day — but those would all be milestones "once removed," where I would be a spectator watching from the sidelines rather than an active participant on the field.

The concert opened with "Last Man Standing," a song from Bon Jovi's most recent album. Its lyrics promised "there's magic in the night" to fans attending the show, and that's exactly what the band delivered. From that first song, I was struck by the complexity of this new music, and it dawned on me that Jon and his fellow performers were approximately the same age as I was. But they were continuing to grow and expand and develop creatively, whereas I had taken myself out of the game. As the concert went on, I began thinking that I should challenge myself to venture off in new, untried directions. If they could do it, why couldn't I?

The following day, I purchased the *Have a Nice Day* CD and played it all the way through, at least once a day, over the next few weeks. I found the song "Welcome to Wherever You Are" especially inspiring since it seemed to speak directly to my situation. The words warned against giving in to doubt and encouraged belief in the power of untapped potential. As I listened, I resolved to stretch my own horizons and push myself toward goals never before imagined.

For me, that meant taking a stab at writing fiction. As a journalist, my background was in newswriting and editorial research, and I didn't consider myself capable of producing creative works. After all, I had always told myself I was a word technician, not an artist, but now the time had come for me to step beyond that self-imposed boundary.

> *Thank you, Bon Jovi, for showing me that creativity doesn't come with an expiration date.*

Within four months — aided by Jon's dulcet tones — I had written and sold my first short story, a piece about a grieving father who copes with loss by helping the homeless. Another sale soon followed, and then a poem I penned about summer giving way to fall garnered a national award. By the end of that year, I had a half-dozen published fiction credits to add to my résumé.

Buoyed by that success, I decided to try something I never thought I could do: write a children's book. It took two years and eight drafts, but I did find a publisher for my tale, and the work remains in print to this day. And it all began at that Bon Jovi concert, when what I thought was a destination turned out to be a crossroad. Taking the unfamiliar path has led to incredible places that I would not have even believed existed before that night, and there is still much uncharted territory awaiting me.

So, thank you, Bon Jovi, for showing me that creativity doesn't come with an expiration date, and that the only limits constraining us are the ones we put on ourselves. The road ahead is as wondrous and rewarding as we choose to make it, and I can't wait for whatever lies beyond the next curve!

~Miriam Van Scott

48

A Trying Time

*All who have accomplished great things have had a
great aim, have fixed their gaze on a goal which was
high, one which sometimes seemed impossible.*
~Orison Swett Marden

I stood in the thin light of early morning, squinting at the buoys in the dark lake. Three different triathlons were being run that day. I was doing the longest one, the 70.3 distance, also known as the Half-Ironman: a 1.2-mile swim, a 56-mile bike ride and a 13.1-mile run. Yet none of the buoys looked very far away. Would we be doing laps, swimming between the two buoys near shore? I was new to the sport. I wasn't sure how it worked.

I asked the people around me, noting their fancy triathlon suits, expensive goggles and waterproof distance-tracking watches. "Are you doing the 70.3 distance?" No, they were all doing the "Sprint" or "Olympic" distances, the shorter options. I started to panic. Everyone was younger and fitter than I was, by at least ten years and twenty pounds, but I was the one doing the longest triathlon that morning. They had zero-percent body fat and calves of steel. I had parts that jiggled. A song from *Sesame Street* popped into my head: "One of these things is not like the others. One of these things just doesn't belong."

I weaved through the crowd until I found someone doing the 70.3-distance, a young man who looked like he could bench-press a Volkswagen. I was old enough to be his mother. He clarified it was an out-and-back course. "There's the turn-around," he said, pointing. I followed his gaze past the buoys visible from shore. In the distance, I saw a floating orange marker. It was so far away it appeared to be in a different time zone. I had to swim to that? And back?

I heard a rumble of thunder as rain started to pelt the beach. "Guess the start will be delayed," said the young man. "Good luck," he called as he ran for cover. I stood for a moment thinking that if I got struck by lightning, at least I'd have a good excuse not to do the race.

My triathlon journey was born from a surge of overconfidence a few months earlier. After finishing my first marathon, I reveled in my post-race high, feeling I could conquer anything. As I rested my sore legs, I read a friend's write-up about a 70.3 Half-Ironman triathlon she'd done. She said the race was fun and would be great for someone doing their first triathlon. Hmm, a first triathlon. I had just done my first marathon. Should I try for another first?

I'd never considered a triathlon. I liked to run, but I was merely a casual cyclist and an avowed non-swimmer. I'd always categorized the triathlon as one of those Things I'll Never Do, like scaling Mount Everest or dancing with the Joffrey Ballet. However, with my post-marathon endorphins surging, I was emboldened. Before I had the sense to change my mind, I found a 70.3 race that suited my schedule and clicked the "Register Now" button on the website. Then I went on social media to tell everyone I'd signed up.

The next morning, I woke up and thought, *What have I done?* I knew nothing about triathlons. Fortunately, my triathlete friend was happy to answer questions and even agreed to serve as my coach. She asked about my goals. I decided they were 1) to finish, 2) preferably upright, 3) ideally without vomiting, and 4) in under seven hours, if possible. She thought if I followed a training plan and did a few shorter "practice" triathlons, I might be able to pull it off, even including the seven-hour limit.

Training, however, was tough. Almost every day, I had a big workout that left me tired. I was hungry all the time and I ate too much. I thought about quitting. I had no free time; I was exhausted; I was gaining weight. What was the point?

But I wanted to try something new, to challenge myself. Plus, I'd told everyone I was doing it. I was too embarrassed to back out. Finally, I found myself standing on the beach in the rain, alternately anxious for the race to start and hoping it would get canceled. An announcer said the weather was improving; the race would begin in fifteen minutes. I made my way to the start. The horn blew. I repeated my mantra as I swam: *Don't drown.* I was behind a woman who seemed to be going the same speed, so I followed her lead. Before I knew it, we reached the buoy — the one that had seemed so far from shore — and headed back. Soon, I was out of the water. The rain had subsided, and the swim was over. My day was looking up, even if I was among the last to start the bike ride.

I forgot to look at the clock as I left the transition area, so I wasn't sure what my race time was. Then it started raining again. In fact, it poured. To make matters worse, the wind picked up. I was riding straight into it. I abandoned my quest to finish in less than seven hours.

> **I was too embarrassed to back out.**

Fortunately, the rain let up by the end of the ride. I sped into the transition area, hopped off my bike and pulled off my wet clothes. Dry socks, dry shoes, dry hat — I was ready to run. I saw the race clock: 4:38. I needed to do the run in 2:22 to make my seven-hour goal. I was sure I could do it. About a mile later, I got to the hill — Killer Hill, as I'd heard several people call it. It seemed endless. Because the course required two laps, I'd have to run it twice. My under-seven goal was slipping away again.

I struggled up the hill. Other runners sailed by me. I tried to push myself, but I faltered. As I began the second lap of the run, I saw the clock at the finish line: 5:54. Could I run the second loop, 6.55 miles, in just over an hour? Maybe. I ran with one eye on my watch, doing the math in my head, my brain working as quickly as my legs while the miles ticked by. I picked up my pace. It was going to be tight. I sprinted down Killer Hill, made the turn toward the finish and looked at the clock. I squinted to make out the numbers: 7:02.

I was heartbroken. My eyes welled up. I stared at the pavement and reminded myself the main goal was to finish, regardless of the time, to show myself I could do it. I held back my tears and kept running.

As I got to the banner, however, I realized I'd made a mistake. I must have read the seconds as minutes on the clock when it was at 6:57:02. It now quite clearly said 6:59:19. My heart soared as I sprinted across the line. I had 1) finished, 2) while upright, 3) without getting sick, and 4) in under seven hours. In fact, I had forty-one seconds to spare. I wasn't the fastest — the winners had received their medals long before I crossed the finish line — but it didn't matter. I'd made it in my own time.

~Sue Doherty Gelber

The Pact

You cannot be lonely if you like the
person you're alone with.
~Dr. Wayne Dyer

I flipped off the headlights, but left the engine running. I wasn't sure if I would go inside the cinema or just drive home. I leaned back in my seat, watching the snow fall, and thinking back to the day Emily and I made the pact.

"Some things are weird to do alone," Emily had said as we strolled down the sidewalk.

"Like going out to eat?" I asked.

"Exactly. It's just too uncomfortable," she said. "I get takeout when I'm by myself."

She put on a pair of dark sunglasses that made me miss her green eyes.

"So, what do you think is the absolute worst thing to do alone?" I asked.

"That's easy," she said. "Going to the movies."

I nodded.

"I guess I would feel pretty self-conscious," I said.

"It's like the epitome of loneliness," she said.

I stopped walking and turned to her.

"So, let's make a pact," I said. "Neither of us will ever go to the movies alone."

She laughed, and the constellations of freckles on her face crinkled.

"That's a promise I can keep."

My mind drifted back to the present. The car vent kicked out heat, but I missed the warmth of the summer sun.

I stared at the cinema. It was the last night the film I wanted to see was showing. I should have asked somebody to see it with me the weekend before. Instead, I had waited until a weeknight, and none of my friends was free. Still, I didn't have to go. I could wait until the movie came out on DVD and rent it.

Keep the pact.

But not all pacts last. Sometimes circumstances change, even when we thought they never would.

I tugged on my gloves and opened the door. Snowflakes whipped by.

When I entered the building, I noticed that only a few people were in the ticket line. I joined them. The small number of moviegoers was both bad and good. I wouldn't be able to melt into a crowd, but I probably wouldn't run into anybody I knew. I might even be the only person here to see my movie. It had been out for close to two months.

> *What if going to a movie by myself wasn't the epitome of loneliness?*

But as I considered that, the couple ahead of me bought a set of tickets to see the movie. The teenager working the ticket booth waved me over.

"Same movie," I said.

"Just one?" he asked.

I was forced to verbally acknowledge that I was here alone, which somehow made that fact much more real.

"Just one."

I walked down the hallway, thinking about the pact and wondering if Emily had kept it. Maybe she hadn't. Maybe *I* wasn't breaking the pact because *she* already had?

When I reached the theater, I picked a seat near the top. The previews hadn't started yet. The couple from the line was sitting off to the side, and a few other pairs of people were scattered around the theater. A pretty blond woman was sitting alone, but she was surely waiting for somebody—maybe a boyfriend who ran out to grab popcorn.

I wished the lights would dim and the movie would start. I felt like I stuck out — as if the word "Loner" were written across my forehead. I surveyed the room again to see if anybody was actually looking at me.

My eyes scanned back over the blond woman, but this time I noticed what I hadn't before: There wasn't a coat on the seat next to her. And she had a lone fountain soda in her cup holder. She wasn't waiting for someone to get refreshments. She was here alone.

Why didn't I notice that before? More importantly, why didn't it seem weird that she was here by herself? She didn't look lonely.

She looked comfortable.

Her posture showed that she was completely at ease with herself and her surroundings. Like going to the movies alone was no more unusual than going for a jog or shopping for groceries by herself.

Maybe I had been viewing this the wrong way.

What if going to a movie by myself wasn't the epitome of loneliness? Maybe it was just being confident enough to do something alone.

I decided it was time for a new pact — one with myself. A promise that I wouldn't let self-consciousness hold me back.

The lights dimmed, and the screen flickered to life. I couldn't see the woman now, but I was grateful to her. I wouldn't always go to movies by myself. But now I wouldn't let the fear of going alone stop me.

~Logan Eliasen

50

No One Could Know

*What lies behind us and what lies before us are tiny
matters compared to what lies within us.*
~Ralph Waldo Emerson

At the tender age of fifteen, with a work-study, poverty-program job two hours a day, five afternoons a week, my weekly check after taxes was $26.51. I was already on my own, so with that salary I secured an "apartment" for $40 a month. The year was 1965, and the "apartment" was really an upstairs bedroom in a ten-room, two-story corner house. The bedroom had been outfitted with a gas stove and an old Kenmore refrigerator.

To me, that huge corner room with big windows that would let the sunlight in all day was a fairy tale come true. A small table stood by the south windows. I parked my schoolbooks there and did my homework, distracted by the beautiful view of the park across the street.

That window was where I saw my future, my dreams floating in the sky like cumulus clouds. Because I was free. Free to go outside anytime I wanted; free to go barefoot in tender springtime grasses; free to walk along the small lake on the other side of the park; free to wear clean clothes every day; free to attend school functions I'd not been allowed to before. I was free to be... normal.

But no one could know. If they knew, they'd make me go back or into child protective services.

The following Monday, armed with my free bus pass, I got on my bus at a different stop.

"This ain't your regular stop," the driver commented. I mumbled without explanation and took a seat near the back.

I assured myself that today would be like any other day; it was tomorrow that I needed to plan out. After all, I wanted to wear a different outfit every day just like the other girls.

And Tuesday, walking around the school halls before class, someone said, "She didn't wear that yesterday."

I yelled back, "Who made you the clothes police?" and raced in the opposite direction.

And at work that afternoon, a co-worker commented, "You look nice today."

Day after day, I reveled in my new life, my new freedom. I wanted to share my happiness. I was independent, earning my way, making good grades. But... no one could know.

After the first few weeks, I felt normal, and the clothes comments ceased. I relaxed — until the morning I was summoned to the counselor's office.

> *If they knew, they'd make me go back or into child protective services.*

"Your teachers have noticed a change in you. You seem less anxious, more self- assured. We're happy for you, but curious about this drastic change. Is there anything you'd like to tell us about?"

I looked at the floor in front of my feet. I sighed and then answered, "Can't think of anything." No one could know.

My junior year ended. No one had found out. Summer came. I secured a full-time position. With some of my earnings, I bought clothes for the next school year. I'd be just like the other girls during my senior year!

The school year began. No longer did my wardrobe bring unwanted attention. There was less opportunity for annoying questions from classmates or my counselor. My senior curriculum was to attend school in the morning and hold a half-time job in the afternoon. By running real fast to the early bus, I added an extra half-hour every day to my paycheck and eliminated another chance for unwanted questions.

The year passed quickly. Spring arrived. My classmates were giddy about graduating and getting their own places. I just smiled. They were excited about leaving home. I was excited about having a home for the past two years. And that no one knew...

Graduation day arrived. The speakers rambled on and on about our futures. Would they ever shut up so I could get my diploma? Finally, I stood four steps from the stage; then three, then two, and then my name was called. I raced to the principal, shook hands, and then grasped my diploma over my chest with hands crossed.

As I descended the steps from the stage, I realized I was finally free... really free. Now, everyone could know.

~Patricia Voyce

51

My Year of "Why Not?"

> *The way to develop self-confidence is to do the*
> *thing you fear and get a record of successful*
> *experiences behind you.*
> *~William Jennings Bryan*

When I was a kid, I had one wish: to have the power to become invisible to the world. Then I turned fifty, and it happened for real.

It happened around the time waiters and salespeople started calling me "Ma'am." My dentist was suddenly younger than me and did that patronizing thing of addressing me as "young lady." Annoying.

I was a professional theater critic for over a decade. It was a great job but it was an invisible one. I saw shows, sat alone in the dark theater, and then, alone with my laptop, typed reviews of the people who were in the spotlight.

I reviewed more than 3,000 shows — way too many *Hamlets* and *Steel Magnolias*. And one night, sitting in a theater, I got an idea for a play.

Now, in the past, hustling to meet deadlines, I would get ideas and file them away with the thought, *Not now. I'll get to that when I have time.*

Idea for a novel: *Not now.* How-to book: *Not now.* Piece of chick-lit that could be a dandy movie starring Reese Witherspoon: *Maybe later.*

Years of "not now" and "maybe later."

Then I attended a workshop where the motivational speaker Mike Dooley talked about not getting hung up in the "cursed hows." He said to see a big goal as reality already in progress.

Something clicked. One of those "not now" ideas — to write a one-woman play and perform it myself — suddenly became a "Why not?" I resolved to spend one year, 2013, saying "Why not?" when I doubted myself, just to see what happened.

> *I resolved to spend one year, 2013, saying "Why not?" when I doubted myself.*

I sat down and wrote the play that January, a solo comedy titled *Sweater Curse: A Yarn about Love*. It's about my love of knitting and an old wives' tale that says knitting for a romantic partner dooms the relationship. I wrote about unraveled sweaters and knotty romances, with snippets of knitters from great literature, including Penelope in *The Odyssey* and Madame Defarge from *A Tale of Two Cities*. The dialogue poured out like I was downloading it from a creative source.

I'm single. Never married. No kids. In relationships, I'm not a "closer." In life, I'm more of an expert knitter and writer with a keen sense of observation and a tendency to go for the laugh. My play uses all of it, plus references to Bette Davis movies in which she knits. I talk a lot in my play about how hard it is to date when we're older: "At my age, we should just call it carbon-dating."

The script was done in four days. Every time I thought of stopping, I'd think, *Why not see where it goes?* When I got to "End of Play," I knew I had something good.

That's when another idea struck: Edinburgh Festival Fringe. It's the biggest theater festival in the world, and it happens every August, drawing thousands of actors doing thousands of performances all over the Scottish capital.

"Why not?" I said, and started the process of getting *Sweater Curse* from my Texas living room to a stage in Scotland.

Let me shorthand the process: To produce my play at the 2013 Fringe, I had to raise nearly $20,000. At the time I finished the script,

I had $700 in the bank. But when I called a community theater and asked if they would like a weekend tryout of my play on their stage, they said, "Why not?" and shared box-office receipts with me. When I offered to perform it at dinner parties and country club ladies' luncheons, I'd hear, "Why not?" and then be handed donations from strangers, sometimes hundred-dollar bills and checks for even more. A friend gave me frequent-flyer miles for airfare from Dallas to Edinburgh. "I'm not using them," he said, "so why not?"

The universe was repeating my new favorite words. The great writer and teacher Joseph Campbell said, "The warrior's approach is to say 'yes' to life: 'yea' to it all." Yes, yes, yes and WHY NOT!

I arrived in Edinburgh on July 27, 2013, alone with two suitcases of costumes and props, including hundreds of tiny crocheted hearts I planned to give to each audience member. *Sweater Curse: A Yarn about Love* opened August 1st at the beautiful Sweet Grassmarket theater. First day: five tickets sold. Second day: none. My lighting guy suggested I perform just for him. You know, why not?

Third performance, a few more people. I didn't know one of them was a major critic. The fourth day, as I walked up to the theater, I noticed my poster had five stars glued on it. Five stars mean it's a hit. The critic's review read like I'd written it myself: "This is as good as it can be, and for that, it's worth a full house — of stars as well as people."

For the rest of the month-long run, the house was packed, often with knitters who brought wool and needles and knitted along. Older women told me I made them feel not invisible anymore, that they related to my stories of love and loss. Young people said they wanted to take up knitting after seeing my play.

I'm so glad I didn't get hung up on the "cursed hows." That I didn't go with "Not now," but with "Why not?"

It all worked into my play. My show, which I've been performing hither and yon since that first summer in Edinburgh, isn't really about knitting. It's about love and hope. It closes with a line about how we have to keep knitting no matter how many sweaters go unfinished and how many romances fray at the ends. Love is lovely at any age, and we have to say "Why not?" when love finds us. Love is, after all, what knits us all together.

My cloak of invisibility has worn off. Back in Edinburgh for my third appearance at the Fringe, I was walking past a coffee shop when a young man came bounding toward me. "Hey, look!" he shouted. From his pocket he pulled one of my little crocheted hearts. He'd seen my show the summer before and still had that little heart in his jacket.

"Why did you keep it all this time?" I asked.

"It makes me happy," he answered, "so why not?"

~Elaine Liner

52

Keeping the Change

Self-care is how you take your power back.
~Lalah Delia

True confession: I love beer. And that was okay back in the day, when I had the metabolism of a frat boy. Me — a mere 125-pound woman — could drink a man under the table and feel great the next day. I never even had a hangover. Didn't even know what one felt like.

And then I hit my late twenties and found out. Ugh.

After that I got married, and kids came along a few years later. No more bar hopping.

But, of course, there's the job. And the stress. And the nightly drinks to deal. To sleep.

Until one day last year when I just got sick and tired of being sick and tired. Plus, I was in the throes of a major writer's block. Something had to give.

And that's when I saw a book on Amazon that changed things for me. It was about a woman with an alcoholic mother. She wanted to be a writer but had trouble finding her voice. The writer's journey to finding her voice helped me to see that the thing that had to give with regard to my writing and my writer's block was my drinking.

With all due respect to Hemingway, or whoever it was who said, "Write drunk, edit sober," I beg to differ. It's just not a good plan. We know more about brain science now. Drunkenness is not romantic;

it's a form of temporary insanity. And hangovers are the body's way of asking, "What were you thinking?"

Alcohol was making my brain fuzzy, and I wanted it back — *needed* it back — in order to pursue my greatest passion: writing. And so, with my new mantra, "Writing is my drink," I decided to go sober.

But how? Drinking beer was a way of life for me. Both my husband and I love nothing more than a tall beer... or six. Our marriage was partly based on beer, it seemed, and our mutual love for it. Some couples are foodies. Some are adrenaline junkies. Some are sports fanatics. We love beer.

> *I prayed to God to take away my taste for beer.*

And so, I needed a plan. I needed help. I did two things: I bought a book on quitting alcohol cold turkey, read it, and outlined it so the information would not just pass through my brain the way booze does, but take up residence there. The second thing I did was a big one — even bigger than reading and taking notes. I prayed to God to take away my taste for beer. That's it. Amazing, right?

I didn't even set a conscious date to give up drinking. Instead, I went to see The Beach Boys in concert, and as a first, I bought a bottle of water at the theater's bar.

I went home that night, went to bed, and decided not to drink the next day. And the next. And the day after that.

It's been a full year with no beer or alcohol of any sort. I've gone through a vacation, birthdays, parties, concerts, holidays, and dinners out, and I'm good.

I don't miss it — not most days anyway. Quitting drinking wasn't a life-or-death thing, and I don't consider myself an alcoholic. I know I could go back to it if I wanted. But I just don't want to drink. I don't even think I will like the taste of it because I asked God to take my taste for it away.

Now, I enjoy mornings. I don't pace to the bathroom at night. My brain is naked. And I'm writing nonstop. Plus, I've lost twenty pounds.

Faith the size of a mustard seed can move mountains. Or dry one's thirst.

Beer may be proof God loves us and wants us to be happy, but sometimes its actual proof—alcoholic, that is—may also be keeping us from being the people we are called to be.

~Susan J. Anderson

53

The Recital

Do the thing you fear to do and keep on doing it...
that is the quickest and surest way ever yet
discovered to conquer fear.
~Dale Carnegie

I sat on stage between girls in party dresses and boys with neatly combed hair, the only adult waiting for my name to be called. I focused on the sheets of music in my hands, not the auditorium filled with parents snapping photos. After the fourth child played, I was introduced. I spotted my friends in the audience waving at me, and I took my place at the piano.

I stood in front of a classroom every day, so I shouldn't have been so nervous. But I was.

This recital was the culmination of a childhood dream — to play the piano. I always wanted to play when I was young, but I struggled with math, and I was afraid of all those half notes and quarter notes — the fractions of music. So I refused the lessons my parents offered me, pretending not to be interested.

When I was twenty-five years old I heard that a piano studio in the neighborhood had opened, and the teacher was looking for new students. I still wanted to play the piano and could almost feel the keys under my fingers.

I recalled my initial fears about teaching. I had majored in education anyway, and I had overcome them. Now I wasn't going to let my fear keep me from learning to play the piano. I called the studio and made an appointment.

When Deb opened the door, I saw that we were contemporaries, making it easier for me to step across the threshold. We talked, and I explained how I had always wanted to play Bach, Beethoven and Billy Joel, but feared the piano. She understood and seemed sincere, so I signed up for three months of lessons. Still doubtful and leery of commitment, I merely purchased a two-octave, tabletop, plug-in organ. Although it wasn't the same feel or sound as a piano, it allowed me to practice some notes at home.

Weekly, I headed down the stairs to Deb's basement studio, often passing students who had their lessons before me. Noticing the textbooks through the opened zipper of my backpack, a child stopped me and asked, "Where's your boy?" After many "ohs" and "wells," I finally answered that I was the student. The children then accepted me, and I would sit in the studio and listen to a piece a child was working on, enjoying the music.

> This recital was the culmination of a childhood dream—to play the piano.

Soon, I felt more comfortable around eighth notes and bought a beautiful Italian fruitwood upright piano. It was given a place of honor in the living room. I lovingly polished that piano each week and had it tuned regularly.

After about three years of lessons, Deb announced it was time for me to play for an audience. "Pianists perform," she said.

Panicking, I said immediately, "I don't." Still fearing those fractions of music, I was uncomfortable playing for people and rarely played for anyone. Only the neighbors heard my scales — through the walls.

Deb persisted. "Look how far you've come," she said. "Let others enjoy your playing."

I shook my head and told her, "No, thanks."

Deb held fast and said it would be a good experience for me, but every time she brought up the recital, I begged off. She finally counter-offered. "You won't have to memorize the music." She promised I could keep the sheets in front of me while I played. We practiced, recorded my playing, listened and corrected errors.

Across the stage, my boot heels tapped their own rhythm. I hoped the audience didn't notice me shudder as I sat down on the piano bench and set up Debussy's "The Little Shepherd." Once my fingers were positioned on the keyboard, I breathed in deeply and played the first four measures well. I slipped on the fifth, and stopped playing. I glanced at Deb seated to my left. She hadn't flinched. She just looked at me as if saying, "Well?"

People waited. How long could I sit there not playing? Unpredictable things often happened while teaching that required me to think fast in the classroom. Now I had to think fast on the piano bench. What if I made the silence a pause Debussy had purposely composed? I let a few more beats pass, then replayed the fifth measure correctly, as if the repetition was part of the music, and then continued smoothly to the end of the piece.

As we had practiced in Deb's studio, I stood with my hand on the edge of the piano, faced the audience, and bowed. Applause rocked the auditorium, validating my playing, showing appreciation that I went on stage and stayed there. My friends were standing, cheering my accomplishment. I smiled and took two more bows. If I had given in to my fear of the piano, I would have missed this moment. I was so proud, thrilled and hoping for the call, "Encore!"

The following year, I memorized the music and played again in the recital. I was a pianist.

~Hannah Faye Garson

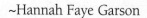

54

The Camera Lens of a Marriage

We are making photographs to understand
what our lives mean to us.
~Ralph Hattersley

grew up in a home where there weren't a lot of family photographs displayed. My sister's and my yearly class photos were still in their cardboard frames atop our stereo. There was a photo of me when I was maybe six months old. And there was a photo of my parents at their wedding, standing in front of a towering white-tiered wedding cake, and a photo of my father in his Army uniform.

There were no photographs of me in a sparkly crown blowing out the candles on the chocolate birthday cake that Aunt Louise made for me each year. No photographs of my piano recital, or photographs of my sister and me opening our Christmas presents. I have to close my eyes to envision the much-loved, perfectly detailed wooden rocking horse my father and mother scrimped to buy for me one Christmas.

I never thought I was missing anything while I was growing up in a home so devoid of photographs. I didn't think that photos were a sign of a happy family. I even convinced myself that my parents decided that money would be better spent on other things besides a camera, such as art supplies, books, piano lessons, and tickets to Broadway plays.

My husband Sam's childhood was just the opposite. Photographs filled every nook and cranny of his parents' home. Every moment of his life, from birth to the day he left home, was captured on camera, and in home movies, too.

I enjoyed looking at their photos, but when the camera was aimed my way—as part of welcoming me into his close-knit family—I cringed and looked for a way to escape. On those occasions when I couldn't avoid it, I'd look stiff and unhappy in the photos.

Standing in front of the camera made me feel too uncomfortable, like a deer in headlights. How should I smile? Was my smile pretty enough? How should I stand? Should it be a natural or forced pose? Would people see the flaws that I so carefully tried to conceal with make-up?

> *I thought myself imperfect, but he saw me as a worthy subject, the woman he loved.*

After Sam and I married, it was inevitable that he would buy a camera to document our lives, but I also knew that my feelings would remain the same each time he pointed the camera my way. I'd find any excuse to get out of being in a photograph.

We settled into being husband and wife, and then parents of three children. I was glad his lens was focused more on documenting their moments and milestones than it was aimed at me. I felt fine standing on the sidelines, wiping sticky smudges off the children's faces, fixing shirt collars or smoothing dress hems and giving instructions to stay still.

As the years passed, and our children grew out of our arms and laps and began to spread their wings, I promised myself I'd change and become one with the camera so they would have more photos of our whole family.

But I still couldn't get comfortable in front of the camera. I continued to step aside when photos were being taken.

This went on until we became empty nesters. I could no longer hide behind the children. Sam wanted to take *my* photograph.

"Sweetheart, look up," he'd say.

"Not now, I'm typing," or "I'm cooking," or "I'm not in the mood," I'd say, turning my head away.

One day, though, I watched him walk away with an ache written all over his still-handsome face — an ache I'd probably glossed over before, not understanding his feeling about photos. I didn't think they were an important part of our marriage — but he did.

It wasn't just that it was a family ritual for him. It was also that we were getting older, and he wanted to have something tangible we could look back on together so we could laugh and cry and reminisce. And I needed that, too — to see me, the woman who had grown from his teenage sweetheart to the mother of his children. The woman who was a sister, a best friend, and now a doting grandmother who still loved to dance. The woman who had been with him through the ups and downs of more than forty years. I thought myself imperfect, but he saw me as a worthy subject, the woman he loved.

That new perspective pushed me past my fears. I learned how to happily pose when someone said, "Smile." I opened my heart to the camera lens and, in turn, opened my heart even wider to my husband.

~Jeanine L. DeHoney

55

My Voice, My Choice

Don't let other people tell you who you are.
~Diane Sawyer

I was that kid who loved to sing. I created makeshift stages on boardwalks or back porches, and dreamt of performing on Broadway. My parents went to see *Les Misérables* onstage, thinking they had never heard the music, only to realize as they sat in the theater that they knew every song because I had sung them in my room so often.

I sang (and danced and acted) throughout my childhood, with musical theatre posters plastering my bedroom walls. In high school, I landed in a competitive performing arts magnet program where, amidst incredibly talented classmates (some of whom are actually working on Broadway today), I came to see my talent as a singer as "not good enough." Not good enough to sight-read sheet music. Not good enough to get a lead in the musical. Not good enough to make the competitive show choir until my senior year. Not good enough to succeed in singing the National Anthem at graduation. (I was so nervous, I flubbed the last line.) My belief in my voice and my joy in singing were fading away.

I tried singing one more time in a gospel choir early in college, but when the college newspaper's review of my solo called it "too quiet," and a college boyfriend told me my singing was "out of tune," I gave in to my insecurities and stopped singing publicly at the ripe age of nineteen. Any evidence to the contrary ignored, I decided I was just "not good enough" to sing and shut it down. Door firmly closed.

More than twenty years went by, and my life went on. I became a writer and editor, got married, and had children. I had let go of my Broadway dreams long ago. I did still sing "just for myself" in the shower or car, and I sang lullabies to my kids, and sang along with the hymns at our Unitarian church on Sundays.

Then one day, our church's music director, who'd heard me singing the hymns, asked if I'd like to sing in a trio for an upcoming service. My stomach erupted in butterflies. I felt shaky and lightheaded. My cheeks burned. That awful voice in my head yelled, "No, not good enough!" But my heart was floating up in my chest at the thought of singing onstage again.

> *It had been two decades since I'd sung in public, and I was terrified.*

As I talked with the music director, she gently encouraged me to give it a try. "A lot of people who sing here hadn't sung in years, and they have found their voices again," she told me. Just the thought of "finding my voice again" made me want to start sobbing right there on the spot.

The little girl in me who simply loved to sing onstage must have won out because I agreed to sing in the trio—though I had major doubts about my decision. The other two women were kind and encouraging as I struggled with reading the music and finding the harmonies. They let me choose which part I was most comfortable with. The song was called "One Voice," an emotional testament to the power of our voices lifted up alone and together, by a Canadian female folk trio called The Wailin' Jennys.

On the morning of the service, I was a jangle of nerves. My mouth was dry and my hands were shaking. It had been two decades since I'd sung in public, and I was terrified. The "not good enough" voice was ringing in my head as the musicians around me smiled and gave me thumbs-up. We stepped in front of the congregation, and it was up to me to start the song with the first verse. I opened my mouth and sang the first verse of "One Voice." The lyrics were remarkably on point for me:

This is the sound of one voice,
One spirit, one voice.
The sound of one who makes a choice.
This is the sound of one voice.

The rest was a blur. We got through the song. I was still shaking afterward when a woman from the congregation came up to me and said our performance was "cute." I felt my face burning again, and the urge to let the "not good enough" critic win and shut me down from singing once more. But others came up and said it was powerful and lovely, and the women I sang with, the music director, and my husband and kids all encouraged me.

Later that evening, I realized that it really was a choice: Whether to let myself be vulnerable and sing, or to let my self-conscious inner critic keep me silent. Whether to listen to one person who might not like my singing versus another person who did. Whether to focus on my successes or my rejections. It was a choice to claim my own voice in the world, no matter what others said, and to claim my joy — my pure joy — in singing for and with others.

So, I made the choice. I chose to sing. That first song was five years ago, and I have been singing regularly since with those two women and six others, in groups and solos, weekly rehearsals and monthly performances. I still may be "not good enough" to sight-read sheet music, but I no longer let that stop me.

Singing has brought a creative joy back into my life. It has stretched me to open a door that I had once closed and to face some wounds within myself. It has reminded me of the immense healing power of our one voice… if we choose to use it.

~Megan Pincus Kajitani

56

The Happy Golfer

Of all the hazards, fear is the worst.
~Sam Snead

When I was sixteen years old my father bought me a set of used golf clubs. "Here," he said, "I think you'll be good at this sport; golf is something you'll enjoy." I'll never forget those clubs. They were Bobby Jones Signatures, made by Spaulding. I loved them, as I loved my father.

His first prediction proved to be somewhat accurate. I did get pretty good at the sport — at my best, I had lowered my handicap to four, a merit few golfers are able to achieve. But it was his second pronouncement where I truly shined. I didn't just enjoy golf, as my father had predicted, I became obsessed with it, fanatical. As my long drive developed, golf became the driving force in my life.

Golf has been an enduring passion since that day. In the six decades since my father first handed me those clubs, the sport has served as both my teacher and my savior. Golf has helped me learn the virtues of patience and steadiness. Golf has helped me cope with the tragic loss of our daughter on her eighteenth birthday. Golf has given me a reason to get out of bed in the morning. On days when the mood is somber and dark, golf has compelled me to get out the door and keep on keeping on. In short, golf has given me a reason for living.

Still, after six decades it was time to stamp a crowning achievement on this sport I so loved. But what could that be? I'd played literally thousands of rounds of golf. What more was there? What challenge was left? I thought about it. There was one other activity that appealed to me as much as golf, and that was travel. Why not combine the two? I pulled out a map of the United States. What about taking that RV of ours and heading out on a golfing extravaganza, a quest to play a round of golf in each of the contiguous U.S. states? Wait, would that even be possible?

I put the map away. That would be impossible.

But the idea possessed me. I kept wondering whether it could be done. The question continued haunting me so I decided to talk to my doctor about it. He cautioned me that attempting such a feat would put a lot of stress on my heart.

"Doc, I'm seventy-two years old. Going to the bathroom puts a lot of stress on my heart. I'd rather go out in a blaze of glory doing what I love, than slumped over a toilet seat."

He advised against it.

I decided to go for it.

But how? Where to begin? I thought about writing a golf company to see if they might be interested in sponsoring my trip. But I was certain that golf companies were besieged with such inquiries about sponsorship. My proposal really needed to stand out. So I decided to propose playing not one, but two, rounds of golf in each of the lower forty-eight states, a total of ninety-six rounds of golf in ninety-six days.

Callaway bought into the idea. They either liked what they heard or were so confused by the math they gave up.

Soon, boxes of Callaway gear started arriving on my doorstep. It was all top-of-the-line and beautiful. They also assisted with some of the coordination, which was quite helpful. And they even agreed to set up a blog for me on the Callaway website, which was amazing, except I was seventy-two years old and had no idea what a blog was. So they found a bright young Millennial to handle that.

There was lots of planning and logistics that went into the trip, and soon maps and guidebooks started piling up in our kitchen. Eventually the mound grew to take over the entire house. Thankfully, I have a very understanding wife.

Anticipation mounted as the day of departure drew near. Finally, the morning came. My family gathered at the house to bid me farewell. As I pulled out of the driveway they all waved and hooted; I felt both confident and comforted by their support. After months of planning and preparation, this would be my Forrest Gump of golf moment.

I didn't get very far. My wife was screaming and yelling and holding something over her head. I'd forgotten my CPAP machine and blood pressure medication. Ah, the delights of growing old.

But from that point forward I never looked back. Thankfully, hemorrhoids aren't one of my problems, because the drive from California to Cerbat Cliffs Golf Course in Kingman, Arizona took seven hours. There were many long drives during the odyssey, some on the golf course but mostly on the roadways. Eventually I got into a rhythm, I found my groove. It went something like this: EAT. SLEEP. DRIVE. PLAY GOLF. REPEAT.

> *Reporters began calling. Soon I had interviews and media obligations.*

As my trip progressed, people started learning about my pursuit and they started showing up at golf courses. They were reading the daily blog updates and my undertaking was serving to inspire them. People started calling me "The Happy Golfer" and golf courses started comp'ing my greens fees and inviting me to pose for pictures in the pro shop afterward. Reporters began calling. Soon I had interviews and media obligations. This whole endeavor was proving to be quite a sensation. I started growing a beard, just like Forrest Gump. I was on a roll.

Then I had heart palpitations and my left shoulder went numb. Next, my right. I checked myself into a hospital. The cardiologist confirmed that my arteries were clogged and I would need surgery. It wasn't a matter of *if*, he explained, but when.

When? It became the defining question of my life. When would I need to have this procedure done? Was it possible to continue onward and realize my dream? Or must I stop? The doctor had his opinion, and I had mine. The two didn't necessarily reconcile, but I decided to play on.

I mostly stayed at campgrounds along the way, or sometimes with friends and relatives, and in a pinch, Walmart parking lots. After the hospital scare, my diet became very regimented. I only ate healthy and wholesome foods, like salads and fresh vegetables. I started feeling better. Maybe it was just psychological, but my scores began improving and I felt less sore in the mornings.

You would think that such a whirlwind tour would be a great blur, but I remember each and every day quite vividly. It was as though someone had granted me a new lease on life so I could fully immerse myself in these grand ninety-six days and experience them to their utmost.

The final day, as you can imagine, was quite emotional. Putting in the last shot on Hole 18 of the Gold Hills Golf Course in Redding, California brought a torrent of feelings and reflections. I'd completed two rounds of golf in each of the contiguous forty-eight states for a total of ninety-six rounds of golf in ninety-six days. Mission accomplished.

It had been an amazing journey, one that required me to overcome many fears and doubts. After seventy-two years of living I finally proved to myself that I was more courageous than I'd ever given myself credit for being. I still don't know what a blog is, but if anyone needs a resource for locating a nice golf course in any state, or finding a Walmart parking lot to camp in, I'm your guy. Beyond that, if anyone harbors a dream of trying something really bold and outrageous in his or her life, think of The Happy Golfer… and go for it.

~Nick Karnazes

Chapter 7

The Power of Yes!

Be Daring

Action cures fear, inaction creates terror.
~Douglas Horton

57

An Introvert on the TODAY Show

Say yes and you'll figure it out afterwards.
~Tina Fey

So, what was a mild-mannered, middle-aged librarian doing on the TODAY show? I'd written an essay, "At Ease with a Body Fighting Gravity," about the fact that I'm more comfortable in a bathing suit at age fifty-eight than I was in my youth, when I actually had the body to rock a Speedo. This, apparently, was so unusual that after it was published in *The New York Times*, a TODAY show producer invited me onto the show to talk about it.

"I'd love to," I replied, "but not in a bathing suit."

I had my doubts about whether a librarian gabbing about an essay would make for riveting TV. While I can be funny on paper, I'm no dazzling wit. You'd never use the words "life of the party" to describe me. Plus, the prospect of being on national television was, to put it mildly, terrifying. At work, I'm always ready to entertain a crowd of toddlers with "The Wheels on the Bus" or "The Itsy Bitsy Spider." But entertaining millions of people on live TV? That sounded more like an Itsy Bitsy Heart Attack.

My library colleagues assured me that I could do it. "If you can handle Tiny Tot Story Time," they told me, "you can handle anything."

So, what's it actually like to be on the TODAY show?

It wasn't my usual day.

A limo turned up at 5:00 a.m. to take my sister Diane and me from my suburban Philadelphia home to 30 Rockefeller Plaza. (Trust me, this isn't how we librarians usually roll.)

After arriving, we were shown to the Green Room (which wasn't green; it was actually orange and purple). There was yummy-looking brunch chow I was too nervous to eat, and wall-mounted flat screens playing the show I was about to be on.

"Toto," I said to my sister, "we're not in Kansas anymore."

Smile like a crazy person. Enjoy yourself.

For the next ninety minutes, I was efficiently passed from one earbud-wearing, clipboard-wielding young staffer to another, each of whom filled me in on what was happening and what to expect next.

"Roz Warren? You'll be here for twenty minutes, and then we'll take you to Hair and Make-up."

Hair and Make-up, it turns out, is just a beauty salon, but at warp speed. Fifteen minutes after I hit the salon chair, my straight blond hair had been transformed into something with shape and body. My face was spackled with glamorous gunk, including burgundy lipstick and heavy mascara—a look my sister pronounced "garish" when I rejoined her.

"But I'm sure it'll look great on screen," she said. (It did.)

We waited in a new lounge with a random assortment of other garishly made-up strangers, again watching the *TODAY* show. A woman who'd been with us in the Green Room earlier was now onscreen promoting a parenting book.

I was, I realized, on a TV-guest conveyor belt, swiftly carrying me toward my three minutes of fame.

"Your segment is scheduled for 8:35," a staffer told me. "It's a beautiful day, so you'll be out in the plaza instead of in the studio."

At 8:15, I was taken to a "dressing room" to change into the Eileen Fisher garb I'd brought with me. To my surprise, it wasn't a room at all, just a curtained-off corner of Hair and Make-up. I ducked behind the curtain, stripped down to my undies and suited up.

Once in Eileen Fisher, I felt more confident. I might soar on my segment or fall flat on my face, but at least I'd be well dressed. (And my local EF store had given me a whopping "She's wearing this on the TODAY show" discount!)

My producer turned up to wish me well. My segment, she said, would start with an upbeat clip of AARP-aged women talking about feeling beautiful. Not only that, but staffers had offered any woman in the crowd watching the show who was over sixty the chance to "background" my segment if she'd stand behind me holding a brightly colored placard proclaiming her age.

Sure enough, when I took my place on a chair out on the plaza, I was cheered by a happy group of middle-aged women (my peeps!). They had no idea who I was, of course. All they knew was that, thanks to me, instead of being stuck at the back of the crowd, they were also about to be on national television.

Two minutes before airtime, Savannah Guthrie, a slim woman in a stunning turquoise cocktail dress, took the chair opposite mine and shook my hand. (Folks have since asked if she looks as good in person as she does on TV. You'd better believe it.)

"I'm Savannah," she said. "I liked your article!"

A writer I know who is often on television had advised me to look as upbeat and animated as possible. "You may feel as if you're grinning like a crazy person," she said. "But it'll come off great on camera."

I wasn't finding it difficult to grin. This was pretty amazing.

Somebody was counting down. Five... four... three... two...

We were on the air.

Savannah Guthrie is, without question, worth every penny they pay her. I am now her biggest fan. Guthrie made sure I didn't make a fool of myself on national television. Every question was calibrated to make me sound well informed and entertaining. And when it became clear that I'd never finish my final anecdote in time, she zipped in, nailed the punch line, and ended the segment on a laugh from the crowd.

Okay, so maybe I'm biased, but I think it was terrific television.

The cameras stopped. Guthrie moved on. "Great job!" said my producer.

Twenty minutes later, my sister and I were back in the limo, headed home. (And by five that night, I was back at the circulation desk, checking in books.)

It was an amazing, incredible, once-in-a-lifetime adventure.

And I'm really glad it's over.

If you ever get invited on to *TODAY*, here's my advice: Get plenty of sleep the night before. Bring your sister. Wear Eileen Fisher. Don't expect the Green Room to actually be green. Smile like a crazy person. Enjoy yourself.

And give Savannah my best.

~Roz Warren

Editor's note: If you look up "Roz Warren *TODAY* show" on the Internet you'll find a video of Roz's appearance. It's fun to watch.

58

A Cardinal Career

As an entrepreneur, you tend to see the
opportunities where others see none.
~Naveen Jain

I was in terrible financial trouble at age nine. On November 1st, I had fifty cents to my name — and only because of a heap of pop bottles I'd found in our back yard. With an allowance of thirty-five cents a week, and seven weeks left until Christmas, I would have $2.95 to spend on presents for the entire family — assuming I didn't spend a cent on anything else.

I was seriously considering going to my dad and asking for an advance on the next year's allowance so I could at least buy gifts for immediate family members. But then, one evening, I was sitting in my room reading the ads in the back *Boys' Life*. Several greeting-card companies were telling us how we could make oodles of money by selling their cards and stationery. Normally, I'd have passed right over the ads, but this time my desperation was such that I felt I had nothing to lose.

The ad that appealed to me most was one by Cardinal Greetings of Cincinnati, Ohio — perhaps because it seemed a bit less hokey than the others. I filled out Cardinal's magazine coupon, typed a short cover note, and found an envelope. I mailed the envelope the next day, crossed my fingers, and waited.

Why did I type the cover note, you may ask? Even at age nine, I already had terrible handwriting. I wanted to make sure Cardinal knew where to send its stuff, and so I used my mother's old typewriter rather than my own pen for the cover note. But the typing of the note, and signing it J. Peirce rather than with my full name, may have been an accidental stroke of genius. For whatever reason, Cardinal was under the impression that I was Mrs. J. Peirce. Very possibly they extended me more liberal terms than they would have given a nine-year-old boy with no previous sales experience.

Whoever Cardinal thought I was, my sales materials arrived within the week. I'd expected something small and neat, but the package looked like a dinosaur's shoebox; it was close to three feet long and nearly a foot wide, and was crammed to the top with stuff. In addition to a thick binder containing a complete selection of the cards and writing paper I'd be selling, generally for $1.25 or $1.50 a box, there were order forms, return envelopes — even a pen to fill out orders. There was also a salt-and-pepper set in the shape of a toaster holding two pieces of toast (white for the salt, brown for the pepper), which I immediately decided to give to my grandmother, who collected such things.

Wasting no time, I stuck two order forms and the pen into the binder and set off on my rounds at nine the next morning, a Saturday. Briskly, I made my way up one side of our street and back down the other, managing to sell three boxes of cards along the way. I felt neither shame nor embarrassment at asking my neighbours to buy my wares. I knew I had a good product, one on which I was quite happy to stake my modest reputation.

By the time I got home, it was lunchtime. I figured I'd done enough for one day. As I ate my sandwich, I decided not to try to sell cards on Sunday. I had no moral objection to Sunday sales, but I reckoned that some of my neighbours might, and in any case, didn't I deserve one day off?

Early the next week, I hit serious pay dirt on neighbouring Sunset Road, which in those easygoing days I could readily access through a neighbour's back yard. The horseshoe-shaped street, over twice as long as my own (Oak Crest), kept me busy for several weekday afternoons and most of Saturday. At one house, I sold four boxes of writing paper;

several other houses yielded sales of two boxes of cards or writing paper. If memory serves, I unloaded at least twenty boxes on Sunset.

Over the next few days, I made scattered sales to the teachers at my school and to neighbours on nearby Brookside Road. By now, it was time to send in my order, for which my customers had already prepaid. This necessitated my going down to the post office and buying a money order for the cost of the cards and paper to send in to Cardinal. My order was handled promptly. Within a week, I was in possession of a second box, this one only slightly smaller than a footlocker, containing the fifty-odd boxes of cards and stationery that I'd managed to sell. Deliveries were completed with but one glitch — the omission of the name on writing paper I'd sold to our local paperboy on Brookside. When he saw the paper, which I had carelessly forgotten to check, he was justifiably annoyed. But I frankly confessed my inexperience and my error and promised to correct the situation, which I quickly did.

> *I wound up raking in over $40—no small change for a nine-year-old in 1954.*

With a commission of around 40 percent on all sales, I wound up raking in over $40 — no small change for a nine-year-old in 1954. Instead of no presents at all, my family members got the finest presents I'd ever given them — a pair of earthenware casserole ramekins for my mother, a special doll for my sister, and a sweater for my dad. Naturally, my grandmother got the salt-and-pepper set, which continued to grace her dining room table until the day she died. I even had $5 left to contribute to *The New York Times*' 100 Neediest Cases, which got me a nice little write-up in that famous newspaper. All of a sudden, life was looking quite good.

"When a man knows he is to be hanged… it concentrates his mind wonderfully," wrote the always quotable Samuel Johnson. Had I not been on the brink of destitution and willing to try almost anything, it never would have occurred to me to write to Cardinal. Having decided to write to them, I was determined to succeed at the venture. Very possibly the fear I felt at my desperate situation inspired me to think more creatively than I otherwise would have — hence the typed note, which arguably made things easier for me with Cardinal. That fear did away with the embarrassment I might otherwise have felt at "cold-calling" my neighbors and teachers.

Who knows… If I'd stuck with business instead of wasting my time doing a Ph.D. in English, I might have become my generation's Warren Buffett!

~Jon Peirce

59

The Jump

Take a chance! All life is a chance. The man who
goes farthest is generally the one who
is willing to do and dare.
~Dale Carnegie

think it all started with a dare. The local vocational college had announced its lineup of adult continuing-education courses. There was a one-day crash course, hopefully not to be taken literally, for parachute jumping.

I dared my friend; he dared me back. I signed up; he chickened out.

I arrived at the county airport early on the date of the class. Two other students were present, both older than me at seventeen, along with our instructor and seasoned jumpmaster Gordon Riner, a former paratrooper for the U.S. Army. We went through a medley of exercises, including how to land, tuck and roll, pack a parachute, pack the emergency chute and many other helpful pointers. Who would've thought foolishly jumping from an airplane at 5,000 feet would be so difficult?

After lunch, the process repeated itself: practice, practice and more practice. My hamstrings were burning from all the tucks and rolls, and we were all a sweaty mess on a hot, humid June day in southern Delaware. But everything was running smoothly, and my confidence was building steadily — until my beloved instructor quizzed me on a key piece of information.

"David, you look awfully young, son. Are you sure you're eighteen?" Gordon asked with arched eyebrows.

"No, sir, I'm seventeen, but I'll be eighteen next month."

"I'm sorry, David, but unless your parents consent to you jumping, I can't let you go up. Can you track them down and have them come out to sign the papers?"

While my two fellow trainees suited up for a mid-afternoon jump, I spent several quarters at a pay phone in the terminal trying to locate my mother and father, both of whom had not been comfortable with me jumping from a perfectly well-functioning aircraft. This was in the late 1970s, well before cell phones. Finally, after I was about to give up and return home disappointed, Mom answered. They had been grocery shopping.

Well, it wasn't easy, but I convinced my mother after much begging and deal-making to come to the airport as soon as she could. Shortly afterward, while I awaited my parents' arrival to sign the waiver form, I saw the plane burst down the runway, lift up into the air and disappear into the clouds. I'd later learn from one of the staff that both students had experienced problems with their jumps, which only added to my growing anxiety.

> **"Son, you sure are looking for an adrenaline cocktail today!"**

It turned out the first jumper missed the landing zone by nearly two miles. He forgot how to steer the parachute and simply drifted until he landed in a cornfield. The second jumper suffered a worse fate. She ended up landing in a dense forest and had to be cut out of her chute and climb down from a large oak. Fortunately, neither was injured.

After my mother signed the paperwork, Gordon announced that I would go up next with a group of seasoned skydivers. I would jump first at a lower altitude, and then the plane would climb higher for the free-fallers. It was at this time I happened to mention with a cracking of my voice that I had never flown in a plane before. I seem to recall Gordon blurting out, "Son, you sure are looking for an adrenaline cocktail today!"

I sat cross-legged on the floor next to the pilot of the small Cessna with Gordon close by. "Remember, when I give you the first signal, we're going to open the door. Then you'll climb outside onto the step and grab the strut. Finally, I'll give you the thumbs-up to go!" I only nodded, suddenly unable to speak.

When the door was opened, I honestly thought I was having a heart attack! I stared down at the passing landscape, a patchwork of squared fields, tiny buildings and miniature moving "ants," which were actually motor vehicles traveling the countryside roadways. I saw the landing zone. It looked to be about the size of a quarter from that vantage point. Now I knew why the other two rookies ended up so far off course.

Moments later, against all common sense and a screaming inner voice that told me to abandon this madness, I found myself nervously shuffling over to the opening, inch by inch, reaching out to grab the strut connected to the underside of the right wing and position my booted feet onto a step about two feet by one foot in size. Miraculously, I successfully and smoothly pulled it off, but once outside I felt what seemed like hurricane-force winds in my face. The plane's engine and propeller were noisy, a cacophony of roaring metal, cylinders, gears and shafts. I couldn't hear myself think, but turned to Gordon, who was yelling at me, preparing me for this moment of truth. And then he gave me the signal. Before I could reason with myself to do otherwise or wet my pants, I arched my back and leapt backward.

At once, in a flash, all was silent. I opened my eyes and found myself floating in the sky, seemingly not moving, treading not water but air. The plane was already well away. Thankfully, beginners start with static line jumps, where the ripcord is connected to a large iron hook inside the plane. If they jump, the parachute automatically deploys. And, in my case, it did.

Slowly, I began to drift, but then remembered the toggle controls to steer, located to the left and right of my helmeted head. I circled the targeted landing zone until, several minutes later, I landed, tucked and rolled, and stood back up triumphantly! A group of volunteers and random spectators, as well as my parents, ran into the field to congratulate me. I had just taken my inaugural plane ride and perfectly executed a parachute jump. I could not have been happier. That jump was a stepping stone of confidence for my future that included being the first member of my family to graduate college, become a multi-published author and later an ordained deacon in the Anglican Church in North America. And it all started with a dare.

~David Michael Smith

60

The Sound of Life

Clear your mind of can't.
~Samuel Johnson

A few years ago, when I was forty, a friend of ours was cast in a community theater production of *The Sound of Music*. My husband suggested that our daughters, then eleven and five, might enjoy being a part of it.

"You can try out for the pit band," he said.

Now, I have nothing against pit bands. In fact, I've played my flute in several. However, *The Sound of Music* is my favorite musical of all time. As a child, I saw an uncle portray Max in a community theater production. I watched with awe and envy as a stage full of children brought the story to life. They sang and danced and had a rollicking good time, just like in the movie, which I've seen more times than I can count. I wanted to be a part of that magic.

"I'm not trying out for the pit band," I answered. "I'm trying out for the show."

There was only one problem with my declaration: I'd never been in a musical in my life. I'd never sung publicly outside of grade school concerts. I'd never taken a dance or vocal class. In high school, I'd auditioned for several shows but made only one. It was a play so riveting that my whole family fell asleep. And it was not a musical.

I'd longed for a part in a musical, and I'd tried out many times, but as a band kid who never sang, I never made the shows. I always worked in the dark, backstage or in the pit band, watching my friends work musical magic under the lights.

My daughters wanted to try out, so we memorized show tunes and prepared to audition.

"Mom," my older daughter said, "I'm nervous."

"You'll do a great job," I said. "You can do anything if you set your mind to it!"

I was full of encouragement. But as our audition approached, I started to get cold feet. My children looked to me for courage and inspiration. Quitting would set a bad example. Since I was auditioning alongside them, I had to exude confidence and optimism.

"Whether you're cast or not isn't important — doing your best is what matters," I'd been telling them. Now I had to live it.

I walked into the audition under my daughters' close scrutiny. To say I was nervous would be an understatement. My last audition had been in high school, after all, and I didn't get the part.

I sang my song, trying to look comfortable and confident. My daughters did a great job during their auditions. And then we waited.

The good news is that we all made it! My daughters were cast as Louisa and Gretl von Trapp. I would have been happy with any role, but the surprising news was that I was cast as the Baroness.

I was elated. Wow. Not only was I cast — I was a lead! Not the most beloved character, but the one with the best wardrobe. Not too shabby.

Then I read the script. In addition to a boatload of lines, I had two solos.

Two. Solos.

I guess I did okay at the audition.

Still, I was relieved that my songs were relatively unknown, since the Baroness doesn't sing in the movie. Except for those who knew the stage version of the show, few people would know if I messed up.

To prepare, I belted out the Baroness's songs at every stoplight and traffic jam in suburban Illinois. When home alone, I sang my heart out to the cat, the shower, and the dishes. I knew I'd have to get over my fear of singing in front of other people, since I'd have to perform my songs on stage. In front of people. A lot of people. With no one else's voice to hide behind.

Reluctantly, I told friends and family about the show. Everyone wanted to see it since I was in it with our daughters. I didn't want the theater to be empty, but I didn't necessarily want it packed either. Nevertheless, if it were full, I preferred to fill it myself with friendly faces.

My mantra was, "I hope I don't stink." A high bar, I know, but there it is.

> *My mantra was, "I hope I don't stink."*

The Sound of Music went off without a hitch. I remembered my lines, my cues, and my wardrobe changes. We sold out eight performances. Friends and acquaintances congratulated us on a spectacular show. At least 100 friends came to see the Lebovic Family Singers.

The most memorable compliment came from an old friend with a beautiful voice. In high school, she sang in chorus and had parts in all the theatrical productions. After the show, she gave me a hug.

"I didn't know you sang!" she said. "Why weren't you in chorus? You have a great voice!"

It was the best compliment ever.

After that experience, I braved more auditions and even learned to enjoy singing on stage. I went on to be a wicked stepsister, a pick-a-little lady, and even a spoiled princess. I filled my life with the sound of music.

~Angela Lebovic

Poolside or Cliffside?

When we say yes, we do more, create more, live more.
~Author Unknown

"**A**n ATV ride anyone?" asks the activities director at the Montana ranch where my husband Larry and I are vacationing with friends. Every hand shoots up but mine.

Only a fool volunteers without the details. "What's an ATV?" I whisper to Larry.

"All-terrain vehicle," he says.

"You go. I'll hang by the pool," I say, not 100-percent sure what I'm rejecting, but confident that nothing good can come from the combination of a moving vehicle, variable terrain, and me. Besides, this trip is about eating, drinking and lounging poolside with a book. Challenging myself is not on the agenda.

"Come on, Hyla!" the group shouts. I shake my head, silently conveying, *It's great that you're such a sporty, spontaneous, go-for-it kind of crowd, but here's the thing: I'm not twelve. Peer pressure won't convince me to ride the Tilt-a-Whirl much less submit myself to the unknown perils of an ATV.*

"You'll be fine," says Larry, who, having prodded me down from more than one icy ski trail and treacherously steep bike path, should know better.

Still, I feel my resolve weakening. I imagine the high-fiving and recounting of exciting near-death experiences that will dominate the evening's conversation while I wait for someone to express interest in my reading material.

"Okay," I say to Larry, instantly regretting my words.

Thirty minutes later, I've traded my poolside attire for jeans, a helmet, leather gloves and giant goggles, and find my incredulous self sitting on a door-free, roofless, four-wheel monstrosity wondering why protective gear is a prerequisite for "fun" activities.

Our rugged, flannel-shirt-wearing instructor gives us an overview of ATV basics and safety tips. I'd listen, but I'm too busy worrying.

"Follow me to the field," says Mr. Rugged. "We'll do a few easy practice turns" (echoing the words Larry once said before leading me down a mogul-filled, black-diamond ski slope).

I rev up the motor. The sound is deafening. The heat from the engine is blazing. I press

> *I press the accelerator, and the ATV surges forward.*

the accelerator, and the ATV surges forward. Panicked, I stomp on the brake. A hundred false starts later, I arrive at the field. "Easy turns" are grueling. I stall. I buck. I sweat.

"We're ready to roll," says Mr. Rugged. "Don't worry, I haven't lost anyone yet."

My heart races as we traverse the mountain. Breathtaking foliage surrounds us, but all I notice are terrifying cliffs. I go slowly, lagging behind. I force my shoulders down in an attempt to relax. Gradually, I get the hang of the accelerator and the brake. I pick up the pace, and a breeze envelops me. In a daring move, I peek at the lush scenery. *Look at me!* I want to shout. *I'm steering and sightseeing!* A strange thing happens: I feel in control. A stranger thing happens: I feel happy. I go faster and faster until I'm on Larry's tail.

"I knew you'd have fun," Larry says during a break, obviously relieved that this is one outing that won't require a rescue team.

Back on our ATVs, Mr. Rugged says, "There's a sharp turn ahead. Take it easy."

Sharp turn? My panic returns. I've barely mastered navigating a straight path.

Suddenly, the turn is in sight. Unable to focus, much less decelerate,

I overshoot my target and drive directly toward the edge of a steep drop. Seconds from tumbling over, I muster all my strength to turn the wheel and whip the ATV back onto the path.

"Whoa," says Mr. Rugged. "You're my closest call ever."

"No worries," I say, feigning bravado. "I wouldn't dream of breaking your record."

Sweaty, covered in grime and feeling fabulous, I rev up the ATV. I drive back at a leisurely pace, taking in the vistas and smiling from ear to ear as I compose the story of my own near-death adventure to share with the gang over dinner.

~Hyla Sabesin Finn

62

No Regrets

I do not regret the things I've done,
but those I did not do.
~Rory Cochrane

I always had a fear of heights. Even with a child's free spirit and curiosity for exploration, a fear of heights held me back. Specifically, I feared activities that involved being above the ground. I would imagine a catastrophe happening, one that would send me plummeting toward the Earth. I avoided roller coasters at theme parks and stayed far away from scenic overlooks on road trips. I would look on fearfully as my younger — and very adventurous — sister went bungee jumping and parasailing on family vacations.

It was my thrill-seeking sister who, of course, suggested hang gliding as our activity in Switzerland during our post-college trip to Europe with two friends.

"Look!" she exclaimed, pointing to a pamphlet featuring tandem hang gliders soaring through the air. "We should all go hang gliding!"

The thought of hang gliding instantly sent shivers through my body, so I quickly scanned the rack of advertisements in the hostel's lobby, hoping to find a safer, ground-based activity. At the bottom of the paragliding, skydiving, and canyon-jumping pamphlets, there was a brochure for a bicycle tour.

"We could rent bikes," I suggested to the group.

My sister and two friends all shook their heads. At this point, she had already convinced the group that hang gliding was the best option for our Swiss activity.

"Fine," I sighed resignedly. Although I agreed to go, I wasn't *actually* going to go hang gliding. I would go along and watch the others.

The following morning, we went to register for hang gliding.

I allowed everyone to register before me, and when it was my turn, I leaned over the counter and whispered to the activities coordinator that I would just be going to watch.

"You still have to pay the fee," she said.

"What?" I asked, shocked.

After hearing that I would still need to pay for the full experience, and sensing that the group was growing suspicious over why it was taking me so long, I said quickly, "Okay," and registered to go hang gliding.

> I scanned the top of the first page and saw the word "Waiver" written in boldface.

Even though I had registered and paid for it, I wasn't *actually* going to go hang gliding.

Once the registration was completed, we piled into a large van to head up the mountain to the launch site. The two male instructors spoke in German to each other as we ascended the mountain. Halfway there, the instructor sitting in the passenger seat turned around and passed out thick packets of paper and pens.

The packets had several sheets of stapled paper that contained single-spaced text on both sides. I scanned the top of the first page and saw the word "Waiver" written in boldface. I gasped.

"This is to sign in case something happens to us?" I stammered. "Is there a lot that can happen to us?"

"You just need to initial and sign each page. That's all," he replied in his thick accent.

I looked around the van and saw my sister and two friends all scribbling their names and initials on the pages.

Finally, after several minutes passed, I forced my clenched hand to sign my name on the waiver. I reminded myself that simply signing papers didn't mean that I was *actually* going to go hang gliding.

Once we reached our destination — the top of a mountain among the Swiss Alps — we climbed out. The instructors immediately began placing the helmets and gear on us. It seemed like it only took ten seconds for me to be completely outfitted for my impending death.

I looked over at my sister, who flashed a wide grin and gave me the thumbs-up sign. "Let's take a picture!" she yelled out, summoning me with one hand as she handed an instructor her camera with the other.

After taking pictures, we were given directions for how we were to run and leap off the cliff with our tandem instructor in order to catch the wind for the hang glider.

I looked around and saw my sister, two friends, and the other brave tourists listening intently to the instructions.

This is crazy! I thought to myself. *I'm going to run off a cliff, with only some aluminum frames and cloth? What if the wind completely stops or we hit a tree or the glider breaks...?*

Once the instructors were finished, I tugged on my sister's arm and looked at her in bewilderment. "Are you really going to do this?" I asked. "It can't be safe!"

She smiled and paused for a moment to gather her thoughts.

"This is probably the safest place in the entire world to go hang gliding. They do this every day," she said, pointing to the instructors.

I continued to stare at her, frozen with fear.

"This is a once-in-a-lifetime opportunity. If you go, you'll get to have the best view of the real thing!" she exclaimed, pointing to the North Face logo on my fleece jacket.

For the first time since we had arrived, I looked out over the cliff and saw the iconic mountains.

My sister was right. I would probably never be back. If I decided to leap off the cliff, I could have the most amazing view of those breathtaking mountains; if I decided to turn around and jump back into the van, I would miss this special opportunity, and possibly regret it for the rest of my life.

And with that realization, I decided to leap off the cliff.

~Anna S. Kendall

63

Trick Riding 101

Everything is theoretically impossible, until it is done.
~Robert A. Heinlein

N ever in my wildest imagination did I picture myself standing on the bare back of a trotting horse. I am not a cowgirl and don't even ride horses for pleasure.

But I was doing a television fitness show, and someone on the crew had the bright idea that we should mosey on down to the rodeo grounds and ask three very delightful trick riders if they could teach me a stunt to do on camera. We could use this footage as the new opening to the show.

I didn't allow myself a lot of time to think this over. I just agreed that the stunt would be eye-catching and demonstrate how flexible a fit person can be.

That was how I ended up at the rodeo grounds with a camera crew, sitting in the bleachers watching the eye-catching performances of three very talented young cowgirls. Once their show was over, we approached them, detailing our ideas for the television show.

The cowgirls were up for it and asked me which particular stunt I was interested in learning. Having watched their act, I especially liked the drama of one stunt wherein one of the girls led a horse to continuously circle the arena in a trot while one of the other girls ran across the arena toward a small trampoline. It was timed perfectly so that she jumped onto the trampoline, up into the air, and then onto the back of the horse. As she landed atop the special flat saddle, she stood up and stretched her arms outward as the horse continued its trot around the arena. It looked magnificent.

They talked me through the necessary moves, stressing the timing since I would need to be in the air at the precise time the horse trotted past. I alone would judge the speed of the horse and my own speed to arrive at our intersection on time.

We were already at the start of my first attempt when I felt a need to give myself encouragement. "I can do this," I repeated to myself to reaffirm my confidence. The important thing was for me to completely believe in myself and concentrate on the task at hand.

Before getting involved in television, I taught dance and recalled the many times I worked to lift up the confidence of the new dancers. I would say, "I know you can do this. Dance is learning new walking patterns, then adding music to blend the two. It takes time, but I have all the patience in the world. So if you are willing to work at this, we will succeed."

> *I had never felt so accomplished, so sure I could tackle anything and succeed.*

In those moments before I left for my first run across the arena, I felt that if these trick riders would bear with me, I would succeed.

The first time out, I miscalculated, hit the rear end of the horse and then the dirt. I walked back to the starting point, and after a couple more tries I had figured out the timing.

Part two was harder than part one. The timing was one thing, but executing the landing and standing on the saddle was another. However, I did finally get it right, even though I fell off almost immediately.

The good news was we could use the footage up to the point where I was standing on the back of the horse with my arms extended as the horse continued its run. We wouldn't show my immediate fall after that!

We had everything we needed for this segment of the new intro. I was relieved and flying high! I had never felt so accomplished, so sure I could tackle anything and succeed. The bad news came from the cameraman. "Ellie, I'm so sorry. I forgot to turn on the camera. It was all so exciting, I just… I'm so sorry."

Okay, we all forget things on the job. "It's okay," I told him. "I'll do it again. Only this time, please turn on your camera."

I repeated the stunt, and this time it was captured on film. I do think this is one of those things I will carry with me always — partly because it still seems a bit unbelievable.

We were all wrapped up by 6:00 p.m., and by 10:00 that night I made a trip to the emergency department of the hospital. The fall I had taken at the end of the first successful stunt had injured my knee. Shock is a strange thing — I had no idea I was hurt even as I repeated the stunt, this time with the camera rolling.

I was incapacitated for a while, but I have no regrets. I am not a trick rider, but belief in myself made me one. For me, it was like doing the impossible. And when the viewers watched it, I wanted them to understand that getting into good physical shape meant they could also tackle the impossible.

~Ellie Braun-Haley

Good to Go

You've got to be closer to the edge than ever to win.
That means sometimes you go over the edge,
and I don't mean driving, either.
~Dale Earnhardt, Sr.

Always the early bird, I awaited the arrival of my friends and fellow racers while sitting in my brand new Mazda CX-5 crossover SUV. It was not exactly a sports car, but I felt pretty cool driving it.

The moment I realized that I might be in over my head was when two ambulances pulled into the lot and parked beside me. They started testing their yellow and red flashing lights. That's when I broke into a cold sweat. A month earlier, propelling myself around a NASCAR track at 100 miles per hour was not on my list of things to do.

"Come on, it'll be fun!" had chided my longtime friend Jack. The problem was that Jack had racing in his blood. His dad, Sammy Tanner, was a World Champion flat track racer known as the Fearless Flea. That name came about not so much for his smaller stature but for his propensity to fly his motorcycle sideways around a dirt track at absurdly high speeds.

"It'll be *more* than fun!" he said. I wondered, is there such a thing as "more than fun?" Needless to say, the apple does not fall far from the tree. Jack had been relentless, so, against my better judgment and with as much bravado as I could muster I said, "Sign me up!"

Now I was on my way into the training facility, where I would sit through an hour and a half class on how best to hurl oneself, without killing oneself, around the 12-degree embanked half-mile oval track. The instructor proceeded to show pictures of past "drivers" who learned their driving skills were no match for the track or the foreboding concrete wall that surrounded it.

"The engine always wins; roll that pedal, don't stomp it; roll it!" he yelled. He then went on with a redundant rant about the 500-horsepower engines, the overly sensitive gas pedals versus the touchy brakes, and finished with the wall and what it would cost were you to hit said wall and have to replace said racecar (assuming you were alive to do so). A voluminous amount of paperwork to sign was my ticket to the track. Not much different from signing a mortgage. The specific amount of the deductible for replacement of said racecar I won't go into.

> "I'm here to keep you alive."

For some strange reason the instructor, Dave, singled me out of the group of nearly two dozen other drivers as a test subject to talk to in front of the class. It must have been the look of total confidence and composure that I had painted across my face. He said, "We don't like losing people or racecars, not necessarily in that order... I'm here to keep you alive." Well, there you have it. I felt much better.

By the time the class ended and we were supposedly ready... I was good to go. As in, I was good to go and get in my Mazda and take nice slow side streets all the way home. Making matters far worse was the fact that a fellow student decided to do just that. Did he know something I didn't?

This was certainly a defining moment, especially given the fact that I am always telling other people to get out of their own comfort zones... although, my zone in this case was really more of a stripe. Or to be more specific a white stripe painted on black asphalt. What could I do? No hypocrisy here. I decided to stay and hurl myself around the track.

Having donned my leathers, helmet and radio headset, I climbed through the window of the racecar #49 and was tightly strapped into a five-point harness as though I were traveling in the space shuttle.

And wouldn't you know it, there was no steering wheel! I was sure Dave hadn't mentioned that. It turned out that the tight confines of the space require the wheel to be removed before you climbed in. Then they put it back once you were squeezed into your seat.

I slowly left the pit and drove onto the raceway. Now I was cruising, albeit at 25 miles per hour while yellow lights flashed around the track. Had it not been for my helmet I am sure the wind would have been whipping through my hair. Did I mention there is no glass in the windows either?

An interesting side fact is that there are "spotters" who bark at you through the headset inside your helmet and they are as important to the success of your drive as you are. They sit perched high atop the grandstands like lonely gods in the sky and direct you around the track. There are no mirrors, so those voices in your head are actually quite useful.

I was handling my racecar just fine until the lights turned green. "Faster, closer to the wall, gas pedal to the floor, push through it, push through it!" my spotter yelled. To the floor? Really, you're kidding me right? Had it not been for the five-point harness I would have been on the floor!

But I did as I was told. I'm not sure how fast I was traveling at that point. 2,000 miles per hour, maybe. And then it all clicked. Although the other drivers, including my friend Jack, were whizzing around me like fleas on a smelly dog… I became a driver! With a smile on my face, I pushed aside the thought of the large deductible, and I accelerated. Twenty laps later I jumped out of the window like Richard Petty on his best day. I had lived to tell about it and better yet I did not hit the wall or the other drivers! Take that, deductible.

I felt fulfilled, restored and maybe even ready for another round. I was good to go and I went. And now I'm good to go on the track of life and business, which can be precarious as well. Sometimes you need to push through it, get closer to that wall, and use the gas pedal… and if you do you will be good to go.

~Stan Holden

Just Breathe

*Coming out of your comfort zone is tough in the
beginning, chaotic in the middle, and awesome in
the end... because in the end, it shows
you a whole new world.*
~Manoj Arora

We were packing for a trip of a lifetime. We would be flying in to Guayaquil, Ecuador, spending a night, and then taking off the following morning for one of our bucket list destinations: the Galápagos Islands.

"Wait! You almost forgot your snorkeling gear," my husband exclaimed as he snatched my equipment from the closet, unzipped my suitcase, and placed it inside with the rest of my travel gear.

"Oh, yeah, how could I forget something so important..." I replied, with more hesitation than enthusiasm in my voice.

"Don't worry, I'll be right by your side the entire time." He bent down and kissed my forehead while he rubbed my shoulders reassuringly.

I grew up in the water, spending nearly every day in the summer at the pool. I was an incredibly strong swimmer, but for some reason, I was absolutely terrified of swimming in the ocean. I felt helpless and out of control in open waters. Plus, I had recently had knee surgery, and trusting my knee was going to be a challenge.

My husband loved snorkeling. On past vacations, he had spent hours swimming around the waters, while I had tried for a few minutes and then retreated to the beach.

Snorkeling in the Galápagos was supposed to be amazing, with a wide variety of sea creatures to observe at alarmingly close distances due to the lack of predators. I didn't want to disappoint him, but I also didn't wish to have a vacation colored by anxiety. But what harm could there be in just bringing the gear? It didn't oblige me to do anything, right?

It was a long trek to our destination, with lengthy layovers, a late-night arrival, and an extremely early flight the next day. Yet, we finally made it to our cruise ship, and the adventure began. We would experience more in that week than we normally do in a year. Okay, maybe that's a little bit of an exaggeration, but we went on a minimum of two to three outings a day to various islands, taking part in hikes, guided tours of endemic species, and wildlife photo ops. It was absolutely incredible.

> *The rocks were sharp, and the sand was shifting under our flippers as the waves rolled in.*

On the second day, we went on a hike, and then there was a snorkeling option afterward. I did not travel all this way to sit on the sidelines and watch. So, I put on my gear, and we chose to begin from shore, rather than the Zodiac rubber raft, to help ease me into the depths and feel a little more in control.

We started wading backward into the water. The rocks were sharp, and the sand was shifting under our flippers as the waves rolled in. I could feel my knee being pulled this way and that, and I started to panic. I looked at my husband and shook my head.

"I don't think I can do this! This is hurting my knee. I don't even know if I can swim with it very well. You go, and I will hang out on the beach," I instructed him, nearly in tears.

"Here." He gently reached out to hold my hand. "Try sitting down." We sat down in the shallow water, and proceeded to scoot back into the water until we could float and begin swimming. He stayed in front of me and constantly checked in with me. There were other people in our group whom we had gotten to know, and they all stayed close to us, which gave me more confidence and security.

At first, all we could see was the murky water and a few fish. I kept pushing and swimming, until the shoreline was far away. The deeper the water got, the colder it got, and I could see more waves coming our way. I felt completely at the mercy of the ocean, and the whole putting-my-face-in-the-water-while-breathing process felt unnatural. I persevered, however, trying to calm my breathing through the snorkel when my head was stuck in the water.

Then came all the beauty, and of course, this was why we were there. There were schools of fish, some blue with black stripes and yellow tails, some yellow with polka dots. We saw sea urchins and rocks covered with red starfish. Then my favorite: the chocolate chip starfish, which literally looked like a piece of cookie dough cut into a star with black spots resembling chocolate chips outlined in black.

I calmed my breathing. It was an issue of mind over matter, but keeping my head in the water for this once-in-a-lifetime experience was overwhelmingly worth it! At first glance, it had all appeared quite desolate, but with time we could see movement, and everything came alive. Stingrays were hidden in the sand, and as I looked to my left, a sea lion went twirling by! An octopus hid among the rocks and sea anemone. The sea lion came twirling back again, this time accompanied by a friend. They would slow down and look at us, and swim through us playfully back and forth. We got to swim with Galápagos penguins; we even saw a hammerhead shark. Once terrified to swim in the ocean, I can now say I have swum with sharks!

Next, we reached a cove. It was dark, and I was absolutely terrified to proceed. My husband pointed, and I saw an entire colony of sea turtles swimming beneath us! Their grace was humbling as they glided slowly by.

The entire outing was breathtaking. It is one thing to see these kinds of creatures behind glass at a local aquarium, but quite another to be swimming alongside these majestic animals in the middle of the

Pacific Ocean. I hate to think of all I would have missed had I remained on the beach. Now I know, when I'm doing something new, I just have to remember to breathe.

~Gwen Cooper

Find the New You

*Your power to choose the direction of your life
allows you to reinvent yourself, to change your
future, and to powerfully influence
the rest of creation.*
~Stephen Covey

Three Years

We must be willing to get rid of the life we've planned,
so as to have the life that is waiting for us. The old skin
has to be shed before the new one can come.
~Joseph Campbell

I had been out of college for eight years. I finally had all my
school loans paid off and I liked my job teaching in a junior
high school and coaching football. In my spare time, I had a
hobby/semi-vocation refereeing high school football games in
the fall and basketball games in the winter. My wife worked as a
nurse at the local hospital, and we had two children — a boy in the
second grade and a girl about to start kindergarten. All in all, I was
relatively comfortable and satisfied.

But since I was a boy, I had had an interest in the law. I watched
every lawyer show on TV and liked the movies that showed the par-
rying and mental sparring of the courtroom. It was always a dream of
mine to call myself an attorney. When an older cousin of mine, whom
I had always admired, finished law school and became a successful
attorney, I knew more than ever that's what I wanted to do.

We were so comfortable, though, and this would be a major
disruption, not just for me but for my whole family. Was I willing to
sell the first house that my wife and I had ever owned? Was I willing
to pull my kids out of school and away from their friends, and my
wife out of her job, just to chase my dream? I knew that the "washout"

rate at most law schools was about half, and I didn't know if I had the smarts or the study skills to go back to school and make it all the way through. I had heard about the Socratic method that they used as a teaching tool in law school, and it truly scared me.

I needed some advice, and I knew where I needed to go. I was part of the "protest about nearly anything," hippie generation, and my dad and I butted heads for a long time about his "old school" traditions. However, like the old saying goes, my dad got awfully smart when I went to college and learned a few things. So I started going to my dad for advice. He was what the old-timers called a "soapbox philosopher," but he always had sage advice for me. He would seldom tell me what to do, but his little lessons always guided me and led me to do the right thing.

> *"How old would you be in four years if you didn't follow your dream?"*

I came into his home one day as he was reading his Sunday paper, one of his favorite things to do. I asked if I could interrupt him for a moment and told him I needed some advice. I explained that it was my dream to become a lawyer, but I was twenty-nine. If I went now, I wouldn't get out until I was well into my thirties. I half expected him to talk me out of it and tell me that I should be happy with the life I had. But he put down his newspaper and said simply, "How old would you be in four years if you *didn't* follow your dream?" I started doing the math so I could answer, and then I realized: That *was* the answer.

So we sold our house and moved into a mobile home in the campus trailer park. My kids started the year in a brand new school, and my wife got a different job.

Those were three of the most grueling years of my life, but I loved the study of law. I was never so robbed of sleep or never spent less time with my family, and I made the library my second home. But I made it through. Two of the proudest moments in my life were when I walked across that stage to get my law degree and my swearing-in as a new attorney-at-law.

I practiced law for twenty-five years, and I was always grateful that my father and my family supported my decision to uproot our lives and try something completely different.

~Doug Sletten

Abolishing Solitary Confinement

Once we believe in ourselves, we can risk curiosity,
wonder, spontaneous delight, or any experience that
reveals the human spirit.
~E.E. Cummings

I can't go camping anymore. That thought came to me a few weeks after my husband's death. Setting up camp and traveling alone were now terrifying. So was dining out. Even attending Sunday services became challenging. The seat alongside me was now vacant, vacant everywhere. Miserable, I spent my time alone.

On the Friday before Memorial Day, watching my neighbors pull their camper down our street, I wished I were headed for a campground, too. Throughout the summer, our Kentucky campgrounds have scheduled activities — for couples and kids, that is. Family swims, relay races, treasure hunts, volleyball, and square dances were designed for couples with children. Then there was me: alone, with grown kids.

That Memorial Day, I sulked, imagining the laughter, the smell of the campfire, the sounds of the night insects, and the occasional amateur guitarist accompanied by friends and family singing off key. And somehow, that did it. I snapped out of it. I told myself, *Whenever I think I can't do something because I'm alone, I'll do it anyway, even if I don't want to.*

I hesitantly went to the AAA office and bought a new Rand McNally

Road Atlas. Then I headed for lunch at O'Charley's, which had been our favorite restaurant. (Free pie on Wednesdays.)

"Parking the car?" our usual waitress said, probably expecting my husband to arrive. I shook my head. She scurried away, but returned with two glasses of water. Two glasses! I resisted the urge to race back to my car. Instead of ordering my "usual" I picked something different. Then I studied the maps and highlighted places we'd been.

"Planning a vacation?" the server asked as she waited for me to move the atlas to make room for the plate she held.

I had no answer. A chill set in. Me alone? The what-ifs began: truck repairs, robbery, lost ID, prescriptions, getting lost. But by the time I'd finished my key lime pie, I had overcome my resistance and knew my answer.

"Yes. I'm going camping." *Alone. To a place I've never been.*

I returned to the AAA office and with trembling hands I bought a Woodall's camping guide for the New England states. Since I'd never visited my mother's birthplace,

> **Whenever I think I can't do something because I'm alone, I'll do it anyway.**

Vermont, I asked the clerk to prepare a TripTik Travel Planner and mail it to me. When it arrived, the package included a list of additional guides and tour books I might get from AAA offices to visit interesting sites along the way.

Hmmm. Frank Lloyd Wright's Fallingwater house, Revolutionary War battlefields, the Houdini Museum, Boston's Fenway Park, the Crayola Factory, New England Candle factory, Lake Champlain, the Kazoo Factory—all drew me out of the solitary confinement I'd imposed on myself.

Against the advice of my grown children and neighbors, I loaded my husband's truck and headed northeast. Did I get lost? Yes. Did the truck burn out a headlight? Yes. Did families stare at me, old and alone? Yes. Did I wonder how crazy this idea was and become tempted to drive straight back home? Yes. Did I enjoy the train ride from Providence, Rhode Island, to Fenway Park? The Red Sox winning in overtime, 13–12? Yes. Did I nearly miss the last train to my car? Yes.

Was I amazed at the enormity of Lake Champlain and the ships on the Saint Lawrence Seaway? Yes. Would I do it again? Do I still face fears? Yes and more.

I now attend college (free tuition over age sixty-five) and hold my own with students forty years my junior. I visit my out-of-state friends. I tutor math and reading. Eating dinner alone at home or at a restaurant feels normal.

Do I still have to take a deep breath, lift my chin and remind myself: "You can do it?" Yes.

~Alvena Stanfield

68

My Pre-Med-itated Career

*Your time is limited, so don't waste
it living someone else's life.*
~Steve Jobs

By the time I turned twenty-three, I had already experienced two massive career failures — and I hadn't even applied for my first job yet! At least according to my parents, who were struggling, Depression-era European immigrants. From the moment I was born, they were set on my future profession. If they could have named me "Doc," they surely would have.

Growing up, I had rebellious moments when I would insist to my parents that I had other career goals in mind. In sixth grade, for instance, I easily won Mrs. Rosenbloom's stock-market contest. The stock I picked from the thousands listed in *The New York Times* was that of a company called TelePrompTer, an early-stage cable television firm that would eventually become the largest cable TV provider in the U.S. The stock wound up quadrupling that semester. Watching that stock's price chart start to resemble a rocket ship to the moon was incredibly exciting, and I recall boldly announcing to my parents that I was planning on becoming a stock-market analyst when I grew up. I'll never forget how flaming red my Austrian father's face turned and how the veins in his neck were popping.

"So, you vant to be a gambler and embarrass your family by losing everything vee vorked so hard for you for?" he yelled. "You vill become a doctor. Dat's a sure thing."

And, indeed, I ultimately did reluctantly pursue the one and only route that would make my parents happy. I entered NYU's pre-med program and slogged my way through four miserable years. Between commuting back and forth every day and studying feverishly, I had little time for a social life. I was depressed as heck, but didn't have enough free time to let it all sink in. Besides, my parents' world literally revolved around my brother and me. I was terrified of letting them down.

But there was one thing that kept me somewhat sane during those awful college years—something I certainly never told my parents about. When I turned eighteen, I yanked out the few thousand bucks that were sitting in the savings account they had set up for me and opened up an account at a brokerage firm. Then, every Wednesday morning, the same friendly, bald Hispanic guy at the nearby *New York Post* printing plant would toss me a copy of that morning's edition. I would quickly leaf through the pages to locate influential stock picker Lou Ehrenkrantz's "Stock of the Week" column.

If the stock recommendation in Ehrenkrantz's column that particular Wednesday morning got me excited, I would call my broker before the opening and invest the full amount of dollars at my disposal to buy those shares at the start of the trading day. Then, like clockwork, I would sell those same shares twenty-four hours later at the next day's opening of trading.

That trading system I developed helped me build a pretty fair nest egg by the end of my junior year. My parents? They never had a clue. All they cared about was that I was achieving excellent grades in my courses and had scored in the top 5 percent in the country on my MCAT exams. My advisors assured me that I was a shoo-in to be accepted by one or more of the medical schools to which I had applied, and I was totally resigned to the path that my parents had laid the foundation for all those years prior.

But a shocking thing happened—not a single medical school accepted me... not a one. To this day, I have not the slightest clue why. Maybe they could sense my lackluster interest through the words of my essay? I don't know, but my parents were devastated. And me? I fell into a deep depression.

With my parents' dreams of medical school dashed, I needed desperately to come up with a backup plan, but I had none. So I had little choice but to dutifully follow my father's suggestion to become, as he referred to it, a "lower doctor." I applied to grad school in psychobiology. At least my mom and dad would still be able to brag to their friends about "my son, the doctor" and not be lying about it. I made up my mind to dive headfirst into my studies as never before.

I ended my second year at SUNY Stony Brook with a perfect 4.0 index and, as importantly, received an "A" on my master's thesis from my curmudgeonly but highly influential advisor/professor, the head of the Psychobiology Department. I then applied to Stony Brook's Clinical Psychology Department and was quickly accepted for their Ph.D. program. My path was, once again, laid out plainly in front of me, and the world was at my feet once more. Well, for a week or so anyway.

> **I will never know why I was rejected by all those medical schools.**

Once my clearly sadistic advisor (yes, the same one who had just given me an "A" on my thesis paper, calling it "exceptional") got wind that I was planning to get my doctorate in a different department area than his, he immediately petitioned the board of the Psychology Department to render my paper invalid as a master's thesis, citing "insufficient originally conceived clinical studies." The department's board subsequently yielded to the power he wielded, and my master's thesis was withdrawn along with my letter of acceptance to the Clinical Psychology Ph.D. program.

Breaking *this* news to my mother and father was even more painful than disclosing my medical school rejections. And as much as I adored my parents (and as much as I know they adored me), I have to admit their reaction was not a pretty one. I recall hearing words like "failure," "disappointment" and, yes, even "loser." My self-esteem was at an all-time low that summer, and this time I was on my own with no Plan B (or, in my case, Plan C) in sight. I felt, at the ripe old age of twenty-three, like my life was in free fall.

After a few weeks of doing little but beating myself up, I found myself contemplating a bold new direction. There had actually been one area where I had experienced the thrill of victory and not the agony of defeat. Unfortunately, this area would involve the one career path (other than maybe "mass murderer") that would upset my parents the most.

So, that summer, I found myself spending several days a week in the Brooklyn Business Library, reading and learning about a subject matter a far cry from the one I had been studying for the past six years: the stock market. And come that fall, armed with a boatload of moxie and a single high-school economics class as my only résumé credentials, I naively began my pursuit of a job as a Wall Street analyst. In hindsight, it was an absolutely absurd notion on my part. But, maybe for the first time in my life to that point, I was actually chasing *my* dream, not somebody else's version of it.

The responses I got from the brokerage firms to which I applied were a consistent blend of, "We love your passion and street smarts," "Won't you consider becoming a broker instead?" and "No MBA? You've got to be kidding, right?" But this time around, I did not fall into emotional abyss #3. For some reason, I knew this was what I was meant to do for a living, and I was going to figure out a way in.

Then one day, while reading—yes, you guessed it, Lou Ehrenkrantz's "Stock of the Week" column in the *New York Post*—I happened to focus in on the fine print at the bottom of the column.

"Mr. Ehrenkrantz has a degree in drama from NYU and a Master's in English from Hunter College."

Drama? English? This dude—this "dean of America's stock pickers," whose weekly recommendations literally built my nest egg during those pre-med years—had nothing even *resembling* an MBA! I decided to hound the one person on Wall Street whom I just knew would "get me"—the drama major himself, Lou Ehrenkrantz.

After three of my calls to him went unreturned, Lou actually picked up his phone early one Monday morning and reluctantly agreed to meet me for lunch at the old Commodore Hotel near Grand Central. After we finished our meal (and what I felt was a fairly impressive pitch for employment on my part), he told me he was sorry but his firm had no analyst job openings at the time. He suggested I go back to school and finish getting my degree in psychology. But just as I was about to get up and leave, Lou grabbed my arm and told me to have a seat once more.

And the next day, in my suit and tie, I walked into the New York Stock Exchange-member brokerage firm of Rosenkrantz, Ehrenkrantz, Lyon & Ross to meet with Lou's partner, Lester Rosenkrantz. The following week, I was hired as the firm's first-ever "junior analyst." Two years later, I became their Senior Growth Stock Analyst. Two years after that, I co-founded the firm's Corporate Finance division.

Today, three and a half decades later, I still happily make my living (out of my home office) doing what I was clearly meant to do: find undervalued stocks. I've never had a losing year after all this time, so I guess my father's prediction about my "gambling" career was not quite on target.

I will never know why I was rejected by all those medical schools. I will never fully understand why my psychobiology advisor needed to be as vindictive as he was. But I don't need those answers anymore. And although I hope I never again have to experience the bottomless pit of despair I felt after those brutal disappointments in my life, one thing is clear: I would not be where I am today if I hadn't stepped confidently in the direction that my heart had intended all along.

~Gary Stein

69

Panic

We cannot direct the wind, but we can adjust the sails.
~Bertha Calloway

Mom died the week before I turned sixteen. She was forty-eight, way too young to die. And, it turns out, she died with a secret.

I thought the worst thing that could ever happen to me happened when Mom died, but I was wrong. It started the following spring. I was at a big family dinner when it hit me out of nowhere. My heart started to race, my head began to swim, and a wave of nausea sent me flying away from the table and out the door. The idea that I could have vomited all over dinner was appalling, but that sudden, overwhelming panic was absolutely terrifying.

That day, I made a decision that would change my life forever: I didn't tell anyone what happened, even when it happened again.

Everything would be going along normally, and then the panic would hit. I'd suddenly leave a restaurant, abruptly walk out of a movie theater, or inexplicably turn around at the door of the shopping mall. I didn't know what was happening or why. I just knew that running from fearful situations seemed like the right thing to do. People don't put themselves in danger for no good reason, right? But in reality, every time I left the table, ran out the door, or turned down an invitation, the world in which I felt safe became smaller and smaller.

I was in my early twenties when I first quit a job because of my attacks. A feature writer for a daily newspaper in a small city, I was traveling all over the county with a photographer, tracking down stories and meeting daily deadlines. I was getting so many bylines that the cashiers in the Safeway recognized my name when I wrote checks for my groceries.

I became quite adept at accommodating my attacks, which were happening more frequently. When on assignment, the first thing I did in any building was locate all of the exits. If I felt trapped, things would start to degenerate pretty quickly so I needed to be ready to flee. Before too long, I would only take seats on the aisle. Then I started standing near the door, and then at the edge of the doorway. Next, I started asking my editor to send a different reporter if I knew a building wasn't "safe." Finally, just walking into the newsroom made my heart race.

I felt like I was losing control, or having a heart attack, or about to throw up all over someone's shoes. My rational self knew I was not going to lose my mind or lose my lunch. But panic's powerful and relentless message overrides rationality: Run! Run! Run!

I ran back home.

Did I explain to my dad why I suddenly quit my dream job to move back into my

> *Within two years, I was a prisoner in my house.*

old bedroom? No. Embarrassed and mystified by the attacks that no one else was having, I told myself they were just something to wait out, like a bad period or getting a cavity filled. Was anxiety even recognized as a disorder back then? If it was, no one was talking about it.

I managed work and life around the attacks, met a young man and got married. My husband and I were not a good match, but by the time I realized it, anxiety was filling my head with words like "trapped" and "helpless." My attacks came more frequently, even when nothing was scary. One minute, I'd be having a nice time with friends, and the next I felt like I stepped off the roof of a high-rise building.

With every new attack, I lost a little more self-confidence and slid a little deeper into fearing the fear. Within two years, I was a prisoner in my house. I couldn't even get the newspaper off the porch. There was no more denying my disorder.

My best friend tried so hard to get me out of the house and back into the world. One day, she said, "I'm taking you to lunch. Don't even think about it. Just step out the door."

I couldn't do it.

"I just don't get it," she said. "It's one step. *One* step!"

"It's not one step," I said. "It's *the* step."

I tried to explain my bizarre behavior to my family and friends, but, really, it didn't even make sense to me. Then one day, my dad said, "This sounds like what your mother had."

Mom was "nervous." She didn't like to drive or cross busy streets, and she especially didn't like stairs. I can still feel the frantic clench of her hand gripping my shoulder as we'd descend into the basement on laundry day, one step at a time. I immediately recognized her fear as mine. I learned that Mom had been prescribed tranquilizers for many years, and that her mother had been given shock treatments for her nervous condition.

I'd love to say these revelations prompted a fast recovery for me, but it took several years. I found a therapist who came to the house for counseling, and after that, a therapist who took me out once a week to help me reclaim unsafe territories. Most people will never relate to how terrifying it can be to walk all the way to the back of the grocery store to get a gallon of milk for their kids. At least, I hope they don't.

In the 1990s, I read an article on anxiety disorder in a women's magazine. I brought it to my doctor. "This is what I have," I told him. "There's medication for this." He waved away the magazine.

"I can't prescribe medication just because you read an article in some magazine." He had no idea how hard it was for me to walk into that building and sit in that exam room; he hadn't checked to see that my heart was beating wildly or noticed that my palms were sweating profusely.

I thought about my future filled with fear and isolation, and instead of letting my anxiety remind me that I was weak and wounded and unworthy, I pushed back. "Write me a referral to a psychiatrist."

The doctor refused.

"Well, I am not leaving here until you do."

Two weeks later, the psychiatrist diagnosed my attacks as an anxiety disorder and prescribed medication. It wasn't the perfect medication, but it gave me the help I needed to start making the world around me safer and to reassert myself as a worthwhile person who should enjoy life to its fullest. And now I do.

As much as I like my new version of "normal," my perception of the world is still modified by the many years I adapted my life to accommodate fear and anxiety. I still walk into a restaurant or a theater or a mall and think, *Wow! Those people don't think this is scary.*

And then it occurs to me: *Neither do I.*

~Grace Kuikman

70

C.R.A.F.T.S.

Our bodies are our gardens to the which
our wills are gardeners.
~William Shakespeare

A few months after my forty-ninth birthday, my life was self-destructing; at least, that was my diagnosis. I was overweight. I had high blood pressure and high cholesterol. My back ached. I had insomnia. Not only did I lose my car keys, but sometimes I couldn't even find my car in a parking lot.

My doctor's prescription was to reduce stress, get some exercise and improve my diet. He gave me a handful of pamphlets to look over, suggesting that something might appeal to me.

When I got home, I flipped through the pamphlets.

Weight-loss meditation therapy. No, thanks.

A mail-order diet specializing in edible seaweed. Nope.

A weeklong exercise program called The Ultimate Extreme Boot Camp Experience. Not for me.

A nutrition seminar at a nudist retreat. Never.

I shuffled to the next pamphlet, entitled C.R.A.F.T.S.

Interesting name, but this wasn't about needlepoint or scrapbooking. The word "crafts" stood for Calming, Relaxing Activity For Tired Souls.

The pamphlet explained that C.R.A.F.T.S. was for people who desired a low-impact, low-pressure, thirty-minute workout in a quiet, supportive atmosphere. Meetings were at the community center on

Monday and Thursday evenings and Saturday mornings. The cost was only $5 per week.

I dropped the other pamphlets in the recycle bin, but I tacked the one for C.R.A.F.T.S. on the refrigerator door.

I had never exercised with other people before; I'd rarely done any controlled, pre-planned exercise at all. I really did not want to attend C.R.A.F.T.S., but I knew I needed to do something, anything, different to improve my health. The pamphlet hung on the refrigerator, continuing to nag at me.

Finally, two weeks later, with more than a bit of trepidation, I made the decision to attend C.R.A.F.T.S. just once to see what it was all about.

The next Monday evening, I stepped into the community center classroom wearing a T-shirt and sweatpants, and carrying my brand new exercise mat.

Tables and chairs were stacked against the wall. A group of women stood together chatting. A CD player quietly played Enya.

"Welcome," said one of the women. "You're here for C.R.A.F.T.S.?"

I nodded. "If there's room available."

"There's always room," she said, reaching out to shake hands. "I'm Janet."

I introduced myself.

Janet pointed to the others. "This is Wendy, Mary, Suzie, Bonnie and Carol."

"I've never worked out before," I said, "but I'm interested in learning."

"You know, there's an ancient Asian proverb," replied Janet. "When the student is ready, the teacher will appear."

"Oh, you study martial arts?" I asked.

"No." Janet shrugged. "I heard it on a rerun of *Kung Fu* last night; I thought it sounded good."

Everyone laughed, and I relaxed a bit.

"Why don't we get started," Janet suggested, and the women spread out.

I took a spot in the back of the room, following the others, bending and stretching when they did.

"Hold your abs tight," Janet called out. "Keep those backs straight. Focus on breathing."

At home, I could wash dishes, watch television and talk on the phone all at the same time, but when Janet called out about tight abs, straight backs and focused breathing, I was overwhelmed.

Then came sit-ups, push-ups, leg lifts and free weights. The session concluded with yoga stretches. The women were intertwining their limbs into knots. I could barely touch my toes.

> **The morning after my first C.R.A.F.T.S. workout, I woke up stiff as the Tin Man.**

"Don't stress," advised Wendy. "In a few weeks, you'll be fine."

A few weeks, I thought. *Only if this initial workout doesn't kill me first!*

After the workout, I handed Janet a five-dollar bill.

She shook her head. "We don't collect money until Saturday."

"Isn't this your payment?" I asked.

"No." Janet smiled. "I don't charge. The room's free, and I get as much from these sessions as anyone."

"What's the money for?"

"Monthly donations," explained Janet. "To the homeless shelter, the food cupboard or the animal rescue center."

"You give the money away?" I asked.

"Yep." Janet picked up her CD player. "If everyone pitches in, we raise over $100 a month."

The morning after my first C.R.A.F.T.S. workout, I woke stiff as the Tin Man in *The Wizard of Oz*, but instead of an oilcan, I groaned for coffee and Tylenol.

I debated not returning after that first session, but for the next few weeks I attended every workout and, as predicted, the pain did eventually disappear. I learned to control my abs, back and breathing and even join in on conversations. It was a good workout and, just as advertised, calming and relaxing, too.

Then came the true test: my next doctor's appointment six months later. Victory! My blood pressure and cholesterol were both down considerably, and I'd lost eleven pounds.

Okay, I still wasn't thin, not even close. I'm certainly not thrilled with what I see reflected in the mirror, but there were some positive changes. My clothes fit better, I have more energy, and I haven't lost my car in a parking lot in ages.

I'd been brave enough to push myself to do something different, something positive for myself that I normally wouldn't do, and I had been happily rewarded with success.

~David Hull

71

Reluctant Writer

I am always doing that which I cannot do,
in order that I may learn how to do it.
~Pablo Picasso

Several days after my forced retirement, I was sitting at the kitchen table feeling sorry for myself. Two severely arthritic hips had made it impossible to continue in my pediatric practice. Now that my life had taken an unwanted turn, what meaningful activity would hold my interest and enhance the rest of my life?

When my phone rang, my good friend Allan tried to coax me into keeping him company in a creative writing class at the Institute for Lifelong Learning at a local university.

"Nah," I said. "I got brung up in Brooklyn and ain't even loined to talk a gooda English."

"Come on, keep me company. I always wanted to write."

"Nah!"

"Please, you'll love it. We'll spend time together."

Just to get him off my back, I said I would, figuring he'd forget about it when the time came to actually take the course.

"Great," he said. "I'll pick you up in ten minutes."

One of the first assignments the teacher gave us was to write the opening sentence of a story about a trip we had taken. We were to make it interesting so the reader would want to learn more. I wrote, "As our ship entered the fjord, the sight of rugged cliffs undulating to the sea, and the sweet smells of multicolored flowers at their bases, presaged the wonders of Norway we were about to see."

"Very good," the teacher said. "Maybe a little overuse of big words, but it grabs our interest."

This really is fun, I thought. *I can do this.* And by the time the class was over, I was hooked.

Several months later, I decided to take a writing course in the university itself. I learned that before I could take more advanced courses, I needed to complete Creative Writing 101. I asked Allan to join me.

"Sounds too easy," he said.

I found myself thrown in with a group of eighteen- to twenty-year-olds. It was interesting to hear about their dreams and passions. I imagined they were not too dissimilar to the ones I had at their age. Could new dreams be formulated at this stage of my life?

One of the assignments was to write a twenty-six-sentence story, each sentence starting sequentially with a different letter of the alphabet from A to Z. I told the story of Abraham Zenobia, an elderly gentleman trying to regain his youth. When I came to the end, I concluded, "Youth couldn't be revisited. Zenobia sadly became resolved to his fate." Then I realized that although youth couldn't be revisited, hopes and dreams needn't die.

The next term, I enrolled in the more advanced class of Narrative Technique. I convinced Allan to join me. When we arrived in class, the professor asked who hadn't taken Creative Writing 101. Allan raised his hand. The professor said all those who raised their hands should leave, as the class was oversubscribed anyway. As Allan marched out of the room, I felt sorry for him. He was the one who always wanted to write, not me.

The accolades I had received in the first two courses for my writing skills were now few and far between. I had no concept of what constituted a good story. Each exercise I handed in was ripped to shreds by the professor. At first, I thought he was doing that because in his mind I was dallying with writing and taking the place of someone who wanted to write professionally. Then I realized what I was writing was generally awful.

"Will I ever be able to write a good story?" I asked the professor.

"How long have you been writing?" he said.

"A long time. At least seven or eight months."

He smiled. "You can't expect to write anything decent for at least five years."

"Really?"

He nodded.

I continued taking fiction classes with different professors, struggling to understand what made a good story. I finally enrolled in a creative nonfiction course because it was the only course being given that I hadn't already completed.

The first assignment was to describe a culinary delight we had experienced. I told a story about my grandmother's chopped liver. The professor's comment on my story was "B+, good."

The second assignment had to do with writing a story about one of the rooms we lived in growing up. I wrote about sneaking into the dining room Friday nights where the male members of my extended family played pinochle. Again the professor's comment was "B+, good."

The third assignment was to go home and write a story about an object in my house. I chose my mother's soup tureen that adorned our dining room table.

I told the story of how, at the age of fifteen, I traveled to Chicago to join my mother, father, aunt and uncle to attend my brother's graduation from a master's degree program at the University of Illinois. I couldn't drive out with them because I had to take several New York State Regents Examinations.

After the graduation, we all drove together in a packed car through Canada, stopping at every antique barn along the way. The first barn we stopped at was a large red structure with aisles laden with merchandise arranged haphazardly. My mother sniffed her way up and down the aisles before smelling out a sterling silver coffee service, tucked between an ornate candelabra and a collection of old English fire irons. I thought it was ugly. My father said we couldn't buy it because there was no room in the car. My brother, who loved it, suggested we ship it, and my father acquiesced. At another large barn — filled with either junk or antiques, depending on one's point of view — my mother waded through the aisles, and like a bloodhound stalking its prey, sniffed out a soup tureen I loved, and my brother hated. "This is beautiful," she said.

My father said it was too big to fit in the stuffed car and too fragile to ship.

"If we buy it, Pop, I'll hold it on my lap till we get home," I said. "Mom really loves the tureen."

My father relented.

I clutched the box the entire trip, as if by releasing my grip I would lose my hold on my mother.

When the professor handed this story back, she wrote "A+, excellent." I spoke to her and said I didn't like this story as much as the other two. I thought I had spent too much time on the description of the tureen.

> *Each exercise I handed in was ripped to shreds by the professor.*

She smiled. "That's easy to correct." She pointed to my manuscript. "Just stop your description of the tureen here, and it will be half as long. Do you see, though, how the story highlights the differences between you and your brother in a subtle way, and shows your feelings toward your mother? The image of you clutching the box on your lap for fear of losing hold of your mother is a powerful one."

I nodded, and really did see what she meant. I finally realized what constituted a story.

I entered the story into the all-university contest, and when it won, the head of the department presented the award to me. He said, "Paul once asked me if he will ever write a good story. I guess this is his answer. I told him it takes at least five years to write something good. If I'm not mistaken, that's how long it has been since he started writing."

As I accepted the award, I thought about how two arthritic hips had prematurely curtailed my medical practice. About how Allan cajoling me into taking a writing course led to a new passion. Saying "yes" to something new and completely outside my world had certainly worked out.

~Paul Winick

Saying Yes to No

Clear clutter. Make space for you.
~Magdalena Vandenberg

S ome people call hoarding a sickness. For me, it was a source of comfort. I always felt safe and secure surrounded by my piles of stuff. I'm sure I can trace my compulsive collecting all the way back to my childhood.

I was raised in a family of six kids, and there never seemed to be enough to go around. My father was the breadwinner while my mother had to stay at home to raise the brood. Nothing was ever wasted. My siblings never complained about anything my mother prepared for dinner. In fact, the only complaint I ever recall was that there was not enough of it to go around.

All of us wore hand-me-downs. Even the oldest kids got clothes picked up at the local thrift store. As a middle child, I never knew what it was like to have an item of clothing that was not well worn by my brother. This didn't always turn out well as I quickly outgrew him. As an adult, I still have toes that display the signs of having been crammed into ill-fitting shoes.

Our general lack of money meant that everything we owned was used to the maximum. Nothing was discarded before it wore out, and sometimes not even then. Unwittingly, my family members were early pioneers of the green movement. Al Gore would have been proud of our efforts. All of the furniture in the house was recycled, usually from relatives or friends. If a piece was discarded in our house, it had already had a long second life and now was impossible to reuse. Even at that, my parents had a problem throwing things away.

Having been raised in this environment, it is easy to see the roots of my hoarding problem. As an adult, I had a deep-seated need to amass as much stuff as possible, just in case it might someday come in handy. My collecting extended all the way from books to discarded building materials. The main problem facing any hoarder is storage, and I was no different. When I lived alone in a large detached house, it was not a big issue. I had a garage for the oversized stuff, and an attic and basement for more manageable items. I always felt comfortable surrounded by things that I expected would one day be useful. Friends in need of an odd thing to finish off a project could always rely on me to have the needed part.

> *Some people call hoarding a sickness. For me, it was a source of comfort.*

Over the years, my hoard had grown quite large. The main source of supply was through curb picking. When I walked to work each day, I scanned through the items my neighbours had deemed of no further use. Anything consigned to the curb was fair game. I saw myself as performing a civic duty, picking up discarded pieces that would otherwise be destined for a landfill. Some days, I could arrive at work laden with treasures picked up on my morning walk. Workmates were tolerant of my habit and would even give me a ride home after work if my load looked too heavy.

I existed in this cocoon of hoarding comfort until I met a woman who was to be more important to me than my hoarding. Looking back now, I can see that my hoarding even spilled over into our marriage. My wife was patient with me up to the time we moved into an apartment. It was then that her tolerance was severely tested. There was barely room in the apartment for us, let alone the products of my years of collecting. Initially, I tried hiding things in our huge basement storage space, but it was not long before overflow items began appearing on the balcony and in cupboards. This was the point that heralded change. My wife never gave any ultimatums, but I knew that she was unhappy. It was important for me to contribute to my partner's happiness. If this meant eliminating hoarding from our lives altogether, then so be it.

In my own defence, I was always selective in my hoarding practices. I had never collected newspapers or magazines. We in the hoarding world look down on the poor souls who feel the need to collect every written word to have passed through their hands. It seems that even hoarders have a pecking order.

Although I wanted to keep my wife happy, I found it difficult to reduce the collection. At first, I could only part with things I thought would go to a good home. As a result, I spent a lot of time trying to gift items to friends and family. Of course, the ideal situation would have been if I'd had a friend who was a hoarder. That way, I could have reduced my inventory in one move. Friends had seen me struggle with my addiction and the negative effects exerted on my life. As a result, no one stepped forward to take on the role.

It took me a few months to get rid of the bulk of my stuff. I was able to do this thanks to my wife's support and encouragement. She gave me the security and stability my life had previously lacked. It had taken me a lifetime and a wonderful woman to realize that I could finally leave hoarding behind. The emotional gap was filled by love and encouragement. Without my wife's gentle and patient coaxing, I would likely have one day ended up an introverted, old man living a cramped existence surrounded by useless treasures.

Now that I'm addiction-free, I find myself in a comfortable physical and emotional space. Every so often, I still get the urge to pick up a discarded item at the side of the road. Knowing the consequences of hoarding, and that I am going home to a loving relationship, I keep my hands firmly in my pockets.

~James A. Gemmell

73

The Sweet Pain of Anticipation

I am not the same, having seen the moon shine
on the other side of the world.
~Mary Anne Radmacher

am gazing at the cover of a passport. It could be any passport — it is blue, with the words UNITED STATES OF AMERICA and the coat of arms embossed in gold.

But then I flip the cover. I see the photo of a twenty-nine-year-old man. He has been a very successful sportswriter. He has interviewed Joe Montana in the bowels of Stanford Stadium after a convincing Super Bowl XIX victory, probed "Bullet Bob" Feller for insight about a 1940s fastball that once got tested against a speeding motorcycle, and traversed the pristine spring training sites of Arizona in search of a captivating story. But he has never really taken a chance. He has lived life within a safe box. Most of what he's done had a measurable probability of outcome.

He is smiling in the photo. He doesn't know exactly where this passport will take him. He just knows that he has to go. He knows that he has lived in conformity for far too long; that he actually has an adventurer's heart that has to be satisfied; that there will be life lessons along the way.

I flip the page and see the stamps. Australia. Thailand. England.

Greece. Turkey. On and on they go, for three years and twenty-one countries.

And my mind clicks back to 1987, just a few months after the passport was issued, and just days before I would hop on a Qantas flight for Sydney — the final step in my migration to Australia.

I had given up a union newspaper job in Stockton, California, packed a big Army duffle bag so tightly that I could barely zip it closed, and prepared to head Down Under. My dad was a very practical, play-it-safe man who had grown up on a farm in the heart of Amish Country in Pennsylvania and married his sweetheart at twenty-one. But I didn't receive any admonishment from him.

He and Mom sent me off with their blessing and this message in a card:

As you journey to a new country, there will be many events to be recorded, many chapters in your life. We're proud of your courage and are very happy that you have this great opportunity. So we wish you well. Have a safe journey. You can bet we'll see you sometime, somewhere in the Outback.

I could have stayed in Stockton. And Sugar Ray Leonard could have stayed in retirement.

Sugar Ray, one of the greatest boxers of all time, retired in 1982, returned in 1983, then retired again in 1984. But on March 10, 1986, he was ringside when rival Marvin Hagler knocked out a nobody named John Mugabi to become the undisputed world middleweight champ. Sugar Ray decided he had to come back again to test himself.

My life and Sugar Ray's intersected in August 1986 when I read a column by sportswriter Dave Kindred, "Sugar Ray must box to live." Kindred described how he had recently hosted a long-time photographer friend who was in town, and they started talking about how life needs mystery, or else everything flattens into a mundane routine.

His friend's drive to work took him past sparkling white fences, horse farms and limestone outcroppings in green pastures. But over time, his friend confided, he inadvertently started ignoring the beauty, for the mystery of discovery was gone.

"Inevitably, it robbed my friend of the spark of imagination that brings a person to life," Kindred wrote. "If we never wonder what's next — if we know the answer before the question's asked — we are less than we could be. We need mystery. We need the sweet pain of anticipation."

> He has lived life within a safe box.

Sugar Ray needed to feel it. Kindred's friend needed to feel it. And after reading that, I knew I needed to feel it.

So I arrived in Sydney on February 7, 1987. One day, I walked into media mogul Rupert Murdoch's building — which housed three newspapers — and was cordially invited to go through a three-day training to become a copy editor. After two days, I was offered what amounted to a full-time job: three days a week on *The Australian*, the national newspaper, and two days on the *Daily Mirror*, the afternoon tabloid. Imagine an Australian walking off the street into *The New York Times* and getting the same treatment.

I took the gift and ran with it. I saw plays at the Sydney Opera House, learned how to scuba dive and ride a horse, and paddled whitewater rapids for the first time.

I wrote a letter to my friends, at one point saying, "There's a real pulse here. Things are happening. This place can steal your heart."

After fifteen months, I used it as a launching pad to discover the world. I started out by doing a sixty-day camping safari around Australia — living mostly in a tent while seeing more of the country than most Australians ever see — and then bought a round-the-world plane ticket, with stops in Bangkok, London, Harrisburg, Pennsylvania, San Francisco, Honolulu, and Sydney.

When I got back to Australia in February 1989, I was rehired on *The Australian*, and even became the paper's basketball writer on the off days of the regular writer. I slipped right back into the dynamic life I enjoyed before.

But after another year there, I had reached a point where I felt I either needed to commit to living the rest of my life there or return to the U.S. There was no Skype, no Facebook, no Instagram. Heck, there wasn't even the Internet. I was relying on a once-a-week international *USA Today* for my news and irregular phone calls to my family at about three dollars a minute. I missed American sports, and I missed my family.

So I shipped my possessions back to the U.S., stuffed my backpack and headed off on one last adventure — a savage journey into the heart of Hong Kong, Greece and Turkey. When I arrived back in the States, I kissed the ground. I still have that photo. It's me saying, "Thank you, Lord, for the blessing of these three years."

And I think of what the author C. JoyBell C. once wrote about growing. She said that the only way we can live is by growing. And that we have to throw ourselves into new experiences.

I did it. I threw myself at life. I bungee-jumped off a bridge in New Zealand, toured the world's greatest museums, and passed through Checkpoint Charlie into East Berlin before The Wall came down. I climbed to the top of Mount Olympus and descended 100 feet into the Coral Sea to get a better view of the Great Barrier Reef. I gained a friend when I met an eccentric Belgian artist named Vollabra and lost an appendix in a potentially life-threatening surgery in England.

After doing all of that, there is no going back to the mundane.

~Rick Weber

74

Twice Their Age

It is never too late to be what you might have been.
~George Eliot

n 2013, I was struggling. I had been diagnosed with morbid obesity, and even though I exercised regularly and tried every diet, I couldn't lose the weight. Meanwhile, my work status was deteriorating. In government, radical changes occur in the work environment when new administrations take over. I saw a tightly functioning family of civil servants disband in a mass exodus due to a toxic work environment. I also faced a reduction in pay and financial hardship for numerous reasons. These challenges forced me to re-evaluate my opportunities. At the age of forty-one, drastic changes to my life began to unfold.

The first opportunity I encountered was investing more in my family than I had in the past. My son had started playing lacrosse, which was a fairly new sport in our Midwestern city. I saw an opportunity to have an athletic bond with my son, so I picked up my own lacrosse stick and started playing with him.

Then I was presented the opportunity to have bariatric surgery. I was actually a very active person for someone classified as morbidly obese. I was always working out. As a former marathon runner, I never stopped running long distances. Playing in sports has always been a part of my life. Regardless of the exercise, I still struggled with my weight; it was in my DNA. I just wanted something to make it a little easier. Hopefully, bariatric surgery was the answer.

As for my career, out went the résumés. After a nationwide search, I received several offers, but none seemed just right until an offer from the land of opportunity. My manifest destiny to the Gold Rush State began with a job offer in Northern California. This was just one month after my surgery. I headed west and prepared to take advantage of my new life, but the opportunities continued to evolve and present themselves.

My new position was for a limited term, so I kept my eye on new career opportunities. Meanwhile, I focused on taking advantage of my weight-loss gift. I followed my post-operative diet and began to run. I was running like Forrest Gump. I had miles and miles of road time in the beautiful, sunny, and warm Northern California weather. I started seeing distances and times I hadn't seen since I was in the Marine Corps twenty-plus years before. I set a goal of running the Marine Corps Marathon on the twentieth anniversary of my first marathon at the same venue, which would occur in 2015. I also continued learning my new love: lacrosse. After a short but beloved time in Northern California, I received a new job offer in Southern California that I couldn't refuse. Off to the City of Angels I went, where I would soon find out how opportunities can snowball and multiply when we take advantage of them.

In SoCal, I found a job that paid well, but I didn't really care for the environment. I had no passion for the job, and it sent me searching for further opportunities. I had always wanted to attend graduate school, but I always put it off in order to pour myself into my job. I began to consider opportunities and applied for the highly prestigious Executive Master of Leadership program at the University of Southern California. I was accepted! I was so honored by the opportunity.

While running and preparing for my marathon, I used the opportunity to multi-task. I ran with my lacrosse stick so I could improve my lacrosse skills while training for "The People's Marathon." On those long runs, I got the opportunity to think; it is my escape, my meditation, my decompression. Sometimes, it wasn't thinking; it was dreaming. One day, the dream came to me. I did my undergrad as a part-time student, and I never played a sport in school. The light bulb flickered.

I have NCAA eligibility! I couldn't... I shouldn't... Could I? Should I? After an Internet search and a phone call to the coach, I got the invite. Come on out, I was told, but I must comply with the rules, which meant I had to be enrolled full-time. It was a dream. For dreams to become realities, sacrifice is required. A full-time graduate student I became.

Now my runs were fueled by my preparation for another dream: I wanted to play lacrosse for USC. In the fall of 2015, it was time for the first team meeting. I was surrounded by men half my age. I must have been asked ten times if I was a coach. "Uhh... no," I replied, accompanied by a nervous laugh.

> **I must have been asked ten times if I was a coach.**

What are they going to think of me? Are they going to run over me? Will I be able to keep up? I am not very good. Can I make it? Am I a liability or an asset? These athletes have been playing since middle school or earlier. I have been playing for two years. I feel as if I am in over my head. There was only one thing to do. Every day, I showed up early to practice, working on individual skills, extra conditioning, proper mental attitude, and employing my major, leadership. I wouldn't be the best player, but I could use my experience and be the best role model.

With my hands full as a husband, father, employee, student, long-distance runner, and lacrosse player, my studies helped me stay focused on opportunities. I saw an interesting job posting that I would be passionate about. It was a little outside my wheelhouse, but I was eager to see if adding the soon-to-be-completed graduate degree to my résumé opened any doors. I got an interview, and a second and a third, and then a job offer. I became the new Director of the American Humane Association's Red Star Emergency Services for Animals. I get to rescue animals for a living!

My new job interrupted my marathon training in the prime training month. I began the new job on October 1st, and the marathon was at the end of the month. I felt completely unprepared. *Do I do it? Is it safe? Will I make it? Randy, you have been blessed with an opportunity to run a marathon twenty years after your first marathon. Just ten months earlier, you were 100 pounds heavier and morbidly obese. Be grateful for the opportunity and honor it by owning it.* After four and a half hours, mission accomplished and Semper Fi. I was a marathon runner once again!

The year turned, and spring lacrosse — the true lacrosse season — began. I continued to be tested. For a forty-three-year-old to keep up with this class of athlete, compounded by the realities of life beyond that of a typical student, it was really unfathomable. However, I have become appreciative of the opportunities before me. I do not know many people my age who can boast that they played college lacrosse in the Los Angeles Memorial Coliseum for the University of Southern California.

With three team goals in our way, I did what I could to be a team player. *We must beat UCLA; we must have a winning record; we must make the play-offs.* At our final game of the season, we were 7–7. We were playing UCLA at UCLA. If we won, we would make the play-offs. We came from behind to tie it in the fourth quarter. USC versus UCLA in overtime, and the winner goes to the play-offs. For USC, we realized all of our goals for the season in this overtime. Was this a movie? No, it was an opportunity, ours for the taking. We won that game and went on to get beat in the first round of the play-offs, but a forty-three-year-old lacrosse rookie was playing in that game, too.

I wrapped up the season and channeled my energy into my new job and maintaining my schoolwork. I had the summer semester and then one elective course left. That would allow me to play fall lacrosse again. And then I was accepted into the Organizational Change and Leadership doctorate program at USC Rossier School of Education. I was able to continue playing lacrosse with the team, and by the end of May 2019 I will have played four full seasons. By then I will be a forty-six-year-old, and will have been the oldest person to play on the USC lacrosse team and perhaps within the Men's Collegiate Lacrosse Association… ever.

~Randal A. Collins

Chapter 9

The Power of Yes!

Give of Yourself

*Love unlocks doors and opens windows that
weren't even there before.*
~Mignon McLaughlin

75

Boldly Going

*No one is useless in this world who lightens
the burdens of another.*
~Charles Dickens

My friend Kate has always been involved in community service. She volunteers at the food pantry and the library; she organizes the blood drive at the fire hall three times a year; and she not only works at, but she and her husband actually founded, their church's clothing center — offering free clothes, shoes, and accessories to anyone who needs them.

Then there's me. I've always been involved in community service, too — if you consider watching too much TV, not littering, and buying way too many Girl Scout cookies to be "community service."

That changed one Tuesday evening last winter, when Kate called me. "I need your help," she said. "What are you doing tomorrow evening?"

"Well," I said hesitantly, "there's a *Star Trek* marathon on TV, so my night is pretty full."

"David, you've seen every episode of that show 100 times," Kate replied.

"That's a total exaggeration," I said. "Some of the episodes I've only seen seventy-five or eighty times."

"Tomorrow, I need your help for a couple of hours at my church's clothing center," Kate explained. "I had a family who signed up to help this week, but they've all got the flu. My husband and I can't run the place by ourselves."

"What?" I said. "I can't do that. No way. I've never even been to your church's clothing center before."

"Well, tomorrow," replied Kate, "I need you to — as one of your favorite TV shows might say — boldly go where you have never gone before."

I didn't want to do it, but since my friend was desperate enough to quote *Star Trek*, I agreed to help.

At 6:45 the next evening, instead of spending time with Captain Kirk and Mr. Spock, I showed up at the clothing center in the basement of the old brick church on Main Street.

"Thank you so much," said Kate when I arrived. "It's really simple. My husband and I will manage the actual clothing room; we just need you to run the welcome table by the door. Have folks line up, make sure they know what they need, give them a bag, and then we'll take them in one at a time to help them. We've gotten a ton of donations the past few weeks, so we should be able to help a lot of people."

The directions seemed clear enough; I figured I could handle it. How many people in my town were going to show up on a snowy Wednesday night for free clothes anyway?

At 7:00 p.m., Kate unlocked the front door, and I was surprised by the number of people who came in.

The first woman was looking for baby clothes. Her daughter had given birth to a baby girl a week ago, and they didn't have any warm clothes for her.

Another woman was there with her two young sons who needed winter coats.

Next was a man who hoped to get shoes for himself and his son. They had been sharing a single pair of size 9s for quite a while; the son wore them to high school during the day, and the man wore them to work at night. But the shoes now had holes in the bottoms, and they needed new ones.

A young woman came in wanting gloves and socks because she couldn't afford the utility payment, and the heat had been turned off in her apartment. Her fingers and toes were getting so cold at night that she couldn't sleep.

An older man arrived who had a job interview the next day and was looking for a shirt and tie to wear because he desperately needed that job.

By 8:45, when Kate escorted the last patron out and locked the door, my head was spinning. I couldn't believe what I had heard. Babies without clothes. Children without jackets. People whose fingers and toes froze at night. This wasn't some Third World, war-torn country—this was in upstate New York, right in my own neighborhood. How could this happen?

> *I couldn't believe what I had heard. Babies without clothes. Children without jackets.*

The next night, on my way home from work, I stopped at the mall to do some shopping, but not for myself; I was shopping for things the church clothing center might use.

One department store had a great sale on baby clothes. I filled my shopping basket, and it only cost me about twenty dollars. A shoe store had sneakers on sale. A sporting goods store had a clearance on children's knit gloves. They were all the same color, but they were less than two dollars a pair.

When I got home, I managed to fill a box with new merchandise for the clothing center for about the same amount of money I'd spend going out to dinner, a movie and coffee afterward.

My friend may have had to persuade me to get involved, but because of that experience, I realized that many people were a lot worse off than me. I also learned that I could help my community through the simple tasks of being aware and donating a little time and money.

Okay, so I'm not saving the world, but I have to admit that it does make life a bit more interesting (and perhaps more rewarding) if we occasionally remember to boldly go where we haven't gone before.

~David Hull

76

Pain Killer

Gratitude is the healthiest of all human emotions.
The more you express gratitude for what you
have, the more likely you will have
even more to express gratitude for.
~Zig Ziglar

I was embarking on my first ever mission trip! We had just taken off, and I was looking out the window at the ground disappearing below, with butterflies in my stomach. I truly had no idea what I was getting myself into. It was spring break, and thirty-six of us from our university's Catholic Student Association were headed to Tampa, Florida to serve the less fortunate.

I had wrestled with the decision to go on the trip for months. My apprehension came mostly from the fact that I had never imagined myself saying "yes" to a week of service away from home. Not that I didn't want to open my heart to help others, but so many what-ifs occupied my thoughts. *What if our interactions with the people we meet are awkward? What if I get all the way down to Florida and want to go home?* And, my biggest what-if of all, *What if cerebral palsy gets in the way of giving my whole heart to our service projects?*

Because of my CP, the muscles in my left lower body are in a constant state of contracture. My pain is unpredictable. Some days, I'm fine. On others, just walking feels as if I'm trudging through sand. The hardest part of living with chronic pain are the days when my heart is saying "go," but my leg is saying "no." Going on this "adventure" (that's how everyone around me was encouraging me to think of it) was already a leap of faith, and not knowing how my muscles would feel added a whole other degree of anxiety. The last thing I wanted was to spend my spring break watching from the sidelines with an ice bag!

On the first morning of the trip, I woke up feeling like a contorted pretzel. Sleeping on an old mattress on the floor had done a number on my leg, hips and back. It wasn't even 8:00 a.m. and I was already feeling defeated. But it was our first day trip offsite to serve the hungry, and I was determined to make the most of it. I made up my mind that I would push through, even if that meant collapsing from exhaustion at the end of the day. I was so nervous, but wanted to be able to meet people and hear their stories.

My personal prayer that morning went something like this: "Hi, God. So I just ask that things can start slow today, okay? Because I don't really know what I'm getting myself into. Lord, just give me one person. If I could hear one story, or maybe even share some of my own… that'd be nice. And, also, I pray that my spasms might go away. But if they don't, allow me to find meaning through this tightness and pain. Please watch over us all and make today meaningful. Amen."

I sent up that prayer, plus a bunch more before arriving at the café. Many of my friends were assigned to be hosts and servers, but I would be behind the counter to help plate the meals. I was thrilled! This was exactly what I had prayed for! I smiled to myself and got ready to scoop corn. The guy I was with was named Xavier, and he was at least a foot taller than I was. Truthfully, his size would've intimidated me if it wasn't for his big smile.

At first, we made small talk. But I also got to hear about the daily workings of the café and how much he enjoyed his job.

"I love it here and what I get to do every day," he said. "Sure, the people we serve don't have much. But that really doesn't matter when you look around. There's a ton of love. You can feel it. This place is so blessed."

He was right. I could feel it. Looking out into the dining room, I saw some of my friends hustling around serving food, while others were laughing or deep in conversation. It felt like something out of a movie, minus the heartfelt soundtrack. At that moment, my heart was so full. It was a deep realization of "Wow, look what we get to be a part of!"

Eventually, Xavier and I started talking more about faith. He told me about his life, and suddenly, I found myself talking about my cerebral palsy. "Oh, please God, give me the right words to say," I prayed.

Xavier seemed truly intrigued and asked genuine questions. Even though I'd only known him for an hour, sharing actually felt natural. I ended my story with a statement I'll stand by until the day I die. "God didn't give me cerebral palsy so I could wake up and feel frustrated by my body… and that's why I do my best to find the blessings in everything."

He looked up and blinked. "Wow. That's…That's super inspiring."

Smiling, I shrugged, glad that what I said seemed to resonate with him. What he didn't know was that those two hours simply being together, talking and scooping food, truly touched me! I loved every minute of it. My prayers were answered in so many ways, and I was overwhelmed with gratitude. God had given me my "one person"… and so much more! But then I realized something else: I was too overwhelmed with happiness, love and the power of community to even think about my pain that day.

> When we open our hearts and put the focus beyond ourselves, beautiful things happen.

It was such an amazing feeling. And as the week went on, that feeling continued. CP was barely a concern of mine; I was enjoying myself too much to care! Friends became like family as we served together and grew in faith. Each night, I went to sleep thanking God, grateful I hadn't missed such a fulfilling experience.

When we got home, people asked me what my biggest takeaway was from going on such an adventure. To me, it was simple: When we open our hearts and put the focus beyond ourselves, beautiful things happen. What are tight muscles compared to learning to have a little faith?

~Annie Nason

77

Take Your Husband to Work Day

One moment the world is as it is. The next,
it is something entirely different.
Something it has never been before.
~Anne Rice, Pandora

W hen I retired, I planned to do more of the things I loved and try new things I never had time for. But after six months, tennis and writing grew stale from overdoing them. Expanding the garden created so much extra produce that I couldn't even give it away. As for new things, well, kayaking hurt my back, golf seemed pointless, and a year into retirement, I had completed every project on my home improvement list.

I began watching more TV, taking up Sudoku, mowing the lawn before it needed it, and even asking my wife if she needed anything done. I sighed and snacked a lot.

One morning, Carol announced, "Today is Take Your Husband to Work Day."

"I never heard of that."

"Because I just invented it. Get dressed — nicely."

I started to protest, but I had nothing. Could I say that I planned to watch *Mutiny on the Bounty* at 10:00 a.m.? I shucked off my baggy jeans and sweatshirt. Khakis and an unwrinkled shirt felt pretty good.

She was on the road visiting clients. I could carry supplies if I wanted to be more than a useless lump. Carol is a retired therapist. Since giving up a salary, however, she's volunteered with the same agency to do therapy, organizational counseling, social work, grant writing, data input, program assessment, and speech making. She latches onto new challenges like a bulldog.

Our first stop was at a rickety boarding house for men. They shared a common kitchen and bathroom, and each man had his own room. The porch steps bounced under my weight. The house paint was curled and cracked. "Have you been here before?" I asked. It was hard to picture my classy wife in such a house.

"Oh, yes. Pull up your socks and roll down your cuffs," she replied. "You don't want anything jumping aboard."

She marched through a dingy hallway and banged on door number three. My skin prickled. I knew she dealt with poverty, but this seemed dangerous. "You shouldn't be alone in places like this," I said.

She shrugged. "I go where the people who need help live."

"Who's there?" a grizzled voice said.

Carol announced herself, and the door creaked open. "I brought you some things."

"Okay." Perhaps sixty, the man was unshaven and wore a sleeveless white undershirt. The room was maybe ten by ten with a card table, two chairs, a TV, and a bed dripping its blanket on the floor. The one window faced the wall of another building.

"Did you get a can opener?" he rasped as he pawed through the box I set on the card table. Eventually, he pulled out a hand-crank opener with a triumphant "Hah! What good's a food pantry if you can't get into the food?"

As we were leaving, I thought Carol's efforts were hopeless. It all drained into a sinkhole. Then the man called after us. "Hey, Mrs. B. That guy you told me about, he's got landscaping work for me. Thanks!"

Back in the car, I said, "I can't believe you go into places like that."

She shrugged. "Someone saw him trying to open canned goods with a brick. That can opener is the difference between whether he eats tonight or not. One thing this job does is make me grateful for everything we have. When I get home at night, I feel like a princess."

I grinned. "Really?"

"I'd feel like a queen if dinner was waiting."

"Uh-oh."

"Another thing. In this job, I'm never bored. Here, use the sanitizer."

Our next stop was at a small but neat house. Carol said, "Two elderly daughters are caring for their mother, and I need to set up respite care to give them a break."

The daughter who greeted us was in her seventies. In the living room, a hospital-style bed with steel sidebars was set up. An ancient woman slept there, snoring. The daughter wept as we watched the mother's chest rise and fall. "Mom's dying, but she just won't let go. She's had such a full life. Seventeen grandchildren, fifty-two great grandchildren, a few dozen great-great grandchildren, and then I lose track. See the picture over her bed? Mom's last birthday—her 99th." A panoramic shot was filled with a huge, waving crowd. I was awed. This woman was like a spring that had expanded into a river of humanity. She was like a biblical matriarch.

> I felt as if some part of myself that had been shut away was stirring.

Right before Carol took the daughter aside to counsel her and discuss practical matters, the daughter told me, "If Mom stirs, just hold her hand. She'll think it's one of the family." Me, hold this stranger's hand? A few minutes later, the mother began to moan, and I tentatively touched her hand. She clutched my hand and held tight. Such strength! Such passion even near the end. And I struggled to fill empty hours? I squeezed back to let her know that someone was here, as she had been for so many others. I felt as if some part of myself that had been shut away was stirring, that this unexpected intimate moment with a stranger was the most worthwhile thing I had done in quite a while. A few minutes later, she relaxed and slept.

In the car, I said, "That was amazing! Think of all the people she's leaving behind, the history her descendants will make! The nurturing she's done. One person can change the world."

Carol nodded. "There's plenty to think about on visits. I never know what I'll face." She shrugged. "Sometimes, it isn't pretty, but it's real life. I need to contribute while I can. You never know what difference a small contribution can make. Don't get me wrong, I like snuggling up with an old movie. And snuggling up with this same old guy I've been with all these years. But dealing with the unexpected makes our quiet moments even more precious."

Take Your Husband to Work Day was a success. I signed up to volunteer that week. Otherwise, Carol would have made me cook dinner.

~Garrett Bauman

I Never Knew That

Dare to reach out your hand into the darkness,
to pull another hand into the light.
~Norman B. Rice

A ll I said was, "Gee, my office has been slow lately. I wish I had something exciting to do." And you know what people say: "Be careful what you wish for; you might get it!"

I was well into my fifties when a couple of my friends, who are nuns, convinced me that I should help them re-organize a local respite center for victims of human trafficking.

"All you have to do is go in the morning to unlock the door, prepare coffee, and handle the phones," Sister assured me with a sweet smile.

By the end of the week, I had agreed to become the office manager for a confidential safe place for anyone looking for help to escape prostitution.

I was given a modest salary so I could still keep my part-time practice as a certified hypnotherapist.

I thought this would be a nice thing to do, to use my free time and help out an overlooked part of my community. I was a little anxious about being in "that" part of town, but I had no idea how this experience would change my life.

I never knew that my original perceptions of these "girls on the street" were so far from the reality of who they truly are: survivors. According to the International Labour Organization, there are about

Give of Yourself | 305

twenty-one million victims of human trafficking in the world. Sixty-eight percent are trapped in forced labor. Twenty-six percent of them are children. And fifty-five percent of these victims are women and girls.

I never knew that one out of five endangered runaways was probably a child sex-trafficking victim. I was shocked to hear how pervasive the curse of sex trafficking is in the Midwest, where middle school girls and boys are picked up at truck stops along the interstates as runaway teens. A free ride from a seemingly friendly truck driver can become a ticket to a whole new world of horrors. A hamburger, fries, cola and a dose of "something to feel better" only cost a little sex act in the cab of a big rig.

I never knew how horribly addictive just one exposure to methamphetamine can be for a young mind. Kids who ran away from their parents' rules became dazed and drug-addled puppets learning sex acts I had never imagined as an adult woman. Clearly, this new job was more than just handing out coffee, condoms and a bowl of soup.

At the time of my tenure, we had several counselors, all of whom were survivors themselves. I was awed by the variations in their personal stories: a massage parlor worker who had been a teenage runaway many years ago; a single mom who escaped from a viciously abusive drug addict. Some of the girls admitted that they were victims of rape in their own family, often facing the horrors of abortion or being a child trying to raise a baby. I was deeply saddened to see the shame and destruction of once beautiful women who had turned to prostitution to support a drug habit, often as part of a wild lifestyle in the music or modeling industries.

> It had never occurred to me that a $1.50 bus pass was an insurmountable obstacle.

Not long after I joined the team, we found a better location in a part of the city closer to our victims. While our guests needed to come to this secret location to get away from angry pimps and drug dealers, they also needed to be able to reach us without having to buy a bus pass.

It had never occurred to me that a $1.50 bus pass was an insurmountable obstacle. I never knew that most prostituted women and young boys are horribly poor.

Our new place was cozy, with sun-filled windows and exposed stone walls. We had a large bathroom with a generous shower and a full kitchen. "The girls," as we lovingly called our clients, were excited to help us set up a large, walk-in closet for the clothes, shoes, and personal items that were donated for them. A generous donor bought us a big freezer so we could accept leftovers from a famous pizza chain. Soon, other restaurants heard of our work, and I created soups and casseroles from their generosity. It was such a delight to see the folks come in, smell home cooking and see the tension leave their faces. Sometimes, all a guest wanted was a warm shower, clean clothes and a quiet cup of fresh coffee. Other times, they needed some one-on-one time with one of the counselors.

One day, I received a call from a mega church in the next state, asking if they could help us on a regular basis. I gave them our usual list of needs, including everything from underwear to deodorant and feminine hygiene products.

"Okay, we can help stock the closet," a kind lady replied. "But we want to do more than just give. We want to serve."

These ladies didn't want to just drop off food. They wanted to personally serve each guest, with love and humility.

"Um, well sure," I stammered, "but let me clear that with management and get back with you."

The staff and I discussed some ground rules to protect the clients:

No verbalized prayers unless requested.
No personal questions unless the guest opened the conversation first.
No touching, staring, whispers or signs of disrespect.

They agreed and assured us that they were truly only interested in being a source of good food, genuine caring and no judgment.

And so they created the Friday Lunch. Each week, a team of ladies would plan, cook and deliver an entire home-cooked meal — from salad to dessert. Each team enjoyed creating a beautiful table. Sometimes, little love notes were tucked inside the napkins with a discreet Bible verse. Often, they added chocolates or a big bouquet of fresh flowers. They thoroughly enjoyed competing with each other to decorate for Easter, Valentine's Day, Christmas and even an indoor Summer Picnic in August!

When the Church Ladies, as the girls called them, insisted on serving guests individually, not in big family-style bowls or buffet lines, something almost magical began to happen. Our clients felt respect and kindness as they were served their own plates, from one woman to another.

I had always thought the "street walkers" on the corners were there by choice. But as one of my favorite survivor counselors once said, "No one wakes up one day and says, 'Gee, I wanna be a prostitute!'" I never knew that... and a whole lot more.

~Valorie Wells Fenton

79

Just Like Me

The challenging part is in the beginning;
it's a leap of faith. But I think the most
important thing is to just do it. Start.
~Tom Szaky

I grew up around the fairgrounds where my grandparents owned and operated the Frozen Whip ice cream stand. The summer I was fourteen, I worked for them on weekends and got to know the other booth owners and game operators.

But our close-knit community changed each year in late September when the fair came to town and the fairgrounds swelled to three times its normal size. Food vendors hawked their wares amid the aroma of fried onions and roasting turkey legs. Operators secured riders in Ferris wheel seats and sent them to dizzying heights. Barkers called, "Step right up. Try your luck!" Carnival workers swept in and set up, worked ten days straight, pulled everything down, and moved on to the next city to do it all over again, leaving behind wisps of trash and tent-stake holes. They were like nomads, a different breed, and we didn't mix.

After my grandparents sold their ice cream stand, I thought little of the fair or its workers except to take my own children each year. Until one September.

That year, I felt drawn to do something for the invisible people who worked the fairs. The fall before, I'd pitched an article about carnival workers to a local newspaper. I worked up my courage to talk to people I'd been warned since childhood to avoid and dragged a friend with me for moral support and safety. Speaking to a game operator, circus ringmaster, reptile display owner, and food vendor, I ended each interview with the same question: "How could people in the towns you visit minister to you?"

"We have no life," one Midway game supervisor said, echoing the others' words. "It would be nice if someone asked how we were doing or if we needed anything."

As fair time drew closer again, her words came back to haunt me. But what could I do?

A meal. Nothing speaks of caring more than a good, home-cooked meal, but I couldn't provide for a crowd of fair workers by myself. My husband and I had just begun visiting a small country church where people barely knew us. I longed to ask for their help, but they had no reason to follow us on such a venture. The fair was only nine days away, and I didn't know if I could even get permission from the fair administration to feed the workers. Besides, my parents were in poor health and required frequent help. I had no time to organize something like this.

It was a crazy idea. But it wouldn't go away.

Finally, I called to talk to the pastor about doing this as a ministry project. He would probably say no. That would put an end to it.

Instead, he agreed right away. "I'll let you make an announcement after service on Sunday."

Several people met me at the front of the church to strategize. One longtime member offered to organize meal donations. My job was to coordinate with the fair administration. Others would check on transportation and table setup.

. We were off.

Phone lines blazed as I tried to contact fair directors. I was dismayed to learn the fair had broken into two separate organizations, both holding events at the same time. One would be located at the old fairgrounds downtown and the other at a convention center closer to where we now lived. The latter was safer and more convenient for our church members, so I started there. But nothing came together. They wouldn't give me a definite answer and couldn't guarantee space for us to serve lunch. Time was running out.

The second director was thrilled at my idea. "I don't think anyone has ever done this before. It will mean so much to the workers. We'll set up a tent with lunch tables and chairs." We were on.

However, the head count the woman mentioned alarmed me. Our small church couldn't feed seventy-five people. I called a friend who cooked for groups at her church.

"I'd be happy to help," she said. "I'll ask my pastor."

By the evening before our big day, everything had come together. Then my dad called to say my mom had fallen. We spent five hours in the emergency room. I collapsed into bed around midnight and slept fitfully.

The next morning dawned windy but sunny with perfect temperatures. We arrived safely at the fairgrounds and found everything as promised. The carnival workers came slowly at first, seeming unsure of why we were there or what we wanted, but things soon picked up.

When I offered to help dish out food, my volunteers waved me away with the flies. "We've got this. You go talk to the people."

Interviewing individuals for an article was one thing, but talking to a table full of fair workers was another. I swallowed and sat

> *I felt drawn to do something for the invisible people who worked the fairs.*

on a bench. Striking up a conversation, I was surprised to learn that many of the workers came from South Africa, recruited to travel nine to twelve months with the fair. Coming from a depressed economy with few job opportunities, they saw it as a way to better themselves and see the United States. But they were young and homesick. Some didn't even speak English, and they missed their families, their girlfriends. Fair work was harder than anticipated, and travel was grueling. Even veteran workers from the U.S. agreed. It wasn't an easy life.

The longer we chatted, the easier it became, and I felt drawn to these people I'd hesitated to approach. A connection grew as we shared experiences. I ventured to pray for one young South African who had fallen from the top of a ride the day before and been rushed to the emergency room. Fortunately, he wasn't badly injured. His friends jostled and teased him to be more careful. They typified young men everywhere, and I could see my own sons in their faces.

Our pastor brought basketfuls of prayer request slips and set them on the tables. More people filled them out than I expected, and I recognized familiar themes.

Please pray for my health. I've been in and out of the hospital for a month.

We're going through a tough time. Please pray we find new jobs when we get back home.

Please pray for Marie. Her best friend in South Africa died while she was here in America.

Pray for my son and my safe return to him.

Universal fears. Universal needs. Universal concerns.

Servers were scraping the bottom of the pans by the time the last fair worker came through. In all, we fed at least a hundred people, but it was more than a meal. I'd found a common bond with people I'd previously thought peculiar. Fair workers may live a different lifestyle, but I could no longer call them a different breed. In many ways, they were just like me.

~Tracy Crump

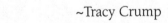

80

An Unexpected Encounter

Look not only to your own interests, but
also to the interests of others.
~Philippians 2:4

swung my car into the parking lot of a large retail store feeling stressed. I had to be in and out quick. "Don't look at anything," I told myself. "Just get the few things you need and leave — or you won't be home on time." We were having company for dinner, and I still had a lot to do.

As I walked toward the store, I noticed a woman sitting several feet to the side of the door. She sat in a slumped position on the cold cement, in front of a short retaining wall. Shoppers bustled by, trying not to look in her direction. I hurried into the store, and as I traveled up and down the aisles, the picture of the woman stayed in my mind. As I placed items in my cart, it occurred to me how lucky I was that I could grab anything I needed. I wondered what she needed.

But I was not an outgoing person. I rarely spoke to strangers, and I certainly could not approach a woman like this. She looked strange and different from me. Helping her could be complicated, not to mention scary, and maybe even expensive. I just couldn't do it.

Besides, I didn't have time. I needed to hit one more store before going home, and the odds were high that she just wanted a handout so she could buy drugs or alcohol. I paid for my groceries and rushed out the door. But before I reached my car, something inside me said, *Go back.*

I put my purchases in the car, and with my heart pounding, I gathered the courage to walk back toward the woman. Maybe I would just hand her some money and leave. That would be fast and easy, and I wouldn't have to say anything. But as I drew near, I encountered something I didn't expect. The woman was young, and a baby was sleeping in the folds of her garment. A tattered stroller was not far away. I had not noticed it earlier.

> *Her grateful eyes met mine, and for that brief moment I felt we were one.*

I caught my breath. "Can I buy you something?"

"Meela," she said.

I couldn't understand her accent. "A meal?" I asked.

She nodded.

"What would you like?"

She looked at the baby and looked back at me.

She obviously spoke another language. After some rough communication, it turned out she wanted infant formula for her baby girl.

"What kind?" I asked.

She made a circle with her index finger and thumb.

"Oh… for a newborn — zero months?"

Her face brightened. She nodded.

"I'll… be… back… soon…" I spoke the words slowly.

Thoughts swirled inside me as I walked the aisles of the large store. Infant formula. She only wanted infant formula. She simply wanted to feed her baby. She was a mother who loved her child.

As I headed up and down the aisles lost in my new thoughts, I had difficulty finding the right aisle.

I asked a store clerk. "Does this store sell infant formula?"

"The baby department's over there." She pointed to the back of the store, looking at me oddly as if everyone in the store knew this but me.

I found the largest size of newborn formula on the shelf and headed toward the checkout. But before I got there, I couldn't resist picking up some soft pink socks, a small stuffed rabbit, and a snack for the mother.

As I stood in the checkout line, I could see the woman through the glass door. She no longer sat slumped over her baby. She sat upright and alert. Her eyes watched the door. She was waiting for me.

It felt like it took forever to get through the line, but I finally paid and hurried outside.

"Is this okay?" I held up the formula in front of the woman.

She smiled.

"Oh… and I also got these." I squatted down next to her and opened the plastic shopping bag.

Our heads were about three inches apart as we looked into the bag together, both of us admiring the cute socks and floppy-eared rabbit. Then she turned and looked at me. Her grateful eyes met mine, and for that brief moment I felt we were one.

"Thank you — bless," she said.

"You're welcome," I said, as a wonderful warm feeling washed over me.

I settled back into my car and watched her from a distance as she carefully placed her baby in the stroller and tucked the package underneath. Then she walked away and disappeared between the buildings.

As I drove away, I felt peace. The stress of the day had melted away, and that warm feeling was still inside me. In fact, it was still with me for the next day or two.

With a little courage, I know I can do this again. I just need to slow down a little. Maybe if I take a small moment out of my own life, I can give a large blessing to someone else. It doesn't have to be complicated or scary or even expensive. And when that person smiles back at me, it's a moment I will never forget.

~Sharon Pearson

81

Chicken Soup for the Soul

Part of the Family

Call it a clan, call it a network, call it a tribe,
call it a family: Whatever you call it,
whoever you are, you need one.
~Jane Howard

My stomach tightened as my husband Darrell knocked on the door of the apartment. *How did I get myself into this situation? What did I know about Africa? Or refugees?* Until the day before, I had no idea that Sierra Leone was even in Africa.

Mariama opened the door. The vibrant colors in her dress and in the cloth tied around her head combined with the boldness of her personality to fill the small, dimly lit room. "Hello!" she said. "Come in! Good to see you!" She spoke English, but with a heavy, unfamiliar accent.

In my mind, I replayed Darrell's comments after he met Mariama last week.

"You'll like her," he said. "She's led quite a life. She's full of amazing stories, and you love a good story."

"True," I had told him, "but you know how I feel about unfamiliar situations. We're talking unfamiliar people, places, culture, language, religion — pretty much unfamiliar everything."

Mariama introduced us to the others in the room. Though not all actually related, they referred to each other as aunty, sister, brother or daughter. One big family.

I struggled to remember names and figure out who was related to whom and how. "And this is my ugly daughter," Mariama said, gesturing to a beautiful teenage girl. Mariama smiled as she noticed my troubled expression at her comment. *Why would a mother say that about her child?* "In my village, if someone knows something is special to you, they might take it or kill it. So we say it is not important," she explained with a wink. I began to think that she took delight in seeing a look of shock on my face.

I sat down on the sofa trying to take everything in. The room was sparsely decorated except for a collection of framed family photos arranged on some shelves. In the corner of the living room was a large black bag.

"It is a goat," Mariama revealed. *A goat?* I smiled nervously as I tried to exchange glances with my husband. Questions flooded my mind. *Why was there a goat in a bag in the living room? What condition was it in? How long had it been there? What were they planning to do with it?* My questions were interrupted by a knock at the door. A line of about six or seven more people filed into the apartment. Some smiled. Some bore no expression at all. Some wore traditional African clothing, and all spoke an unfamiliar language. Mariama spoke to them in hushed tones, and they disappeared into the bedrooms, leaving us alone in the living room with the goat.

Mariama and her visitors returned to the living room. We sat for what seemed like hours in uncomfortable silence. Finally, she spoke. "We buy the goat from a local village (a nearby farm), and we share the meat." They divided up the (thankfully already butchered) goat into bags, and then the friends filed out the door just as they had arrived earlier.

I practiced in my mind the conversation Darrell and I would have on the way home. "I think I won't be coming back next time. How can I relate to someone so different from me? I just don't think I can do this."

Mariama began to share bits of her story in a mix of English and Krio. I could not understand every word, but I clearly understood her enthusiasm for life even when hers had been so difficult. I could also see her "mama's heart" for her own children and for the many others she had cared for along the way. Maybe we did have some things in common.

By the time Darrell and I left that afternoon, we had learned a song in one of the six languages Mariama knew, and we had been invited to visit her again the next week. Well, maybe I would go back one more time, but I wasn't making any promises after that.

That next visit led to another and another until weekly visits with Mariama and her family became a regular part of our lives. Each week we helped them with practical things like reading lessons, filling out paperwork, finding jobs, and getting to appointments. And each week was filled with stories just as my husband promised. Mariama told funny stories from her childhood, stories of wisdom passed down from her grandparents and, sadly, tragic stories as well. We heard of the atrocities she witnessed during the war in her country, the uncertainties of ever seeing some of her children again when having to flee, and the miseries of living in refugee camps. We also heard triumphant stories of the day she reunited with two of her young children, including the "ugly" daughter, after a five-year separation, and of the day when Mariama became a citizen of the United States.

> Instead of simply helping a refugee family, we became part of it.

Instead of simply helping a refugee family, we became part of it. Mariama's children and grandchildren called us Aunty Cindy and Uncle Darrell. We saw that playful look in her eye as she delighted in shocking her family back in Africa with pictures of her and her tall white American brother. We came together for graduations, church services, Thanksgiving dinners, and backyard barbecues complete with drums and African dancing. I even made an overnight road trip with Mariama to take her son to camp.

It's interesting that "familiar" and "family" come from the same root word. Once the unfamiliar became familiar, we became like family. A photo of all of us together made its way to the shelves in their apartment. And later, when Mariama told stories, she often told one about us and a certain goat.

~Cindy Jolley

82

No Longer the Retiring Type

We must remember that one determined person can make a significant difference, and that a small group of determined people can change the course of history.
~Sonia Johnson

A friendly buzz was coming from the first-floor dining room. People were engaged in lively chatter. The clatter of dishes echoed from the kitchen, and hearty laughter occasionally rose above the din.

I could hear it from my secluded office on the second floor of the historic, brick building that had originally been the city's first high school when it was constructed just prior to the Civil War. In recent years, it had been pressed into service as the senior center of a small city on the coast of New England.

An introvert by nature, I was very comfortable in my office, tucked away off a narrow corridor at the far end of the building. My new job there had kept me mostly desk-bound for the first couple of weeks, and I was quite satisfied with the solitude.

I had been hired to facilitate programs for senior citizens, a position I expected to be my last. I was of an age, after all, when the prospect of retirement had begun to whisper in my ear, and I was very inclined to listen.

The senior center, largely neglected for years, had begun a slow decline into disrepair. There were moments when I felt the same way — run down and a little creaky. My plan was to spend my waning work years behind my desk, quietly handling paperwork to support programs that would keep senior citizens engaged in life.

The noise from downstairs, however, piqued my curiosity, and I left my desk to see what it was all about. Standing at the edge of the dining room, I saw a dozen round tables, all occupied with senior citizens chewing on pizza, salad, and each other's stories of days gone by.

At the front of the room, a musician was setting up his keyboard, preparing to play a selection of old favorites — a little Perry Como, a little Doris Day, and a lot of Sinatra. With the first notes of "It Had to Be You," a few couples left their tables, walked hand-in-hand to the middle of the room, and began to dance.

It was, I learned, a monthly pizza party, one of the activities at the senior center supported by my desk duties. I took some satisfaction in having played a role in giving so many people a decent meal and a chance to socialize, but I had an uneasy feeling on the way back to my office.

Residents of the city I worked for were racially diverse, with close to 20 percent being Latino. At that party, however, there wasn't much of a mix. As the months went by, and my paperwork became more routine, I was able to circulate more among our elderly guests. The reality became clear: There were no Latinos in our building. We weren't attracting a single one.

I had grown up in a white, middle-class neighborhood in northern New Jersey in the 1950s and '60s. My adult life had not been entirely without challenges, but they were few and far between. As a senior citizen myself, I was able to look back on what had been a very comfortable journey through life, with all my pathways paved and well lit.

It would have been easy to overlook the fact that none of the city's Latino senior citizens were at that pizza party, nor any other programs we hosted. Not one was using our transportation service, joining us for lunches or attending our activities. The reason was obvious. We just weren't speaking their language, quite literally.

None of our newsletters included information in Spanish. None of our web pages. None of our presentations. After asking around the building, it also became clear that none of our fifteen staff members could do much more than find their way around a menu at a Mexican restaurant.

I was no exception. I had never shown any interest in learning a foreign language. I had to take two years of French in high school, but failed miserably. I always justified my poor grades by narrowly insisting I was never going to visit France, so why bother learning the language?

> *I had never shown any interest in learning a foreign language.*

Not once, since bidding *adieu* to high school, did I ever have a shred of motivation to communicate in anything other than English. My reasoning, as a teenager, made sense at the time, and my premise was accurate. More than fifty years later, I still haven't gone to France.

I never imagined, though, that Spain would come to me. Or Guatemala, Paraguay and the Dominican Republic. Our small New England city, I calculated, had nearly 1,000 Hispanic senior citizens living within its border, hailing from more than a dozen countries in Central and South America and the Caribbean.

It stood to reason: If we were ever going to serve them, we were going to have to reach out to them in their native language. Since we had a cooperative arrangement with the local community college, I registered for a Beginner Spanish course and slowly started to learn how to introduce myself and ask, "*Cómo está usted?*"

I was, by decades, the eldest member of the class and probably the most anxious. I stumbled my way through the semester, though, and signed up for the next level.

Then, one day while standing in line at my favorite coffee shop, I overheard an elderly man in front of me speaking Spanish. I silently dared myself to practice my shaky new language skills on the stranger. I was panicky, of course, that my pronunciation would be off, and I'd say something entirely inappropriate.

Finally, I mustered up enough nerve to try a greeting. At first eye contact, I smiled, choked out my best "*hola*" and asked how he was in Spanish.

"*Bien,*" he said, with a curious smile. "*Y tú?*"

"*Bien, gracias, amigo.*"

Minutes later, after he'd bought his coffee and turned for the door, I felt emboldened to try one more phrase.

"*¡Que tengas un buen día!*" I blurted. Have a good day!

He glanced back over his shoulder. "*Igual,*" he said. Same to you.

To anyone in line at the coffee shop that morning, our brief exchange was of no significance, and I never ran into that friendly gentleman again. Yet it was my first opportunity to take what I'd learned in a classroom and use it to greet a stranger in his own language.

No longer was I bound to a textbook, memorization, repetition and weekly quizzes. I had passed my most important test in the coffee line that morning. Encouraged, I found the spark to take several more classes, reached out to a few Latino community leaders, and began to hear Spanish voices in our building.

Within two years, dozens of Latino senior citizens were showing up regularly, joining programs and even offering their time and talents as volunteers. My Spanish still wasn't perfect, but it didn't have to be. All I had to do was try. Eventually, those new guests at the senior center became my informal Spanish teachers and, far more importantly, my friends.

I spent far less time tucked away in my office after that, and far less time thinking about retirement.

~Bill Woolley

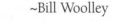

Learning to Ask

The strong individual is the one who asks
for help when he needs it.
~Rona Barrett

arrived early, dressed in black slacks and a white top as
requested, and tried to calm my nerves as I approached the man
and woman standing at the kettle. The greeting was not what I'd
hoped for. "You were supposed to be here yesterday, not today,"
the man told me after I introduced myself. "We wondered what happened to you."

I could not have felt worse. For weeks, I had geared up for this. I
put the instruction sheet on my refrigerator and re-read it many times.

I was volunteering for a few shifts of bell ringing for the Salvation
Army. That probably doesn't seem like a big deal. Every Christmas,
people in shopping malls, grocery stores and on street corners collect
donations for the Salvation Army's programs for those in need.

But in addition to helping raise money for an organization I believe
in, I decided to volunteer for a personal reason. I find it difficult — in
fact, ridiculously hard — to ask people for anything, even though I
quite enjoy helping others when they need a hand.

My friends will tell you that I'm outgoing, independent, even
adventurous. Yet, when I'm sick I'd rather stagger out the door half-
dead to buy some chicken soup than ask a friend or neighbor for help.
When I sign up for a run to raise money for cancer, I donate the cash
myself rather than asking others. The thought of asking a friend for a

ride to the airport is way too stressful, even though my rational mind knows the answer would be yes.

So, I decided one Christmas I would take a baby step in learning to ask. I'd do a few shifts as a "bell-ringer" to see how it felt to ask perfect strangers to give.

By the time I returned for my shift the next day, I had learned that the mix-up wasn't my fault. There had been a computer scheduling error for which the supervisor of volunteers apologized profusely.

The man I'd met briefly the previous day was there again. He was a driver who made the rounds collecting money from each kettle every couple of hours to deliver to the local headquarters.

> *I'd do a few shifts as a "bell-ringer" to see how it felt to ask perfect strangers to give.*

He gave me a few friendly pointers, since he had been a kettle volunteer for a decade or so before being hired as a seasonal driver. He also revealed that he had gotten help from the Salvation Army years ago, which had changed his life.

That gave me something to think about. This cheerful guy, with the responsibility of handling thousands of dollars in cash, was one of many who had been helped by the donations dropped into the Christmas kettles.

As I slipped on the Salvation Army vest and took my spot beside the kettle, I consciously tried to follow the "tips" provided to volunteers. Stand (don't sit), smile, make eye contact, and don't ring the bell too loud or too often. (That can get annoying to those in nearby stores.)

It felt awkward at first. My location on the second floor of a shopping mall wasn't a busy spot, so I tried to smile and catch the eyes of every passerby. Most quickly glanced away. I worried I was making them feel guilty. I didn't like that at all.

I was starting to wonder whether this bell-ringing thing was for me when a man emerged from a store some distance down the corridor and marched purposefully toward me. "Well, this won't do," he said as he slipped a twenty-dollar bill into the slot of the clear plastic globe that topped the collection kettle. "We can't have this sitting empty."

I thanked him for his donation and for "seeding the pot." The smiles we exchanged were more than polite. It was like we were on the same team.

Even then, it took me a while to relax. When people walked by with nothing but a quick glance and then turned away, I felt like I wasn't doing this right. Should I smile more? Say "Merry Christmas?" Try more eye contact?

But little by little, I began to see that people who had passed me once, or even two or three times, were coming back later to drop money into the kettle. It was a revelation to me that many of the people whom I thought were dodging me weren't doing that at all. Whether they needed time for the idea to percolate, or felt pressured to get their shopping started first, I cannot say.

For a while, I tried to guess who would return to donate later. But I gave up. There was no "typical" donor, at least, to my unpracticed eye. They came in all ages and apparent income levels, and for their own reasons.

By the time I had my last two shifts, in the week before Christmas, I had relaxed and enjoyed watching people bustling by. I still stood tall, looked people in the eyes, smiled and occasionally rang my bell. But inside me something had changed.

I no longer felt I was "targeting" people, or that my success or failure depended on whether they gave a donation. I felt much more like I was part of the cheerful, busy crowd. Once people noticed my presence, their own circumstances and feelings would determine the rest.

It was surprising how many people came to talk to me. One woman shared how her brother had been helped with addiction; others told how they look forward to helping the Christmas kettle campaign each year. Quite a few parents took their small children aside for a talk about the kettle, and then gave them coins to drop in.

A few dropped money into the kettle without a word. That was the case with my biggest single donation. A middle-aged, casually dressed man stopped a short distance from me and began pulling bills from his wallet. He walked over, dropped eighty dollars in the kettle and quickly walked away.

The weirdest donation came from someone in a group of twenty-somethings, dressed in elf costumes, who were racing around the mall early one morning. I thought they were Santa's helpers, doing a few errands before the Santa House opened.

But it turned out they were on a scavenger hunt. Once they spotted my bell — a musical instrument was on their list — they beseeched me to ring it and sing "Jingle Bells."

"I just donated!" one of them shouted cheerfully, as if to urge me on. I would have done it regardless, of course. We sang with gusto, if not with perfect pitch, as one of them recorded it on his cell phone.

There was a lesson for me in this little venture into uncomfortable territory. It has given me a great appreciation for the good feeling that comes with giving, not just for me but for everyone. So it follows that asking for help is not such a bad thing. It is just another side of living in a caring community.

I'll try to remember that next time I'm down with a cold and in need of a little chicken soup.

~Kristin Goff

Chapter
10

The Power of Yes!

Go for Adventure

You have to leave the city of your comfort and go into the wilderness of your intuition. What you'll discover will be wonderful. What you discover is yourself.
~Alan Alda

My Geriatric Vacation

Let us be grateful to people who make us happy,
they are the charming gardeners who
make our souls blossom.
~Marcel Proust

"'ve got a great idea for your mom's birthday present," I told my husband, Eric. "Her friend, Sue, moved to Florida last year, and she really misses her. We should send her down there for her birthday gift."

But Eric shook his head. "She wouldn't go. She'd be too nervous to travel by herself."

"I know, and that's why I'm going with her." I shrugged. "I love your mom, and I love Sue, too. It would be really fun."

Sue was my mother-in-law's friend first, but she and I became fast friends as well. Despite a twenty-five-year age difference, Sue and I clicked. We are both writers, and we both met our husbands on the dating website eHarmony. A few years ago, Sue and I attended a writers' conference together, and we had a blast. Sadly, her husband passed away in 2011, and she moved to Florida to be closer to her children. My mother-in-law had been talking about visiting her ever since.

When we told Judy about the birthday trip, she was thrilled. She even suggested inviting her sister, Barb, who was also recently widowed.

So, it was decided. The three of us would fly down to Florida to visit Sue. Several people told me that it was sweet of me to accompany the ladies on their trip, and I jokingly dubbed it "my geriatric vacation."

At age forty-one I was going to cruise around Florida with three senior citizens. I expected it to be fun, but in a quiet, relaxing sort of way.

I was wrong. It was fun in the *best* sort of way.

Sue picked us up at the airport, and although we hadn't seen one another in more than two years, our friendship picked up right where we'd left off. We talked into the wee hours that first night.

The next day, we walked downtown and shopped — not for clothes or souvenirs, but for attractive older men for our two single ladies.

"Look at him," I'd say. "He's a nice-looking guy."

"Him? He's too old for either of us," they'd say.

"But he looks about seventy," I'd say. "How old do you want him to be?"

"We don't care how old he is," they'd say. "We care how old he *acts*."

I nodded, but I didn't really understand. But as the days went on, it became clear to me. These ladies might have been pushing seventy, but they weren't old.

We took an airboat ride and spotted several gators and dozens of bird species. We laughed at one another's wind-blown hair after the ride.

We had a seafood lunch and went shopping — for clothes this time. I bought a dress that was so-not-me because these ladies told me to. I even bought the matching shoes.

That night, we took a walk around the lake at Sue's condominium complex. It was a beautiful trail, and the walk gave us more time to talk about things that really matter. Things like love, and self-image, and finding purpose in life. Important things, no matter how old you are.

It was refreshing in a way that touched my soul and brought tears to my eyes. It reminded me how rare and precious true friendship is, and how blessed we are when we find it — even when many years or many miles separate us.

The next day, we took another boat ride, this time to an island to hunt for shells. On the way to the island, a pod of dolphins played just feet from our boat. We found tons of beautiful shells and sand dollars. As I walked on that island, I thought it would be the best part of the trip.

Again, I was wrong.

On the last day of my stay, we went to a manatee park. I love manatees, and it was really neat to see them, but it still wasn't the best part of my trip.

We did fun things and ate yummy food. We relaxed and enjoyed nature. It was an amazing trip. But the most amazing part wasn't what we did; it was the lessons those ladies taught me.

I couldn't have enjoyed myself anymore had I gone with women my own age.

I went on a trip with three women, each old enough to be my mother, but it wasn't that way. They gave me advice, but as friends, not maternal figures. We enjoyed girl talk, and I never felt like anything but "one of the girls."

We were four friends on a trip together. I had a blast, and I couldn't have enjoyed myself anymore had I gone with women my own age.

The trip wasn't what I'd expected. I learned how much fun it is to do things we don't normally do, even things that seem a little scary at first. I learned that stretching our expectations of ourselves is a good thing at any age.

And although it's a cliché, I learned that age really *is* just a number, and we truly *are* as young as we feel.

~Diane Stark

85

Game, Set, Cure

Nothing diminishes anxiety faster than action.
~Walter Anderson

My friends were trying to get me to ride a roller coaster — any roller coaster — at Wonderland amusement park in Toronto. But the *click, click, click* of the cars climbing up the tracks hammered spikes of fear into my heart. The anticipatory pause at the crest, before descending in a fall filled with chilling screams, seemed more tortuous than exhilarating.

They were still trying to convince me, and I was still saying no, when I suddenly saw a familiar face, one I had never seen outside a television set. It was Jennifer Capriati — a popular tennis star at the top of her game, already winning titles at the age of fourteen. I scrambled through my backpack, pulling out a pen and the only paper I could find — the Wonderland brochure. It would have to do.

She was weaving through a zigzag of rope that led to a ride called the Jet Scream. I was running on adrenaline because I didn't want to pass up meeting her face to face, but I was also a bit nervous, so I waited at the exit to calm down and approach her as she came off the ride.

I watched her climb into a giant spaceship that started to gently rock. It was soon swinging around in nearly a full circle, putting the screaming riders at unnatural angles. The Jet Scream is the type of ride that could easily make me throw up in two seconds, and I couldn't bear to watch.

To take my mind off the horror of the ride, I fumbled around for an appropriate greeting, since I had never been taught proper celebrity-meeting etiquette. How should I introduce myself? What should I call her?

My time for preparation ran out. She trotted down the exit ramp, laughing and talking with her brother. All thoughts of etiquette vanished. I focused on her walking toward me. I looked down at the ground. She walked past. It was more difficult to talk to a celebrity than I thought, but I had to seize the opportunity.

I whirled around, calling her name, not very confidently, but more as a question, "Jennifer?"

She turned around. Her eyes met mine. Our eyes actually met!

"Jennifer Capriati, right?"

"Yep." She spoke to me. I was dazzled.

"Would you mind if I asked for your autograph?" I asked, nudging the brochure and pen toward her. Her hand scribbled over the paper.

"You're playing in the… ah… Toronto tournament?" I stuttered, as she dotted the two i's in her last name with record-breaking speed.

"Yep." Her pronunciation of a single word stunned me. She was actually answering questions that I asked.

"That's cool," I said.

She flashed me a glowing smile and walked away. No crowds of screaming admirers flocked to her, and I felt good that someone so famous could enjoy her time here without being interrupted. That led me to feeling guilty for disrupting her. But on the other hand, I was proud of myself. I may have been just one of the many fans who crossed her path, but I had broken out of my shell by approaching her, and I felt emboldened to follow her around for a while. I started shadowing her about twenty paces behind. When she got in line for another ride with her brother, I followed. My friends caught up to me.

"You do realize this is a roller coaster?" one of them asked. "This isn't a line for snow cones."

"I know. Jennifer is doing it, so I think I should, too," I said.

My friends were dumbfounded; they had spent years trying to persuade me to do exactly this. The fears of heights, moving too fast, and vomiting in public seemed unimportant now. I was ready to be thrilled, to have my breath taken away, to do what before had been unimaginable. I didn't even consider not going on this roller coaster. Through some twist, I had replaced my terror with a new sense of curiosity.

The line was for the Wild Beast, and it became my first roller coaster ride ever. I had known it would become a contest of mind over matter, and my mind won — even though my stomach reeled and lurched in ways I didn't know were possible. And I did survive, albeit screaming the entire time like a sorority girl being chased by an axe murderer. I thought I was nervous getting a signature from a famous athlete, but that was before I stepped off the Wild Beast and felt my knees buckle from the anxiety that I had just experienced.

> *Through some twist, I had replaced my terror with a new sense of curiosity.*

Jennifer then moved on to a roller coaster that corkscrewed through the air, taking curves at heart-pounding speeds. And I trailed right behind. It was called Dragon Fire, and afterward I knew why. But Miss Capriati was not slowing down, so neither could I. However, when she darted into line for a stand-up roller coaster called the SkyRider, I sensed that I might have met my match. Even more than sitting in a roller coaster, standing in one gave me even more reason to throw up, but I had come this far, so I couldn't back out now. Standing in line, all I could see was a huge loop of track that took a group of thrill seekers and turned them upside-down while strapped into a standing position. I could not believe I had become a card-holding member of this mentally unstable group of roller coaster enthusiasts.

That chance meeting with Jennifer Capriati instantly cured my phobia. I can't say that I enjoyed those roller coasters. I was terrified standing in each line; I was shaky stepping into each car; and I was petrified as I clutched the safety bar as we climbed each hill. But I had crossed a threshold, and now I live in a world where I am a bit braver because of it.

~Darin Cook

86

But I Can't Touch Bottom

Courage is like a muscle. We strengthen it by use.
~Ruth Gordo

W hen I visited Israel at age eighty-one, all I really wanted to do was support my daughter Crystal and her husband during a difficult crisis in their lives. However, Crystal wanted me to have some fun, so she took me to Eilat, the oasis in the desert at Israel's southern tip. We visited a bird sanctuary and an aquarium, and lounged on the beach.

"I want to take you snorkeling along the coral reef," she told me. "You'll love seeing the tropical fish and having them swim around you."

I wasn't so sure. I swim, but only in a pool where my feet can touch the bottom. On my one trip to Hawaii, I'd tried snorkeling and panicked in the deep water. Though I was perfectly capable of swimming, the fear paralyzed me. I thrashed about in the water until someone helped me back to the boat.

"You'll be fine," Crystal assured me. "We'll take a foam noodle for you. It will keep you afloat, and I'll stay right by you."

I really wanted to go, so we put on all the equipment. Crystal secured the noodle around my middle, and looking like women from space, we walked down the beach to the pier. When we started along the long pier, my mouth felt dry. The farther we walked, the more nervous I became, and the slower my feet moved. Near the end of the pier, I stopped. "I'm not sure I want to do this," I whispered, almost shaking with fear.

Again, Crystal assured me I'd be okay. I looked at the rope that stretched from the end of the pier to the next one about 1,000 feet away. "I can hold onto the rope, right?" I asked.

"Yes, yes, of course," she assured me.

Slowly, I descended the steps at the pier's end. "Oooh. It's very cold," I said, as shivers like icicles went up my legs. "I don't know if I can handle this."

"You'll get used to it," Crystal assured me, so I kept going. When I reached the last step, I took a deep breath, reached for the rope and stepped tentatively into the deep water. With my face underwater, I took another breath and discovered that the snorkel really did work. Only then did I look around me. I saw red, yellow, blue, purple and black fish of all sizes, and some with multiple colors, too. Some fish sported polka dots, while others had stripes. In and out of the coral they darted, totally unconcerned about me.

After a few moments, I began edging along the rope. As I moved along, I noticed the coral, as well as the fish. The different colors and shapes fascinated me. What wonderful hiding places the porous openings provided for the fish.

When I was about halfway to the next pier, Crystal looked at me and said, "Your goggles are taking on water." We stopped, and she helped me dump it out. A little farther, I realized the water was filling into the nose area of my goggles. I ignored it as long as I could, but soon we had to dump it out again. I looked at the next pier. It seemed a long way off. I looked at the one I had come from. It was even farther.

> I hope I'll never stop accepting the challenge of a new adventure.

I breathed a prayer and slowly edged ahead, holding onto the rope. A couple of times, I almost lost my foam noodle, but Crystal tightened it around me again.

I was getting tired, but the pier ahead appeared larger each time

I looked. At last, I was beside it. I took a final look at the brightly colored fish, grasped the pier, and let go of the rope.

"You did it, Mom! Look how far you came," Crystal exclaimed. "I thought you would stay by the first pier, but you kept on going. I'm proud of you."

I looked back along the beach to the first pier. I knew I wasn't much of a swimmer, but with the help of my daughter, a rope and a snorkel, I'd accomplished something I never would have guessed I could do.

I may be getting older, but I hope I'll never stop accepting the challenge of a new adventure.

~Geneva Cobb Iijima

Spiders or Mountains

A journey of a thousand miles begins with a single step.
~Lao Tzu

The sun was setting as I approached the Sierra Nevada mountains in California, and I was in serious trouble. I had just been given a military assignment in California and was driving across country to get there. But this was before GPS was a standard feature in cars or cell phones.

My only map was a 2002 road atlas my grandfather had given me as I set out on my trip, along with the instructions, "Just call us when you stop for the night, girl. Deal?"

"Deal," I had said.

I had left Ogden, Utah, early that morning when it was still dark, anticipating that I would be in San Luis Obispo, California, by nightfall. But I had badly miscalculated my mileage and actual drive time.

Along with that error in judgment, I made a terribly wrong turn along the way during a stop for snacks and gas. Instead of ending up back on the interstate, I ended up on Highway 50.

Highway 50 cuts straight through the Sierra Nevada mountains.

I tried to fight my rising sense of panic as the sun sank over the mountains, and I navigated a nasty track of hairpin turns. I took stock of my situation. I had a full tank of gas. I had water and reasonable food. I also had all of my worldly belongings packed in the back of my Jeep Wrangler.

Okay, I reasoned, *I also have a cell phone. I can call someone and pass the time.* I decided I would call my dad, and then my grandparents, and let them know I was still driving — and might be for a while.

That's when I discovered I had zero service. None.

I became so panicked that I pulled over to the shoulder of the road and tried to catch my breath. I felt as if I were on the verge of hyperventilating.

I had not seen another car for miles, let alone a house or a business. At this point, I wasn't even sure if I was still on Highway 50.

I shook my head at the sequence of events that had led me here, in the middle of nowhere, facing a mountain range.

An insurmountable mountain range.

In many ways, those mountains could not have been more fitting. I had been fleeing one life and running full tilt for another one. Before I got in that Jeep, a life had been cut out for me, if I wanted it. I had a long-term relationship, had finished college and had job prospects that wouldn't catapult me across the globe.

> *I had been fleeing one life and running full tilt for another one.*

But, for me, a number of slow deaths waited down that path. It was a life during which I would never leave my hometown. Children would be expected immediately after marriage. It was life that would fit everyone else's definition of a life — but not mine.

I craved adventure, change and new things, and I went out into the world looking for them. An Air Force commission and an assignment to California were a good start.

My steady, secure, long-term relationship fell apart. Several members of my family thought I was intentionally abandoning them by joining the service. Although I had made new friends, it meant I had to leave others in search for a new life.

And now, as a final test from the universe, these mountains were blocking my path — rising high above me as if to say, "See? You are no match for us. You need to turn around, admit defeat, and go home."

At that moment, a couple of tarantulas scuttled across the arid road, illuminated just a few feet away from me by my Jeep's headlights. I leaped back into my Jeep, brushing myself all over, and praying one hadn't hitched a ride on my pant legs.

Spiders or mountains?

I decided I was way more afraid of those tarantulas! I dropped my Jeep into low gear and headed up the mountains, my headlights barely illuminating the pitch-black road.

Up one hairpin turn and down another I went, swinging left, right, and back left again. I guessed I could see maybe fifty, a hundred feet in front of me — that was it.

I paused a few times. *Keep going?* I asked myself. Either that, or go back and see what the tarantulas were up to.

And that was when it dawned on me: If I stayed on the road and just kept going, I could make it through the mountains with just a few feet illuminated in front of me. I didn't know how I was going to reach the end, but if I just kept going, I knew I could.

I think life tends to unfold for us like that, too. We never truly know what is around the bends and curves. We can make plans, but we never really know. But if we just keep pressing forward, our path will unfold, just a little bit at a time. If we keep faith and keep moving forward, no matter how slowly, our path will light up for us.

After midnight, I saw reflective green traffic signs down the road, glimmering like an oasis. My breath caught in my throat.

And sweet mercy, I came upon a T-intersection. If I turned left — Los Angeles. Right — San Francisco. A navigational point I could actually locate in my state-of-the-art atlas!

My goal had been San Luis Obispo, but I settled for San Jose that night. It wasn't quite my intended goal, but I was definitely going the right way.

I finally checked into a hotel room for the evening, my entire body shaking with adrenaline from the experience.

It would be just past two o'clock in the morning at my grandparents' house, but I called anyway. My grandfather picked up on the first ring.

"That you, Wonder Woman?" he hollered into the phone, his hearing long gone, making him think he needed to shout.

I smiled at his nickname for me, Wonder Woman, because he said he always wondered what I was going to do next.

"Yeah, PaPaw, it's me."

"Did you get lost or something?" he wanted to know.

I took a deep breath as I thought about that question. I did, and I had been — in so many ways, I wanted to say.

Instead, I said, "I did. But I found my way."

~Kristi Adams

88

Travel Buddies

We travel not to escape life, but
for life not to escape us.
~Author Unknown

"Y ou don't even know her?" my daughter shrieked into the phone. "Are you crazy?"

"But I do know her," I said. I met her on the Amazon trip that Dad and I went on last year. He liked Elaine."

"Come on, you spent a few days on vacation together. Now you're traveling to Egypt with her?"

"Not really, she's flying from Chicago; I'm going from New York. We'll meet in the hotel room."

"This gets worse," my anxiety-ridden daughter lamented. She had misgivings; I had none, at least none that I would admit.

I later learned that her daughter had the opposite reaction. She was ecstatic that her grandmother had found a travel companion.

Elaine and I had connected over a glass of wine as we floated down the Amazon River. Our conversation had turned to travel.

"I've always wanted to go to Egypt," I told her.

"I don't," my husband, who was sitting between us, announced. "No Third World countries for me."

We ignored him. "Egypt's a place Jim and I wanted to see, too," Elaine said. "But he died before we could get there."

"Let's go together," I said as casually as I might say, "Let's have another glass of wine."

"YES!" she said. And so our wine-fueled discussions began. Over the next few evenings, we discussed travel times, tour companies, and cost. At the end of the trip, when we hugged each other goodbye, it was with the words, "See you in Egypt."

Funny how quickly one leaves the vacation mode behind.

What was I thinking, I asked myself now, *to consider flying halfway around the world to travel with a stranger? It seemed like a good idea at the time, but it's just not realistic. Plus, much as I want to see the world, this is too much of a stretch for me — a retired teacher whose life was spent in a classroom.*

In weak moments, I allowed myself to dream of this venture; I asked my travel agent for the names of good tour companies, and I e-mailed these to Elaine. Her return e-mails were brief. They didn't sound all that enthusiastic, but she was still planning on going. How easy it would have been to pick up the phone for a real discussion; somehow, we didn't. Were we afraid that one of us would back out?

> **"Let's go together,"
> I said as casually as
> I might say, "Let's
> have another
> glass of wine."**

We settled on a tour that fit our calendars. I made my deposit, and then I forgot about the trip until one morning when I received an e-mail from Elaine — a copy of her plane reservation. Panic! After a few days on the phone, I finagled a ticket using my frequent flyer miles — New York to Heathrow, seven-hour layover, Heathrow to Cairo.

I paid the final deposit and tried to hush the "what-if demons" that continued to haunt me. This would be my first solo plane trip, and it was to a country where I didn't speak the language.

Everything went smoothly, as it turned out. My driver met me at the airport. I found my way around the hotel and spent the next day exploring a museum. It was late afternoon, and just as I stretched out on the bed, I heard a card sliding into the lock on the door. It opened.

"POLLY!"

"ELAINE!

We hugged and jumped up and down like school kids. We high-fived each other, yelling, "We did it! We did it!" The bellboy was nonplussed. He forgot about hanging around for a tip.

I'd told Elaine when we were on the Amazon about a trip I'd taken a few years ago with Barbara, a gal I didn't know well. It turned out she was less than neat, co-mingling our toiletries in the bathroom, using all the towels, and dropping her underwear and shoes throughout the hotel room. But I'd told Elaine this saga before we'd mentioned traveling together.

I'd forgotten about this discussion; Elaine had not. I noticed that she was excessively neat and solicitous to the point where she was getting on my nerves. "Do you mind if I take a shower now? Is it okay if I hang my cosmetic bag on the back of the bathroom door?"

I assured her each time, "No problem," but I began to wonder.

On the third day, I'd had enough. "Am I intimidating you? What will it take for you to stop tiptoeing around me?"

Then she mentioned the Barbara story. Uh-oh! "There's nothing not to like about you as a roommate," I assured her.

We discovered we were more alike than different. We took copious pictures, bought gifts for our grandchildren, sent a few postcards, and collected the mini bottles of soaps and shampoos to take home. Both of us liked to be punctual, respected each other's quiet time and turned off our bedside lamps within minutes of each other. We reveled in every sight we saw, meal we ate and picture we took. Neither one of us was a big spender, nor a cheapskate, which made it more comfortable.

I e-mailed my doubting daughter. "Put your worries to rest. I've found the world's best travel companion."

The two weeks sped by. We planned another trip the following year. Elaine left for her flight home at 2:00 a.m., whispering, "See you in China."

"China," I mumbled before going back to sleep.

Fast forward to the next year and the next and the next. We're working our way down our bucket list. We've met in hotel rooms in Beijing, Mumbai, and Sydney. Despite the threat of terrorism, I'm no longer fearful of flying alone to foreign countries or working my way through their airports.

When my husband and kids question this travel, I tell them, "If something happens to me, remember I'm doing what I want to do." When I was in fourth grade, I saw photographs of exotic places in my geography book, but it never occurred to me that one day I'd scramble along the Great Wall of China or climb onto an elephant's back to see tigers in the wild, but I have. If I hadn't taken the chance and gone to Egypt, I would probably still be sitting at home watching TV with my husband and our dog.

Elaine and I hope to never run out of world to explore, and to never lose appreciation for how fortunate we've been to be able to push life aside and travel together. Questions loom: Can we save enough money each year to go on these trips? Will a family issue demand we stay home? My fingers remain crossed as I turn the pages of the travel brochures in search of next year's trip.

~Polly Hare Tafrate

89

Mic Drop

Nothing is impossible — the word itself
says, "I'm possible!"
~Audrey Hepburn

I started to sweat as soon as I saw the e-mail. It was from Acme Comedy Company, the comedy club in Minneapolis. It wasn't unusual to receive e-mails from the club, as I was an "Acme Insider" and one of the first to receive offers on discounted show tickets or upcoming events. In this e-mail, however, the subject line read: "Are You Funny? Do You Like Money?" They were hosting their annual "Funniest Person in the Twin Cities" contest. I quickly closed my laptop, as if someone on the other side of the screen was gauging my reaction, seeing if I had the nerve to fill out the attached application.

Should I do it? *Could* I do it? I did have a knack for making my friends and family laugh, but they didn't count, did they? They were just being polite… for the past twenty years.

I didn't have the time for it, anyway. There was way too much going on in my life. I was busy raising a preteen, separating from my husband of thirteen years, starting a job after many years of not working and, to top it all off, I had quit drinking.

Hmm. I had quit drinking. I had no way to escape the seemingly overwhelming obstacles of life or get that rush… that "high" that helped me to escape, however temporary that was. But I'd gotten a small dose of adrenaline just from reading the e-mail. The prize, in addition to a lifetime of bragging rights, was $1,000 cash. I did need money….

Slowly, I lifted the screen of my laptop, peering into the darkness until the computer came alive with that question: "Are You Funny? Do You Like Money?"

It was then I remembered a recent conversation I'd had with my therapist. "Go on a roller coaster," he suggested. "Try bungee jumping. See a scary movie… Those are things that will raise your heartbeat in a safe way."

I remember rolling my eyes at him.

Now, here I was — about to hit the Start button on the metaphorical roller coaster.

The application itself was simple: name, date of birth, phone number, e-mail address and tell them how you heard about the contest. That was the extent of it.

The guidelines were straightforward, too.

"The Contest: Be as funny as you can be in 3 minutes on our stage during our regular shows.

"The Rules: The rules are simple. The contest is for amateurs only. If you have ever been paid for your comedic talent, you are not eligible to participate. Material must be original. Contestants are judged on stage presence, creativity and audience response."

My hands shook as I entered my information and hit the Send button.

I reminded myself that just because I signed up didn't mean I actually had to show up. I could think about it. There was plenty of time to talk myself out of it.

I didn't want to tell anyone. I didn't want to get anyone's hopes up or have people expect anything of me….

As much as I wanted to keep it that way, I just couldn't keep it to myself. I started out telling my best friend. She was so excited for me! She offered to help in any way she could. She was a great help when it came to proofreading my material. I could tell by her laughter (or lack thereof) what had the best chance of working on stage. She gave me valuable feedback in a gentle way, saying things like "I find this hilarious, but I don't think it will appeal to a broad enough audience…

This is too risky for a competition… Let's try this…"

I told a few more friends and got similar responses — excitement mixed with wanting to help and support me.

I immersed myself in television — commercials, specifically. They were rife with stand-up material! The drug advertisements, complete with their possible side effects listed, were gold mines! "Side effects may include heart attack, stroke or death." Guess what, guys? Go back to the drawing board!

Then there was Pinterest.

And the fact that I was working with the general public in the food-service industry.

I was going to have trouble getting my set down to three minutes!

But the writing was only half the battle.

I've heard it many times before: People's number-one fear is public speaking. I'm not normally afraid of public speaking. In fact, I won an award in high school for it, but doing stand-up? That's public speaking *and* having to be funny. Getting people to laugh? Strangers? No pressure there!

Thankfully, Acme has an open mic night every Monday. People who mentioned they were in the contest could get time on the stage to practice.

I was a wreck. I couldn't eat. I couldn't sit still. I didn't want anyone to come with me. What if they didn't laugh? What if they laughed at the wrong parts? I wanted to do this dry run solo.

Monday night came, and I clutched the lineup of amateur comedians, noting I was third on the list. I tried to focus on the person on stage, but I was too busy trying to figure out my strategy for getting to the stage without tripping or having to squeeze between two tables while reciting my set in my head.

"Next up, we have Melanie Celeste! Give her a round of encouragement, folks. It's not as easy as it looks up here…"

God, was I that obvious? That apparently clueless?

I put my foot up on the platform and stepped into the spotlight. I looked out at the crowd and couldn't see a thing! It was amazing. I was worried about the microphone stand being too tall, which it was, but I even made a joke about that!

Once I was on stage, it was incredible. It was like something else inside me flooded me with calm and took over the rest. I grabbed the microphone and strode around that stage as if it were my own living room, completely at ease.

> *I grabbed the microphone and strode around that stage as if it were my own living room.*

While I couldn't see anyone's face, I could hear the laughter. It was roaring and in surround sound. It filled me up and carried me the rest of the night. I felt for one of the few times in my life that this was what I was meant to do.

Despite my earlier promise to myself that I didn't have to go on stage, no one could stop me.

The night of the contest, I was up against four other comedians. Surrounded by friends and people who supported me, I won my night. I then had to wait to find out if I'd advance to the semi-final round. Two and a half months later, the e-mail came: "You Made the Cut!" Out of 300+ people, I'd made the Top 20.

While I didn't win the contest, I had ventured outside my comfort zone and found that I never felt more at home.

~Melanie Celeste

90

Six Years Before the Mast

Your mind is a ship; it can sail across the universe as
long as you don't allow negative thoughts to sink it.
~Matshona Dhliwayo

I ran off to sea on a tall ship. This may conjure images from Melville, Dana, and Darwin, or perhaps *Master and Commander* and *Pirates of the Caribbean*. The golden age of sailing. The romance of the sea. But there's nothing like an open-ocean passage to turn a romantic into a realist, and I was on a 125-foot, wood-hulled Baltimore clipper halfway between Virginia and Bermuda before I realized that I was absolutely terrible at this job.

I went to preschool at age two, where I failed "pouring," which was a motor-skill activity that involved transferring dried lentils from one cup to another. But I could already read, and I'd dictated my first short story with Snoopy on the cover. From then on, my teachers wrote things in the margins of my papers like, "Although you clearly misunderstand global ocean circulation, you misunderstand it beautifully. You should be a writer." Or, "If you conducted the experiment this way, you'd have blown us all to smithereens. But your description of the process is lovely. Perhaps that's where you should focus your studies." Or, "Maybe it's best if you describe here how the game of volleyball is played rather than attempting to actually play the game itself."

And so, like most people, I gravitated toward what I did well. After eleven years of postsecondary education, I was in an English/writing department, a journalist, and editor. I worked hard, but I worked in a world I knew. I was comfortable. I had a community of like-minded friends, two cats, lots of plants, a retirement plan, and a long-term relationship. I showered every day, my summer tan was sprayed on, and I certainly didn't know how to sail. I would have told you that I needed eight hours of sleep, that I couldn't function without coffee, and that I needed my personal space and large amounts of time alone in my own head.

But as I built my writing career, newspapers and magazines folded in the wake of the Internet boom, and journalists by the thousands lost their jobs. Just as I left adjunct teaching behind to pursue a tenured position, universities stopped hiring and turned to their part-time faculty, sans benefits, to stay afloat. Just as I settled into editing, my relationship of many years came to an end, and on my salary, I could no longer afford to stay in the city I loved.

When things spiral out of control, many cling to what they know. This makes perfect sense. I could have moved to a smaller city, returned to adjunct work, and learned best SEO practices to write for the digital age. Instead, when the universe seemed determined to shake up my life, I responded by shaking back. I not only stepped out of my comfort zone, but also gave up comfort all together.

From a distance, a sailboat is grace, beauty, and slow, luxurious travel. Up close, sailing is physics and geometry, spatial relations, rigid schedules, hierarchy — and motor skills. I was an academic, used to learning from books. On a sailboat, we learn on our feet, when others are already impatiently relying on our competence. I knew I was entering uncharted territory, but I wanted a challenge. I thought I could learn.

As a deckhand, it was my job to stand watch, and when running on a skeleton crew, this meant four-hour rotations: four on, four off, around the clock. The Atlantic sloshed across the deck and poured into our living spaces; everything was covered in salt, and our clothes grew mold. I lived in the fo'c'sle, a 15-foot triangular space around the foremast, with seven other people and a marine toilet. I slept in my bright orange Grundéns and thick rubber boots. Getting undressed was an energy expenditure I could no longer afford. Hauling on a traditional rig strained a rotator cuff, and I had plantar fasciitis. I couldn't curl my fingers into a fist; even my palms were swollen.

And yet it was my job to know where dozens of lines led and how to use them without hurting myself, others, or our floating island. It was my job to climb aloft on an 80-foot mast that swayed and jerked with the wind and waves, and once at the top, to let go so both hands were free to furl sail. It was my job to steer by the compass and eventually the wind, to calculate the relative angles of the wind, swell, rudder, and sails, all at once. It was my job to be on time to the minute, to hand pump the bilge against steady leaks between the planks separating us from the sea, and to complete all manner of projects requiring motor skills, from splicing line to scraping old, soot-filled Vaseline from the forward mast and slushing it with new.

If I made a mistake in my job as an editor, there might have been a misunderstanding. If I made a mistake in gale-force winds in February in the mid-Atlantic, someone — maybe me — could die. And I made mistakes all the time.

I stepped where I shouldn't have stepped. I hauled when I should have let the line run. And when I did see something, like a line misled inside the shrouds, I was too unsure to speak out. At thirty-five years old, with a fully developed sense of my own mortality, I climbed the rig more slowly than the twenty-year-old boys with whom I worked. I couldn't afford to volunteer my way up the hawsepipe and instead was trading skills I did have — building the social-justice programming on board — for minimum wage and a chance to learn to sail. But on a ship, the only work that counts is the tangible kind.

Once we reached Bermuda, the captain called me aside. "Are you happy?" he asked. "Is this everything you wanted it to be?" What I wanted was to cry. I wanted to quit. I wanted, more than anything, a friend to patiently explain how to set the main gaff-topsail again. (Even seeing the hyphen placement would have helped.) But sitting there, hot coffee in hand while the wind that would keep us in port for three weeks sunk smaller boats in the harbor, I knew my answer was "yes."

I'd left behind a life in which I was confident and skilled, for one in which I not only lacked knowledge, but struggled to learn. It was a challenge to stick with what I didn't know. It was humiliating to repeatedly reveal my weaknesses, and frustrating to get it wrong again and again. But I loved being at sea: the changing light, the salt air, and riding the wind to our next destination. I loved the simplicity of life when stripped down to the elements, and I'd discovered the deep sleep that comes only with physical exhaustion in the rocking cradle of a hard-working ship. To stand watch was to train one's physical and mental awareness to the present moment, to focus on what one can see and hear and smell. It was, in its way, a meditation.

> *It was a challenge to stick with what I didn't know.*

And I was, however slowly, learning.

I spent six years before the mast. By my second year, I ran the galley aboard an educational/scientific research vessel. I taught myself to cook for forty people from locally sourced island produce. I read what the students read and woke in the middle of the night to sort through the plankton we pulled up in the nets. I learned the lines on that boat, too, and earned the U.S. Coast Guard license of Able Seaman, or AB Special.

If I hadn't been willing to be as terrible a sailor, I wouldn't have visited some of the most remote places on earth. I wouldn't have jumped into the ocean halfway between Canada and Ireland, or watched pods of humpbacks breeching in the Alenuihaha Channel, or high-fived a manta ray, or dove with reef sharks in an atoll lagoon. I wouldn't have eaten palusami, poisson cru, breadfruit, or fafaru, and I wouldn't be able to sell with confidence my skills as a chef, despite never having gone to culinary school or worked the line in a commercial kitchen. I wouldn't have met the man who is now my partner. I wouldn't know how far I can push myself. And I wouldn't know that I can do something I'm bad at, in front of everyone, until I'm not so bad anymore.

I've since returned to land. It felt good and right to go back to my desk, where I spend hours in still and silent solitude. My time is my own, but I don't sleep nearly as well. I miss the heel of the ship, and I ache for the sounds of the waves lapping the hull, for the kick of the wind in a sail trimmed just so.

With my new partner, an oceanographer, I bought an antique 44-foot Swan, born the same year I was. I so readily put up my life savings for this project that he was shocked to learn how little I knew about overhauling and restoring a boat. I've had to reveal my ignorance multiple times as we've cleaned, stripped, sanded, scraped, patched, painted, varnished, and oiled her — as we build our future home at sea.

~Sayzie Koldys

91

The Chapter Called France

Retire from work, but not from life.
~M.K. Soni

n the cold, early days of January 2011, if anyone had predicted that I would be spending most of the next school year in the south of France, I would have laughed and said they were crazy. But that's where I went for eight months — six time zones and several comfort zones away from Wisconsin!

For more than thirty years, I worked with young children. When I made the decision to retire at age fifty-five from teaching kindergarten, I had no idea what would come next. I just knew it was time to begin a new chapter.

"What are you going to do now?" asked my friend Sue.

"I have no idea. I'll have to work at something, but I don't know what." Actually, I was a bit shocked by how absurdly right, yet crazy, the idea of quitting my job seemed.

"Have you thought of house-sitting as a transition?" Sue continued. "I know someone who is spending time on the coast of Spain and staying at a really nice place in exchange for taking care of a cat."

I never had taken my semester abroad when I was in college. Working three jobs and going to school full-time landed me in the hospital with a bleeding ulcer two weeks before I was supposed to go. This could be like a semester abroad! I warmed to the idea quickly and started searching online.

Lots of websites popped up. Amongst the entries, I saw one called HouseCarers.com. I liked the idea of caring for someone's place. I had done farm sitting before, caring for four cows, hundreds of sheep, chickens and even a llama. Certainly, I could care for a house and a pet or two.

"Where would you like to go?" the website asked.

My answer came quickly, "France."

Two opportunities appeared on my computer screen. I was blind to the second offering after reading about the first — a house- and garden-sitting gig in the south of France in a little village called Bormes-les-Mimosas, right on the Mediterranean Sea. "That's it!"

> *"Have you thought of house-sitting as a transition?"*

But what about the fact that I didn't speak French? And what about my own house, and not being home for Christmas?

"Honey, how would you feel if I wasn't home for Christmas?"

"Where would you be?" asked my only daughter, now married and a career woman in her own right.

"The south of France."

"Well, as long as I could come and visit, I'd say go for it!"

I applied for the job and was invited for a working trial holiday. If it didn't work out, I would consider the three-week trip a retirement gift from me to me.

I had only traveled abroad on my own once before, to Venezuela to visit an exchange student. Flying wasn't my favorite pastime, and if I was offered the position for the winter, I would have to return to the States and then go back to France again three weeks later.

The chance for adventure, and my desire to fill the void of retirement, got me going. The owners of the house, Nicky and Mick, became great friends during my summer trial. They offered to let me stay in this, their second home, while they were back in California teaching at UCLA. I would care for the house and garden in exchange for a place to live, lots of vegetables from the garden, and Wi-Fi.

"Je regrette de parler un peu le français." "I regret I speak French a

little bit," was the somewhat incorrect phrase I uttered most during my first weeks in France. I had taken two weeks of French lessons in Hyères before returning to the States to pack more bags and say "*au revoir*" to family and friends.

My experience in Hyeres was full-blown French immersion. I've heard time and again that it is the best way to learn a language — to jump right in and start swimming — but I felt way over my head. Everyone in the beginner's class had at least a year or two of French.

There were people from Spain, Venezuela, Japan, Norway and Germany in the class. After the first day, my priority changed from understanding the French language to understanding people. At every break, and most afternoons, we gathered, cobbling together bits of every language we knew, including using charades to communicate.

Two weeks is barely enough time to learn to dogpaddle through a French conversation. So, I began private lessons once a week when I returned.

Until those lessons began, I tried my best, sounding like Tarzan when he first met Jane, but in French. Everyone was gracious, though, and appreciated my efforts.

One late September day, I attempted to tell *la madame au bureau de poste* what was in the package I was collecting. "*Libre,*" I began erroneously. The Spanish words that I used with my kindergartners from Mexico were more ingrained than my *français nouveau*.

"*Livre!*" Madame corrected. "*Libre, c'est liberation,*" she continued.

"*Merci.*" I thanked her and left.

Two blocks from the *bureau de poste*, an elderly tourist approached me for directions. "*Où est le bureau de poste, s'il vous plaît?*" he asked.

"*Tout droit, monsieur. Sur la gauche.*" Straight ahead. And on the left.

I walked away smiling with the knowledge that my personal world had grown a few blocks and a few words wider.

~Deb Biechler

92

The Birthday Present

*Every great move forward in your life begins with a
leap of faith, a step into the unknown.*
~Brian Tracy

t was his birthday, and our oldest son and his wife gave my husband Randy a power tool. A woodworking magazine was tucked in with the gift, and it just happened to be one he had subscribed to years ago. As he sat on our front porch, thumbing through his new magazine, he commented to no one in particular, "Hmm, that's interesting." Of course, I took the bait and asked him what he had found.

"They're looking to add an associate editor to their staff. That would be my dream job."

Randy had always been a woodworker. From his childhood days of handing nails to his dad while they built a room addition, he has loved working with his hands. Over the years, he gained skills that allowed him to build fine furniture as well as do many projects around the house.

But woodworking was just a hobby. Randy had a good job in the computer industry. The only problem was that it required a tremendous amount of travel. Sometimes, he was gone from Sunday evening until Friday evening for months at a time, leaving me to raise the six boys who were still at home.

"Maybe I should apply for this job," said Randy. "What do you think?"

I shrugged. "What have you got to lose? I'd say go for it."

We turned our attention back to our party guests. But after the last guests drove away, and we were getting ready for bed, the subject came up again. We reread the job requirements. Randy was definitely qualified. The opportunity to do what he loved and get paid for it was a big draw, but there was also a major downside: We would have to relocate.

We had both lived in the same county in central Ohio for more than forty years. We'd grown up there and were now raising our sons in a house that we'd lived in for twenty years. It was the only home our boys knew. If this job became reality, we would be moving almost 700 miles from everything we knew — to Des Moines, Iowa. We had never even been to Iowa.

A few days later, I took the boys to ride their bikes at the park. As I walked along a path talking to God about this huge decision we needed to make, my eight-year-old son came up beside me and got off his bike to walk with me. I had been asking God to give us some sort of sign if this move was right for our family. As my son and I walked, a man came jogging toward us. As he drew closer, I saw that his shirt had words on it. Of course, we always feel compelled to read what people wear, so both my son and I did so automatically. After the man passed, my son stopped and looked at me with his eyes wide open.

"Mom, did you see what his shirt said?" I had. The man's shirt said: JUST DO IT — IOWA. I have never seen that on a shirt in the twelve years since that day. I would have thought I'd imagined it if my son hadn't also read those words. It seemed a little silly, but it was the sign we needed.

Over the summer, there were phone interviews. Finally, in August, an offer was presented. Randy and I flew to Des Moines to look for a home. We spent days searching, but we found nothing in our price range that would house a family of eight comfortably.

Randy began working in Iowa in early September. A couple of weeks later, I took another trip to hunt for a house. This time, I traveled with two of my older sons. We spent almost a week looking at dozens of homes. Nothing seemed adequate… until the night before we needed to head back to Ohio.

We were tired of seeing other people's houses that couldn't possibly feel like home. Just before dusk, we met the real estate agent at one last house. As soon as we walked in, we knew it would be perfect. Huge picture windows in the dining room overlooked a lovely park with a pond. There were plenty of bedrooms and bathrooms. The process to buy this house began.

> **We trusted that we would have an address by the time the van arrived in Des Moines.**

But that process bogged down. Our home in Ohio hadn't sold. We could do nothing until that happened. We discussed a different arrangement with the seller, but were getting nowhere. Finally, our home sold, but we still hadn't made the deal we needed for the Iowa house. There were no other buyers in sight, so we tried to be patient. But the days kept passing, and we needed to get moved.

Finally, in the middle of October, Randy flew home to help with the final packing and sale of our house. When moving day came, we watched the moving van leave our driveway and head for Iowa. We had no address we could give the driver. He would take three days to make the trip, and we trusted that we would have an address by the time the van arrived in Des Moines.

The next morning, we roused our boys, loaded our pets into the van and left for our new home, wherever that was. The trip took twelve hours. Randy was on the phone most of the day still trying to make the deal to buy the house. Just as we were crossing the Mississippi River into Iowa, the deal came together. We would have an address for the moving van and, more importantly, we would have a place to sleep that night. We arrived late in the evening, and the eight of us slept together on the floor in the living room of what was to become our new home.

It was a daring decision for us to move from a place where we had deep roots to a place we'd never even visited — with a houseful of boys. But it was the right decision for us, and we have wonderful memories of raising our boys in Iowa.

~Sheryl Maxey

Chapter
11

The Power of Yes!

Let Yourself Trust

Trust your instinct to the end, though
you can render no reason.
~Ralph Waldo Emerson

93

Buy the Book

Live life with no excuses, travel with no regret.
~Oscar Wilde

don't know why it was Bali. I just felt called to go there for years. But I always pushed it off to "someday." *When I have more money, when I have a partner to go with, when terrorism isn't such a threat... then I will go to Bali. Then I will see the world. Then. But not now.*

Then one warm spring morning, my anxiety and discontent were overwhelming. So I sat under an apricot tree and meditated. In the quietude of my mind, thoughts of Bali came to me. My inner voice said suddenly, *Go buy a Bali guidebook.*

The critic within me retorted, "We can't spend money on that right now!" Money was really tight, so spending on anything other than absolute necessities would only make me more anxious.

But the inner voice gently nudged, *Just go to the bookstore. If you get there and don't want to go in, then you don't have to. But just go.*

I didn't know what had come over me. It made no sense for me to be buying a book. I couldn't afford the book, much less the actual trip.

I walked into that bookstore feeling like a crazy person, wondering what I was doing buying that book — especially because when I found the book on the shelf, the price was about twice as much as I expected.

I put the book back on the shelf. Then I picked it up again. I held it in my hand and debated for a while. I told myself all the logical reasons why I shouldn't buy that book. But then my inner voice piped up, gentle but firm, *BUY THE BOOK.*

I walked toward the register and handed it to the cashier, riddled with anxiety, still thinking I was crazy. When I walked out of that store, I felt like I was making my way to a getaway car. When I backed out of my parking spot and saw the book sitting on the back seat, I thought, *Oh, my god! What have I done?*

I knew in that moment that what I was looking at was not merely a book; it was a step. It was the first step in my journey of 8,327 miles.

I took my book to a nearby coffee shop where I sat and explored the pages. I thought about when I might want to go to Bali, and October was my first thought. That gave me just under six months to figure out how to make it happen. When I referred to what the book had to say about October in Bali, it mentioned the Ubud Writers & Readers Festival happening that month. That was just the green light I needed. I knew then that this was actually going to happen. And it terrified me.

I'd never traveled anywhere before, other than a few family vacations as a kid and a small road trip with a friend in my early twenties. And now I was planning to go to Indonesia — a woman, alone, with no travel experience.

All I could think of was a long list of fears — some valid and some totally outrageous. But I'd done enough inner work to know that I could trust the voice that prodded me to buy that book, to take that step. And even though each step closer brought up new anxieties, I knew I could continue to trust that voice.

I managed to scrimp and scramble and save. I found old, inactive bank accounts that had small amounts of unclaimed money in them. I got clever and resourceful, and somehow I managed to get enough money together to spend six weeks in Bali.

When it came time to buy the ticket, I had yet another anxiety attack. I called a friend who talked me down and helped me take that leap. I purchased the ticket, and it was official. I was going to Bali.

By the time I boarded the plane, my anxiety about flying had diminished, and I remembered how much I loved flying as a kid.

When I woke up my first morning in Bali, the voice in my head said, *I am so happy!* Over the following six weeks, I rode motorbikes through rice fields, with the wind in my hair. I saw sunsets and full moons. I participated in ceremonies and processions. I hiked to the top of a volcano. I tiptoed through a cave. I ate wonderful food and met the most incredible people. And I fell in love… with Bali.

Before I embarked on my journey, I was riddled with fear. But what I was really scared of was anything new and different, which also happened to be the exact thing I craved.

> *I spent so many years making excuses instead of making plans.*

I spent so many years making excuses instead of making plans. But when I think of the happiest times in my life, they are all direct results of saying yes to new things and leaving my comfort zone.

That means facing my fears, and I know now that the only way to exorcise those fears is to act in spite of them.

I was afraid of losing my luggage, but I ended up getting rid of a lot of baggage.

I was afraid of communication barriers, but I ended up amidst people who really "spoke my language."

I was afraid about money, but I actually got a lot more comfortable, confident, open, and loving in my relationship with money.

I was afraid of getting lost, but ended up finding an even deeper sense of self.

I was afraid of monkeys, but I ended up getting the monkey off my back.

I was afraid for my safety, but I ended up feeling a deeper sense of safety there than I have felt since, well, I can't even remember when.

There was a special gleam in the eyes of the Balinese people that touched my heart in an inexplicable way. I'd do it all again just to feel that. I may just sell all my possessions and move back there one day.

~Julia Rebecca Miron

94

The Distance Between Fear and 5'5"

One of the greatest discoveries a man makes,
one of his great surprises, is to find he can
do what he was afraid he couldn't do.
~Henry Ford

My fingers curled around the rolled concrete rim of the swimming pool, pressing them down as hard as I could in an effort to get a better grip on the smooth, flat surface. To my right was Lori, doing her best to persuade me to advance toward her into deeper water. On the left was the shallow end of the pool.

Awash with fear, I wanted nothing more than to scuttle back toward the 2-foot depth and out of the pool, never to set foot in water again.

Why did I ever think I could do this?

I thought I saw a hint of exasperation at the corners of Lori's eyes, but maybe it was the reflection of the feeling in my own gut. I kicked myself inside.

Don't be such a coward.

We were finishing up a half-hour of lesson time, just Lori and me. We had mostly just stood in the shallow end of the warm therapy pool, giving us a chance to get to know each other a little and begin to build trust.

It gave her a chance to evaluate my fear, too. The enormity of it was mortifying, and spending time with the swim teacher in the water made me feel like I was wearing my entire insides on my skin for the world to see.

We had spent that first lesson taking baby steps. She had led me down the shallow wheelchair-access ramp into the pool, encouraging me to take a step deeper, and then another. I was up to my mid-calves, and then my knees, and then my mid-thighs. When the water was touching the lowest reaches of my swimsuit, I tried to remember the last time I had stood in water that deep.

I had been afraid of water my whole life. At age forty-four, I had no memory of ever enjoying any body of water. Even walking around the edge of a pool was unsettling.

As if that wasn't crippling enough, shame and humiliation had come along with it. All those times I had feigned being too busy to attend get-togethers when I found out they were going to be held at the pool, all those invitations I had declined for lakeside and boating events—I had long since stopped admitting I was uncomfortable around water because there was always someone who would try to cajole me. "Oh, it will be fine." And, "You can wear a life jacket." And, "Don't worry, we won't let you drown."

> I hid my terror in order to save face, and few people knew I was afraid of water.

They didn't get it. They couldn't understand that phobia happens from the neck down and pays no attention to reason or reality. The combination of emotions seemed to spin into such a dark vortex—being embarrassed led to more fear, and being afraid increased my shame. I hid my terror in order to save face, and few people knew I was afraid of water.

Lori urged me deeper as I slid my toes gingerly along the pool floor, trying to decide if it was suddenly dropping off more steeply than it had before.

What if it gets too deep? What if I slip and lose my balance? Oh, dear God, why can't we be closer to the wall of the pool?

When the water reached my ribcage, Lori could tell I had reached my limit. She switched tactics and began working with me to put my face in the water — not to submerge in it, but merely to lean in enough to let the water touch my face.

I pinched my nose shut with one hand and held Lori's forearm with the other. It unnerved me to feel the way her body seemed so fluid, undulating like waves of grain in the flat shallow water. I managed to get my face wet, and we called it a day. I had gotten through my first ever swimming lesson. I breathed a sigh of relief and turned to walk back out the shallow end.

"Let's try going this way," Lori said, guiding me the few feet over toward the edge of the pool. I was aghast as I understood what she meant. She wanted me to hang onto the rim of the pool and work my way along it to the stairs at the opposite end. I had seen the blue-painted block numbers as I walked in, taking care to leave ample space between me and the edge of the water. Five and a half feet? *No way. No freakin' way.*

"Just try it," Lori pressed. I tried it. I advanced a few inches. Then a foot. Then another.

At 4'6", I was struggling to keep my heels on the pool floor. I felt like I had forgotten how to breathe. As the water depth increased, I moved more and more slowly. As we neared the 5-foot mark, my progress was so labored that Lori wavered. But we inched on.

It felt like hours later when I reached out and closed my white knuckles around the handrail on the stairs at the far end of the pool and scrambled up the steps.

I stood dripping on the floor, trembling with relief and exhilaration. *I did it. I did it!* But — could I do it again? Could I come back for another lesson next week? Would I ever be able to dunk my whole head under the water or let go of the wall, much less actually swim?

Somehow, right then, I knew I could. I had been inspired by a series of sermons about courage to place a call to my local YMCA and inquire about private swimming lessons for fearful adults. Now that I had signed up, and then actually followed through and showed up, I felt like I could do anything.

I kept coming back. Between lessons, I spent time in open swim sessions, splashing around and gaining confidence and skills. Five months later, I let go of the wall at the deep end and swam the length of the pool, amid cheers and applause from fellow swimmers.

Being able to swim might not be a huge deal to most people. But the big deal is not so much in the swimming, but in the overcoming. In the daring and trying and being afraid, but doing it anyway. The really big deal is hanging on when we cannot let go — until we are able to let go and not hang on. The huge deal is support and encouragement and persistence. And sometimes the biggest deal of all is to walk into the shallow end and come out a winner at the deep end, no matter how long it takes to get there.

~Kathy Bernier

95

Pedal Power

Life is like riding a bicycle. In order to keep your
balance, you must keep moving.
~Albert Einstein

"**D**on't let go!" I bellowed as Graham sprinted down the alleyway after me. His long hair flapped on his neck alongside me as he tightly grasped the silver bar attached to the side of my shiny new bicycle.

While the other Peace Corps volunteers whizzed in and out of the busy Sri Lankan streets, I was forced to walk back with my newly purchased bike from the tiny shop on the Colombo-Kandy Road. I was the only one who didn't know how to ride a bicycle.

"Please, don't let go," I pleaded. Graham, a kind volunteer, promised to be my teacher.

"I won't, Elana. I promised," he said. Even though we had met only a few months earlier, I felt completely safe with him.

In the middle of our lesson, I saw locals standing in groups, staring at me. I looked up and saw my fellow Peace Corps volunteers coming out of our hostel. They were photographing my lesson and cheering me on.

It was so natural for all the other volunteers. They had been riding since they were children. "It's easy," Myah chided. But when I tried, my legs quickly turned to Jell-O, and I simply could not get my balance right. As if joining the Peace Corps wasn't difficult enough, learning how to ride a bicycle in less than an hour seemed inconceivable.

As a city girl, I had managed to escape this rite of passage. My alibi was always the same: City kids didn't do such things. Or so I claimed. The truth was that lack of motor skills had plagued me for years. My whole life, I had wanted to conquer that fear, but how? Graham was my answer.

After a few practices getting on and off and only falling twice, I ended up wobbling, nearly falling and then, eventually, I was riding. I was actually riding a bicycle! I couldn't believe it! I looked behind, and Graham was running diligently like a track star, keeping pace until I told him he could let go. At that moment, I knew what it meant to fly. I understood the rush of bungee jumping and skydiving and all those adrenaline-related sports. I finally got it!

> *No training wheels. No kneepads. No shame.*

I learned how to ride a bicycle at twenty-four. No training wheels. No kneepads. No shame. I felt invincible. It was the beginning of a long battle with overcoming fears that I can't really explain in words. Just as I cannot truly express the joy a young woman felt when, for just a moment, she was able to do the impossible.

Once I began to ride, I was often seen on my bike swerving in and out of my village. It became my trademark, my icon. In the beginning, I wasn't sure how to stop or brake properly; we never got that far in my training. Instead, I often used a ditch near a hairpin turn to cushion my fall. Somehow, I always managed to land on the same exact spot of my right kneecap. I have the scars to prove it — a slight star formation that remains like a tattoo on my leg. It is somewhat malformed as a result, and I love that. I turn to this imperfection when I lose my confidence and need to remember what it's like to take chances. It symbolizes all the risks I took during those years abroad. It reminds me of what I am capable of — even when I think it might be too late.

Graham and I are still friends. Bonds like that are unbreakable. I saw him in person recently, and we hugged firmly. He rearranged his schedule to meet me. He wanted his wife to meet the sassy volunteer from all those years ago. I asked if he remembered that day. "Of course," he said. "You sent me a picture of you riding a bike in your village. I still have it; it's my favorite picture." It meant something to him, too. "You were so brave," he said. I was. I still can be. Sometimes, we just need that special person to give us a push and help us as we start down the road.

~Elana Rabinowitz

96

Empty No More

Friends are the family you choose.
~Jess C. Scott

M y husband had abandoned us, moving to the opposite side of the country, and leaving me with thousands of dollars of unpaid bills, a cleaned out bank account, an empty doghouse, and a car that wouldn't run. But, worst of all, my son's room was empty. My husband took him, too.

It was just my daughter and me. The emptiness was overwhelming.

I stood in my rental house feeling terribly alone, anxious, angry, even desperate. I so wanted to give my daughter some measure of strength and stability during this terrible time by keeping her near her friends, in the school she loved, and in the home she knew. I contemplated taking in boarders, but I really didn't want strangers to invade our broken world and see our pain.

I had other fears about boarders as well. Could I adequately judge the character of strangers so I could allow them into our home? I was also concerned that my daughter might be exposed to negative influences from them. Most of all, I wasn't sure I wanted to have relationships forced into our lives as we tried to heal from the past. And I was brokenhearted at the thought of filling my son's empty room with anyone other than him.

Yet I had to be realistic. If we were to stay in our home and maintain any measure of continuity in our lives, I had to be brave — and find the courage it would take to become a landlady. I decided that I would sublet our empty bedrooms only to young, single women.

I knew it would be a risk. First, I made sure there weren't any legal issues with subletting. Then I talked with others who had done this to find out how they chose people who could be trusted.

I decided not to advertise to the general public. Instead, I passed the word around to my friends and colleagues, and I cautiously posted an advertisement at church. I drew up an application and rental agreement that included a security deposit, the monthly rental fee, late fees, and damage fees. I also included house rules—no smoking, drinking, overnight male guests, etc.

With each applicant I interviewed, I asked for references and verified her character as best I could by talking with their friends and employers. And before I gave the final okay, I made sure my daughter met each woman so we would both be comfortable with the choice.

> *I found healing and joy in their companionship and friendship.*

Once we chose a housemate, then two, many unforeseen challenges arose, and I had to be strong and set additional boundaries. Quickly, I realized that my plan was not without flaws. My empty bedrooms were full, but my broken heart was still empty.

My daughter and I tried to respect our housemates' privacy, and we expected them to respect ours. But that wasn't always easy. One snuck in her boyfriend for the night, even though that was against our agreement. The other was a busybody and annoying. I had to ask them both to leave, and though we were relieved, I felt like I had failed—and my bedrooms were once again empty.

I tried again and I got better at choosing our tenants. Usually, we could work out our differences, resolve the issues, and move on, and I continued to grow in strength, faith, and courage over the years that I was a landlord. Over an eight-year period, I had ten different housemates move in and out. Along the way, we shared our lives together, and they became much more than rent payments. They became friends, and thanks to them, I started to laugh again, play again, and even cry with others as I journeyed through the healing process.

We became a community. We worked as a team, and we played together, too. We had a "Girls' Night" where we shared meals, played games, or watched movies. We celebrated one another's birthdays and holidays. We participated in each other's weddings as bridesmaids or wedding coordinators, and later on we blessed the birth of babies and more. We built lifetime relationships, and even today we continue to "do life together" even though most of us are married and live far from each other.

Today, one former tenant is an accountant in France. Another does microfinance in South Africa. One is a busy mom of three in Nebraska. Another is raising twin boys in Missouri. Just three of us still remain in Colorado Springs. Yet each woman is an important part of my life. They are family — people who have healed my heart, taught me to trust again, and changed my life.

All these women were instruments of grace who helped bring me to where I am today, and I am grateful that I found the courage to fill my empty rooms and welcome these women into my life. Each one taught me important lessons along my single-again journey, and I found healing and joy in their companionship and friendship.

My life is empty no more. Through all the ups and downs of doing life together, I learned so much about myself as well as living with different people, and I learned to be brave. Our friends and neighbors often accused us of having too much fun for our own good. They were right.

~Susan G. Mathis

97

Chicken Soup for the Soul.

A Teacher in Thailand

*Just try new things. Don't be afraid. Step out of your
comfort zones and soar, all right?*
~Michelle Obama

My flight arrived in Bangkok late at night, just in time
for me to clear customs and make my way to the adjacent station where I would board an overnight train to
Nong Khai in the far north, near the Vietnam border.
That's how it was supposed to work anyway.

I was a little nervous but more tired than anything after the twenty-
hour, sleepless flight. I hadn't yet focused on the reality that I was in
Thailand and could not speak a word of Thai or read many of the signs.

I arrived at the ticket counter breathless from carrying and drag-
ging my big bags. I presented my printout from the train reservation
website to an unsmiling agent who stared at it briefly, ran his fingers
down a handwritten list on his desk, shook his head and told me in
curt, halting English, "No, Madam. Train is full."

"But what about my reservation? A sleeper seat. I made it online.
See, right here." I pointed to my wrinkled piece of paper. He shook
his head more vigorously, but then said something unintelligible to me
that seemed to suggest I could wait and see. There might be a regular
seat available, but definitely not a sleeper. The train would be coming
shortly from the main terminal in Bangkok and making its quick stop
at the airport terminal sub-station. Dazed, I sat down.

About a dozen travelers were seated near enough to hear my

conversation with the agent.

"Why you want to go Nong Khai?" asked a woman, shyly. "Not for tourists."

I explained I was going to the headquarters of a charitable organization where I would go through orientation and be given my volunteer work assignment in another town. I would be teaching English for a few weeks.

"Teach" was a magic word. Another woman, well-dressed and speaking excellent English, immediately made a fuss over me, announcing excitedly in both Thai and English to the other waiting passengers, "She is a teacher! She must be on the train!" Then they had an animated conversation I could not understand with the ticket agent. The next thing I knew, he was telling me, "Okay, Madam. You can have a sleeping seat."

The young couple sitting across from me in the waiting area had offered to give me their sleeper in exchange for regular seats, which the agent found somehow. It didn't seem quite fair, I thought. I hesitated briefly but, exhausted from the long flight, I accepted gratefully.

I began to relax. The same kind woman offered to help me get to the correct car and find my space. We soon heard the train approaching and made our way to the platform. As it pulled in, we realized we had not exchanged contact information. Quickly, I pulled a notepad from my handbag. I scribbled my name and e-mail address, tore out the sheet of paper, and exchanged it for her business card, which she had pulled from a coat pocket.

Then it was a quick scramble to climb aboard the train — it would be there only long enough for these few passengers to enter. She pointed to my car. We shared a quick goodbye as she ran down the platform to her car and hopped on, and the train began to pull away.

Just as I sat down and began to wonder how to convert the seat into a reclining bed for my all-night ride, a smiling young lady approached. Apparently, she had also just boarded the train. She was pushing her bag down the aisle in front of her but holding out one hand toward me. Puzzled, I looked down. In her hand was my billfold. In that moment of total panic, I realized it had fallen from my bag and onto the platform while I was swapping numbers with the friendly Thai woman.

My feeling of foolishness and carelessness was immediate. Here I was, in Thailand for less than an hour, and I had almost missed my train. Even worse, I'd lost my wallet. I felt grateful but vulnerable.

Finally, I fell asleep, and the train rattled its way toward my adventure. A coordinator met me in Nong Khai, and I spent that day with other volunteers from around the world, learning about local customs such as when and how to "wai" (dip knee and hold hands together in front of me as a sign of respect) and basic guidelines. We would be assisting English teachers and letting their students practice English pronunciation with us.

> **I found myself facing twenty-five or thirty inquisitive faces.**

The following day, I traveled by bus to Loei, encountering my first-ever squat toilet. I was shocked to enter the small room labeled Toilet and see nothing there but a hole in the floor.

I was met in Loei by Nat, the young teacher I was going to assist. She took me to her parents' home to spend the night. Although they spoke no English at all, they were cordial. So far, so good. Very early the next morning, we drove to the rural village where her school was located. I was excited and eager.

After the 8:00 a.m. outdoor flag ceremony, Nat escorted me to the first-grade classroom and introduced me to a teacher. Without discussion, Nat left the room. Fine, but then the teacher left the room also, and I found myself facing twenty-five or thirty inquisitive faces, peering at me over their crisp navy-blue-and-white uniforms. They were silent — and I was stunned. I looked around and saw colorful posters and signs in Thai. Above them, stretching all around the room, was a banner bearing large letters I could read. Thank goodness, a Roman alphabet. There were also a few short words: B-boy. D-dog. K-key.

Speaking slowly, I said, "Good morning, children." To my relief, they responded in unison, "Good morning, teacher." We were on our way, and I was as timid as they. We recited the alphabet together, and then I tried pointing to objects and parts of the body, providing the

English word, which they repeated obediently. After twenty minutes, I was running out of ideas, but still the teacher I was supposed to help was nowhere in sight.

I taught them "The Hokey Pokey" and danced to demonstrate the words I wrote on the blackboard and pantomimed — arm, foot, head, in, out, shake. We pointed together to noses, mouths, eyes, and elbows. Left and right. It felt like an eternity!

After that terrifying first class, I explained to my host that I was prepared to help, not lead, and that I needed someone to translate for the young children. Things got better in the days that followed, and with the older students I found that I could teach all by myself!

I will always treasure my memories of that Thailand adventure. My only regret is not having a video of that first class when I performed "The Hokey Pokey" for a class of Thai first graders.

~Ruthanna Martin

98

Standing in the Doorway

*The meeting of two personalities is like the contact
of two chemical substances: if there is any
reaction, both are transformed.*

~Carl Jung

I was hunched over the desk in my office, grading student papers and looking forward to a lonely evening when a gentle tap sounded on my door. It was Sarah, my colleague in the professional writing department, whom I'd known since our freshman year of college. But seeing her didn't brighten my day. She and I had been rivals since the day we'd met, and only the day before she had been accepted into a writing program and I was rejected.

"Are you doing anything tonight?" She stood just outside my office doorway, her hands holding both ends of a pencil as she angled herself toward the hall.

"I don't have any plans," I said reluctantly.

"Would you like to meet at Starbucks tonight? We can edit each other's essays for the writing seminar."

No, I didn't want to go.

She knew I'd been rejected, so her invitation had to be pity. She hadn't invited me to do anything in the past eight years we'd known each other. Our only interaction had been passing "hellos" in the halls of the English department. So, no, I didn't want to go or have her read my essay, but I heard myself saying, "Yeah, sure, sounds good."

I dreaded the Starbucks meeting all afternoon, feeling my gut tighten every time I pictured Sarah reading my essay. I imagined her thinking, *Yeah, no wonder they rejected you. This is garbage!*

When I arrived at Starbucks that night, I found her sitting at a small table with several drafts of her essay. I ordered a latte and sat across from her. Sipping the foam silently, I determined to stay for only one hour and pulled out a stack of papers to grade. Hoping she'd forget about reading it, I pushed my essay to the side and started grading while she penciled edits on her already-perfect essay. I'd heard her tell someone that she'd included this essay in her portfolio for the writing program — obviously it was good enough as it was. I hoped she wouldn't ask me to read it; I couldn't emotionally handle the inevitable comparison I'd draw between my writing and hers, knowing I'd fall short.

"Did you have a good day?" I asked without looking up, just to break the awkward silence.

"Yeah. Yeah, it was fine. You?"

"Yup." I wiggled my foot in nervous rotations. We fell silent again, each pretending to focus on our work, until she finally asked the dreaded question.

"Is this your essay?" She lifted the paper and fixed her eyes on its inadequate pages.

I tensed. "Yes."

I felt like the kid at the science fair with the sloppy solar system whose planets won't stay glued in place. Pretending to grade, I kept my head lowered and periodically glanced at her face for signs of contempt or possible sneering. But she remained stoic and unreadable while I tormented myself over what she must be thinking, especially when she started penciling on the draft. I crossed, uncrossed, and recrossed my legs, then cracked my knuckles and bounced my foot. I flicked at the lid of my pen and chewed on my lip. Thinking I'd go insane, I searched for anything to preoccupy my tortured mind when I noticed her essay again.

I read the title: "My Little Box."

I had to read it. She was expecting me to.

"Is this your essay?" I was so unprepared to ask that question that my voice stuck in the back of my throat like Kermit the Frog.

"Mm-hm," she said. From her tone and the look in her eyes, I wondered briefly if she felt as insecure as I did or if it was just that the Kermit voice had startled her.

Something enchanting occurred as I read her essay. I'd known her for eight years, but suddenly I was meeting her for the first time. Her simple descriptions of herself on the beach as "a freckle-faced terror" chasing sand crabs and the poetic images of her seeing the ocean for the first time entranced me, warping time into a peaceful lapse in which all felt normal and right. Her little box in which she couldn't recreate the ocean mirrored her little box of unmet expectations. "But if all expectations met actualization," she wrote, "we'd have no dreams, no spontaneity, no impetus."

> *I could hardly breathe, fearing if I did, the magic would vanish.*

She'd poured her spirit into those pages, and it reached out and touched my own. I could hardly breathe, fearing if I did, the magic would vanish.

"You okay?" she asked.

I cleared my throat and answered, "This is how I want to write." I slid her draft back across the table.

"What?"

"You are the kind of writer I imagine myself to be," I said. Then I tapped my essay. "This is just what I happen to be at the moment."

"No, this is who you are," she said. "Our styles are just different. You focus more on characters and humor; my style is more meditative."

"Meditative sounds so much more purposeful than humorous," I said with a half-smile.

"You can't change who you are," she said. "Where would we be if Lucille Ball had wanted to be Audrey Hepburn?" Sarah handed me back my essay. "You should apply to a different writing program."

She smiled hesitantly, as if she could see my battered spirit and wanted to medicate it. Still caught in my moment of enchantment, I heard myself spending the next hour and a half unloading my goals, failures, and disappointments while she listened with the intensity of a lifelong friend, commenting, encouraging, and sharing her own thoughts and concerns. The conversation flowed so easily that I'd forgotten the novelty of this moment until the Starbucks barista told us they were closing soon.

I didn't want the night to end. I didn't want to go home and end the conversation. "Let's do this again," I said as we walked out.

She nodded. "It's a plan!"

I did get accepted into a different writing program, and Sarah and I encouraged each other through the rough road to MFAs in writing. It's been five years since that night in Starbucks, and we're still the driving force of encouragement in each other's lives. It feels commonplace sometimes now. A story from a long time ago.

But I'll never forget the picture of Sarah standing just outside my office, angled toward the hall, ready to run away if I'd rejected her Starbucks invitation. It makes me wonder how many friendships I've missed because I was too busy to accept or wasn't brave enough to be the one standing in the doorway.

~Laura Allnutt

99

I Could Never Do That

Being brave isn't the absence of fear. Being brave is
having that fear but finding a way through it.
~Bear Grylls

n 1990, the music ministry at our large church had many choirs, including ones for children of all ages, a mixed ensemble, a bell choir, an orchestra, and a melodious 150-voice adult choir under the leadership of Jane Parker.

I admired Jane and the talented music makers from afar, since I was not gifted with any natural vocal ability. It would be truthful to say I couldn't carry a tune in a bucket, I didn't know what a pitch was, and I didn't have a clue as to what the black dots on the music pages meant. "Profoundly singing-challenged" might be a politically correct term to use today.

But I loved music. So, I expressed my love for music in a unique way — by singing to the top of my fingertips with the use of sign language and movement. When I was five years old, I taught myself to "sign" to music. It was my way to obey my parents when they said, "Children should be seen and not heard."

One Monday, I was leading our regular church exercise class. The beautiful Sunday anthem replayed in my mind, and I wanted to try my hand at signing it. So, I waited patiently to tackle the song until after class when everyone had left. I was technically a "closet signer."

I was only comfortable signing for an audience of one.

But that day, there was an audience of two. Jane Parker happened to walk by the room and witness my silent efforts to sing praises and worship without words. She approached me. "I see you like to sign songs." Oh, no, my closely guarded secret was out. She continued, "I am looking to visually enhance a song that lends itself to sign language and movement. Would you be interested in signing a duet with one of our singers?"

"Sorry, I'd have to pass," I replied. "It would be too stressful for me to sign in front of people. Signing is how I communicate with God privately."

"I see," she said, seeming to understand. "But would you be willing to at least pray about it before making a final decision?"

"Sure, I could pray about it, but I already know I could never do that," I said. I went home with an unsettling stirring in my soul. This insecure, shy person who regularly sat in the back row at church had been asked to do the unthinkable.

Obediently, I prayed about the proposition. My prayer went something like: "Oh, Lord, you know how impossible it would be for me to sign in public. You know how I only like to sign to you. I could never sign in front of the church. And I'm sure you don't want me to, right?"

It wasn't an audible voice I heard as God spoke to my heart, but it might as well have been. "People need to *see* what a love relationship with me looks like. Do this for me."

I was dumbfounded. I shared with Jane what I felt God was instructing me to do. She was delighted. I was petrified.

The singer/signer duet was arranged. It happened.

I lived. But I do have to admit I was immensely relieved when it was over. I could go back to obscurity, worshipping in private.

The following Monday, Jane came to the church room after our weekly exercise class. She wanted to tell me how grateful she was for the duet on Sunday and how much she appreciated my courage to overcome my fears to sign in public. She shared that the response from the congregation was overwhelmingly positive. She went on to say that she wanted to start a Signing Choir at the church, which would be considered a part of the music ministry.

I supported her awesome vision and creativity. I told her that someday, if I were brave enough and could get good enough, I might even consider joining such a choir.

"Oh, no," she said. "You've got the wrong idea. I don't want you to be *in* the signing choir; I want you to direct it!"

Laughing, I stated firmly, "Thanks for the vote of confidence, but I *know* I could never do that."

"Would you pray about it?" she challenged.

"I could pray about it until the cows come home, Jane, but the truth of the matter is that I am not a music director by any stretch of the imagination. I can't sing, I'm not a certified sign-language interpreter, and I'm not qualified."

"I'm just asking you to pray about it," she reiterated calmly.

I went home and once again prayed fervently, "Oh, Lord, you *know* I can't do this."

> **"Oh, Lord, you know I can't do this."**

I felt an immediate response hit my heart. "I know *you* can't. That's why I chose you. You can be my vessel."

Tentatively, I agreed to try to start a signing choir. We put an announcement in the church bulletin that a sign-language choir was starting. I told Jane, "If no one shows up, we should abandon the idea." She agreed. Eight people showed up.

The eight of us decided to call the choir LOVE IN MOTION Signing Choir. We thought our little band of signers might be asked to sign a song once or twice a year. That was more than twenty-seven years ago, and now we average twenty-eight appearances worldwide yearly.

Each time the choir performs, people ask if they can join. Over the years, more than 400 people from twenty different churches have been through the choir and learned the art of song signing.

In 1998, the multi-generational LOVE IN MOTION Signing Choir became a traveling choir as we went to Washington, D.C. over Memorial Day weekend to minister at a conference for those who had experienced the death of a loved one in military service.

Through word of mouth, we were invited to share our inspirational ministry in other churches, local happenings, and regional, national, and international conferences of The Compassionate Friends, Bereaved Parents of the USA gatherings, and Umbrella Ministries. We have appeared in thirty-four states and thirteen countries, and signed in Christian and secular arenas to audiences of up to 6,000 people.

I am humbled as I look back in awe and wonder at what I would have missed if I hadn't prayed about it and said "yes" to God's nudging. He had abundant blessings in store for my life and the lives of thousands of others. Because of this, I still enjoy signing for an audience of one.

~BJ Jensen

100

Butterflies and Pterodactyls

Encourage, lift and strengthen one another. For the
positive energy spread to one will be felt by us all.
For we are connected, one and all.
~Deborah Day

I was struggling and had committed myself to doing thirty Al-Anon meetings in thirty days. It seemed doable in the beginning, but between work and life, I found myself with four days left and ten meetings short of my goal. I had nearly reconciled myself to being a failure when I saw a notice for a weekend Al-Anon/AA convention at the Hilton in Burbank. It was the solution to my problem!

Except that I don't do crowds. I don't even like big meetings. My max is about twenty people. I had been trying to stretch myself and share at every meeting—which was hard because I much preferred to sit there and pretend I was invisible. Still, I convinced myself to go to the convention. I just wouldn't be talking to anyone.

I took a deep breath and searched my closet for something that would make me look more confident than I felt. A cape and fancy underwear would have been nice; I settled for jeans and a pretty shirt.

When I walked into the convention center, I nearly turned around and left. It was packed! It looked like the whole Valley was there—holy cow! I took a deep breath and went in search of my first meeting. When

I walked into the room, all I saw was NOPE. It was a BIG room with a LOT of chairs. There was a podium. With a microphone. Oh, hell no.

I don't remember the topic of that first meeting, only the feeling. I sat in the last row, in the very last chair. I listened, but mostly I just soaked in the vibrations around me. I started to relax a little. When it was over, I slipped out quietly. I made a note about the meeting and mentally patted myself on the back — only nine more to go!

Halfway through the third meeting, I realized I wanted to share. I wanted to tell some part of my story to these people who were sharing theirs. I wanted one of the little butterfly pins they were giving out to people who shared.

It happened in my fourth meeting. As I made my way up to the front of the room, I was shaking from head to toe. My throat felt closed; I wondered if I would even be able to talk. When I reached the podium, I stared at the microphone and the hundred people in the audience, and wondered briefly if anyone had run out of the room screaming yet or if I would be the first. I took a deep breath, gripped each side of the podium until my knuckles turned white, and began to speak.

"They are giving out little butterfly pins to people who share today, and I have to tell you that I don't just have butterflies — I have pterodactyls. I find it hard to share in a meeting with a couple dozen people. I have no idea what I am doing here!" The ensuing laughter did a lot to quiet my nerves. Laughing at myself was my best defense against embarrassment; inviting others to laugh with me was like calling for backup. I smiled at my audience — these people I didn't know but who wanted to know what I had to say — and launched into a story about my relationship with my mother. I saw smiles, a couple of tears, many laughs, and so many nods of understanding and commiseration.

When it was over, I received applause and hugs, and then I got my butterfly pin!

I shared twice more that day and a few times the next day. I talked about my mom, my dad, relationships, feelings, and challenges. Almost every meeting I went to, no matter the topic, it touched something inside me, and I had something to offer.

It did not get easier. I still sat in the back of the room. I still didn't talk to anyone. I still trembled as I walked up to the front of the room. I still left sweaty handprints on every podium I touched. The butterflies in my stomach were still as big as birds. But time after time, I was able to quiet them with the promise of what came after. The euphoria of success was like a natural high, and I could see that I was not the only one experiencing that feeling. There were just a few smiling people on Saturday morning, but by Sunday afternoon, almost everyone was grinning ear to ear!

> *I still left sweaty handprints on every podium I touched.*

The topic for the last meeting was, fittingly, gratitude. I forced myself to sit in the front row. When I got up to speak, the giant birds in my stomach flapped their wings but didn't cry out. And I discovered that having a shorter walk to the podium gave me less time to freak out. I wish I had realized that sooner!

When I stared out into the crowd, I didn't grip the podium for dear life, and I didn't take a deep breath to calm myself. Instead, I smiled, feeling my lips tremble because this was still really hard! Several people smiled back, silently encouraging me. I began to speak. It went something like this:

"One month ago, I committed to do thirty meetings in thirty days. I did great for a week, and then I got off track. I am so grateful for this convention because I can't think of any other way I could do ten meetings in two days! But more important than the tally sheet is the magic happening inside. If someone had told me three days ago that I would be standing here at a podium with a microphone talking to a crowd of strangers, I would have laughed and probably made some self-deprecating joke. Basically, unless I was tied up and wheeled in on a dolly, this was not an option. In fact, when I shared for the first time yesterday, I made a joke about having pterodactyls instead of butterflies. And I still do, but I have butterflies, too. Look at my butterflies!" I pointed to the pins on my shirt.

"When I go home tonight, I am going to put these pins on my wall so I can see them every day. I want them to remind me of this weekend — not just that I made my thirty in thirty, but that I stepped outside my safe, sheltered, little world and didn't die. I did things I didn't think I could do — things I DID NOT WANT TO DO! Things I thought would feel terrible but instead felt wonderful. And, yes, I am also going to crawl back into my shell, but now I know I can come out again if I want to. That's pretty cool. I am grateful to you all — for being here, for listening to me, for laughing in all the right places, for blocking the door when it looked like I might run. Okay, seriously, that only happened once. I just want to say thank you for giving me exactly what I need right now. Plus butterflies."

~Linda Sabourin

Full Circle

One's destination is never a place,
but a new way of seeing things.
~Henry Miller

It had been almost a year since my father passed away. We'd all gone through what I thought was a normal course of grieving, but I was unable to shake the sense of loss. I was restless and depressed. "I need to get away," I kept telling my husband, but he was working so he had no time for holidays.

I felt like I needed to do something I had never done before — travel alone. Some of my girlfriends, mostly the single ones, did so on a regular basis, and I had tons of admiration for them. I didn't even go out for dinner alone!

I never did anything spontaneously either, but finally, one morning, I called a travel agent. When she asked me where I wanted to go, I didn't know. I told her I wanted to go somewhere alone, somewhere I could practice both yoga and Spanish. She booked me into a hotel on the Maya Riviera, in Mexico.

My husband and son drove me to the airport late at night, and it hit me like a ton of bricks that I was going toward the unknown. *What if the plane crashes? What if I never see my family again? What If someone gets sick or dies while I am gone? What if I get mugged? Or lose my passport?* I started to cry while we were waiting in line.

My husband smiled and teased me, "Boo hoo, poor me. I'm going to Mexico on a holiday. Poor me. Come on, sweetheart, this is a happy thing. Cheer up."

I was being childish. Meanwhile, my teenage son stood back a few steps in hopes that no one would connect him with this middle-aged woman in tears.

So, off I went and boarded the plane. I sat next to a lovely couple — well-seasoned travellers. While we chatted, I realized I was on a chartered flight and that, when we landed, I might be the only one not getting on the bus to whatever resort all these passengers were going to. My anxiety peaked when the plane shook in midair, so I held onto the woman's hand as if my life depended on it. "You don't fly much, do you?" she said.

We landed in Cancun at 1:00 in the morning. After all the other passengers left, I stood there alone outside the arrival terminal. I waited and waited, and was about to go inside the terminal when, lo and behold, a pink van pulled up, ejecting a small fellow who was holding a sign with my name on it. We exchanged our "holas," and I sat in the back of the van.

> Yes, I was dining alone and enjoying every moment!

In the middle of the night, I was whisked away in a rattling pink van with no seat belts. We drove through what looked like construction, then along a highway, and all the while the driver was chatting away in Spanish. I just nodded and repeated, "Si, si."

After an hour or so, we pulled into what looked like a palace. Someone offered me a glass of wine, but I just wanted to sleep. I was taken to my room in a golf cart. I dropped the suitcase by the bed, ignored the lizard on the wall, got undressed and lay down. By then, I was numb, drained of all fears and worries. That night, I slept soundly. I had surrendered.

The next day, I woke up to sunshine, room service, saltwater, and giant iguanas, followed by evenings of concerts on the beach and gourmet meals. Yes, I was dining alone and enjoying every moment! My Spanish improved. I attended yoga classes every morning and fed the fish in the pond. My anxiety dissipated. When I phoned my husband, he was pleased to hear an enthusiastic traveler on the line, not a sniveling, homesick, forty-year-old wife. "Soon, you'll be travelling the world alone, just like your dad," he said.

On Thursday, I came across what the Mexicans call a *temazcal*, an ancient sweat lodge made from volcanic rock that is used for purification ceremonies to cleanse mind, body and soul. Of course, I was skeptical, but curiosity got the best of me. I signed up for the ceremony, expecting only to be mildly entertained.

The shaman looked ancient. We were a small group of six, all tourists from different parts of the world. One fellow from Germany told us he had lost his wife a few months earlier. Before we knew it, everyone was sharing a personal story. When my turn came, I began speaking about my father. And then I cried a river. I cried like I hadn't cried or allowed myself to cry since his funeral.

I came out of the *temazcal* feeling serene, feeling confident and strong. Nothing horrible had happened to me. The world was not a strange and dangerous place preying on lonely gals. On the contrary, I would continue to travel alone without fear. I had become my father's daughter.

~Julie de Belle

Meet Our
Contributors

Kristi Adams is a travel writer who has written about llamas in Europe, the trials of using German GPS, adventure caves, and more. She lives in Germany with her husband, serving on active duty, and a curmudgeonly rescue cat. She is a proud six-time contributor to the *Chicken Soup for the Soul* series. Learn more at www.kristiadamsmedia.com.

Laura Allnutt completed a Master of Fine Arts degree in creative writing at Fairfield University in 2014. She recently completed a novel and is seeking publication. She currently lives with her friend Sarah and their mini Dachshund, Dudley.

Susan J. Anderson is a recovering teacher of English who now writes full-time. She holds a Master's in creative writing from Towson University, and blogs at foxywriterchick.com. She enjoys reading, swimming, and spending time with her husband and three sons.

Andrea Atkins is a writer whose articles and essays have appeared in national magazines for the past twenty-five years. She teaches personal essay classes and workshops in Westchester County, NY, and is a graduate of the University of Massachusetts/Amherst.

Jo-Anne Barton lives in Oxford Mills, Ontario with her husband and two dogs, Rocky and Billie. This is her first published work, and she hopes to continue to write and get published. She has numerous hobbies;

international travel is her favorite. E-mail Jo-Anne at jotours2015@ gmail.com.

Garrett Bauman has published fifteen stories in various *Chicken Soup for the Soul* books. His work has also been in *Yankee*, *The New York Times*, *The Chronicle of Higher Education*, and many other publications. He and his wife live nearly a mile off the nearest road in rural New York.

Nancy Beaufait has lived in Michigan all her life, and loves her mitten state. She enjoys reading, knitting, and has always enjoyed writing. Nancy is looking forward to retiring soon from her nursing profession and living in their little cottage on the lake.

Richard Berg is an author, artist, and advocate. He hosts and produces a Poetry and Music TV series, co-hosts two additional arts venues and performs as Edgar Allen Poe. His poetry and photography appear in publications and galleries and he is a Health and Safety Advocate in Massachusetts.

Kathy Bernier is a Maine author and blogger. Her love of the natural world and concern for the planet and all its inhabitants is evident in her writing, which runs the gamut from nature articles to fiction to homesteading how-to's. Find and follow her at www.facebook.com/ kathybernierwriter.

Deb Biechler is a retired kindergarten teacher and freelance writer from Wisconsin. She loved housesitting in France as her segue into retirement, and encourages the readers of her story to say YES! to their own invitations to adventure.

Family is key to happiness, says **Ellie Braun-Haley**. She continues to write/talk on miracles and goodness. She's a regular contributor to the *Chicken Soup for the Soul* series and the author of books, two on creative movement for children, one on miracles, and a co-author on a book about spousal abuse with husband, Shawn.

Eva Carter has a background in finance. She is a freelance photographer and a frequent contributor to the *Chicken Soup for the Soul* series. She and her husband live in Dallas, TX with their cat, Ollie.

Nebula-nominated **Beth Cato** is the author of the *Clockwork Dagger* duology and the new *Blood of Earth* trilogy from Harper Voyager. She's a Hanford, CA native transplanted to the Arizona desert, where she lives with her husband and son. Follow her at BethCato.com and on Twitter @BethCato.

Melanie Celeste is a Minneapolis-based freelance writer and stand-up comedian. She lives with her teenage daughter and two fat, ungrateful cats.

Geneva France Coleman is a freelance writer from Eastern Kentucky. Having grown up in Louisa, she moved to Pikeville when she married her husband, Mike. Although always Appalachian at heart, she and Mike recently moved to the beautiful Bluegrass region of Lexington, KY to be closer to their children and grandchildren.

Randal A. Collins is the Emergency Manager for the city of El Segundo and is the President of AHIMTA. He is a doctoral candidate at USC in Los Angeles where he also plays lacrosse. Randy has held positions with American Humane, the Indiana Department of Homeland Security, and as a U.S. Marine. Randy has a Master of Leadership from USC.

Ginny Huff Conahan taught for fourteen years in Los Angeles schools and sixteen years in Fort Collins, CO, to kindergarten through college-level students. She has a doctorate in Education from the University of Southern California. She enjoys reading, crafting, and volunteering. E-mail her at gcona@comcast.net.

Darin Cook received his Bachelor of Arts in 1993 and has been writing and editing ever since. He draws material for his travel writing and works of nonfiction from all of life's experiences, whether travelling the globe, journeying into his past, or exploring the challenges of being a parent.

Gwen Cooper received her B.A. in English and Secondary Education in 2007, and completed the Publishing Institute at Denver University in 2009. In her free time she enjoys krav maga, traveling, and spending time with her husband and Bloodhound in the beautiful Rocky Mountains. Follow her on Twitter @Gwen_Cooper10.

Jennifer Crites is a writer/photographer whose work has appeared in magazines and books worldwide, including *Islands*, *Fodor's*, and *Travel + Leisure* among many others. She loves to explore far-off places like Thailand, India, Dubai, and Argentina. Her travel blog can be found at jennnifercrites.wordpress.com.

Tracy Crump has published two-dozen anthology stories and numerous articles and devotionals. She co-directs Write Life Workshops, speaks at conferences, and edits a popular writers' newsletter, "The Write Life." But her most important job is Grandma for two completely unspoiled grandchildren. Visit her at TracyCrump.com.

Kaye Curren is a retired event planner. She has returned to writing after thirty years of raising two husbands, two children, two teenage stepchildren, three horses, umpteen dogs and cats, and several non-speaking parakeets. Find her essays, articles, and humor online at www.writethatthang.com.

Priscilla Dann-Courtney is a psychologist and writer living in Boulder, CO where she and her husband raised their three children. She is the author of *Room to Grow: Stories of Life and Family*. Her family, friends, work, running, yoga, baking, and meditation keep her aligned with the beauty in life.

Born in Ottawa, Ontario, but living in Quebec, **Julie de Belle** is a poet, teacher and freelance translator. She spends her time writing, cooking, skiing or cycling depending on the season. She lives with her husband and their dog on an island off of Montreal.

Jeanine L. DeHoney is a wife, mother, and grandmother and former preschool teacher and Family Services Coordinator. As a freelance writer her work has been published in several anthologies, magazines, and blogs including *Parent Co.*, *Brain Child* magazine, *Wow! Women on Writing Blog: Friday Speak Out!*, *Rigorous Magazine*, etc.

Katie Drew is a frequent contributor to the *Chicken Soup for the Soul* series. Writing as Susan Kimmel Wright, she's also published mysteries for kids, and is currently working on a cozy mystery series for adults. Please visit her on Facebook at Susan Kimmel Wright, Writer, or on Instagram @susankimmelwrights.

Logan Eliasen is a third-year law student at the University of Iowa College of Law. He previously graduated from Wheaton College with a Bachelor of Arts in biblical and theological studies. Logan enjoys spending time with his four younger brothers and reading in his hammock.

Sara Etgen-Baker's love for words began when her mother read the dictionary to her every night. A teacher's unexpected whisper, "You've got writing talent," ignited her writing desire. Sara ignored that whisper and pursued a different career; eventually she re-discovered her inner writer and began writing memoirs and personal essays.

Victoria Fedden received her MFA in Creative Writing in 2009. She lives in South Florida with her family and teaches college writing. Her memoir, *This Is Not My Beautiful Life*, was published in 2016. She enjoys yoga, poetry, cooking, and the beach.

Valorie Wells Fenton, Ph.D., has been a Certified Hypnotherapist for twenty-five years. She has written articles for *Huffington Post* and been featured in articles in *New York Magazine* and *Women's Health*. Valorie has appeared on ABC, CBS, NBC, and PBS TV stations in Kansas City.

Hyla Sabesin Finn's personal essays have appeared in *Self*, *Parents*, *Working Mother*, *The New York Times*, CSMonitor.com and others. When not writing about the trials and tribulations of everyday life, she is a private college admissions consultant. Hyla lives in Chicago with her husband and twin daughters.

Marianne Fosnow lives in Fort Mill, SC. She enjoys photography, reading, and spending time with family. She is thrilled to have her story included in the *Chicken Soup for the Soul* series.

Dave Fox is a travel writer, writing coach, and life coach based in Ho Chi Minh City, Vietnam. He teaches writing and offers his coaching services online, helping people around the world to successfully pursue their passions and live more fulfilling and adventurous lives. Learn more at Globejotting.com.

Victoria Otto Franzese has degrees from Smith College and New York University. She owned, operated, and wrote for an online travel guide for fifteen years before selling it to a major media outlet. Now she writes about a variety of topics and all of her travel is for fun. She lives in New York City with her husband, two sons, and a Goldendoodle named Jenkins.

Hannah Faye Garson taught special needs children in New York City's public schools for thirty-five years. She is currently a docent at the Kupferberg Holocaust Center in Queens, NY, where she continues to educate students of all ages. Her articles, puzzles and short stories have been published in newspapers and magazines.

Sue Doherty Gelber is a New Englander turned Chicagoan now living in Colorado, where she's still recovering from her last triathlon. Her work has appeared in the *Chicago Tribune*, *The Examined Life Journal*, *Purple Clover* and *Realize Magazine*, among others.

James A. Gemmell's favourite hobby is long distance hiking. He can be found most summers walking one of the Caminos de Santiago in France or Spain. His other hobbies are writing, playing guitar, drawing/painting, golfing and collecting art.

Tammy Nicole Glover writes short stories and devotionals. Her works have been featured in *Believers Bay* online publication. She has an inspirational blog, "Balm4theSoul" and she currently works in the mental health field and lives in Detroit, MI.

Kristin Goff is a retired journalist, grandmother of five, plodding runner and slow triathlete. She enjoys travelling, trying new things and is grateful for the love and support of friends and family, who may laugh with her but not at her.

Dr. Shari Hall is an internationally recognized physician, speaker, singer/songwriter, and writer. From New York, and educated at Yale and Columbia Universities, she now resides with her family on the beautiful Sunshine Coast of Queensland, Australia, where she owns SCeNic Real Estate. E-mail Shari at sharihallinfo@gmail.com.

Erin Hazlehurst is an award-winning screenwriter and self-published author from British Columbia, Canada.

Steve Hecht is a 1972 graduate of Duquesne University. He is retired from the *Pittsburgh Post-Gazette* where he was a writer and copy editor for thirty years.

Christy Heitger-Ewing, an award-winning writer and columnist, pens human interest stories for national, regional, and local magazines. She has contributed to eighteen anthologies and is the author of *Cabin Glory: Amusing Tales of Time Spent at the Family Retreat* (www.cabinglory. com). She lives in Indiana with her husband, two sons, and two cats.

Stan Holden is an art director and author and has created work for many Fortune 100 companies. As a prodigy, he was first published in a national magazine in the fifth grade. He is a graduate of Cal State University Long Beach and his critically acclaimed best-selling book, *Giving Candy to Strangers*, is out at bookstores now.

David Hull is a retired teacher who enjoys spending his days reading, writing, working in the garden and spoiling his great-nephew. He's had many stories published in the *Chicken Soup for the Soul* series. E-mail him at Davidhull59@aol.com.

Geneva Cobb Iijima lives in the Northwest of the U.S. and has four books and over 100 stories and articles in print. She is currently researching and writing a new book, *Amazing Youth of WWII*. She enjoys her children, grandchildren and friends. Visit her website at genevaiijima.com.

Robyn R. Ireland is writing her third novel. She has published fiction and nonfiction regionally. Working in the aerospace industry by night, she enjoys reading, writing, and nature during the day. She has a B.A. degree in English Literature from the University of Iowa. E-mail her at writerrobyn@gmail.com.

Leah Isbell is the mother of two sweet kids who keep her busy and exhausted. In her free time Leah enjoys reading, writing, cooking, and going to the movie theater. Someday, Leah would love to write Young Adult novels. Until then, Leah is taking each day in stride.

Aviva Jacobs is an accountant, writer, photographer, chronic traveler, and scrapbook addict. She and her husband have five adult kids and share their Victorian-era home in Wisconsin with two obnoxious cats.

BJ Jensen is an author, inspirational speaker, dramatist and music-signing artist. She is the Director of LOVE IN MOTION Signing Choir (www. signingchoir.com), which travels internationally. BJ is happily married to Dr. Doug Jensen and they live near their son, daughter-in-love, and three granddaughters in San Diego, CA. E-mail her at Jensen2@san.rr.com.

Nancy Johnson is a freelance writer living with her Schnoodle, Molly, in northeast Ohio. When not writing or working at her beloved retail job, she can be found on a yoga mat.

Cindy Jolley is a former elementary school teacher who lives in Grapevine, TX. This is her second story to be published in the *Chicken Soup for the Soul* series. In addition to writing short stories and devotionals, Cindy is also following her heart to write and illustrate stories for children.

Megan Pincus Kajitani is a writer, editor, and educator. Her writing has appeared in several anthologies, including the *Chicken Soup for the Soul* series, and publications such as *The Chronicle of Higher Education*, *Mothering* magazine, and *Huffington Post*. As Meeg Pincus, she also writes nonfiction for children.

Nick Karnazes (AKA: The Happy Golfer) is an avid golfer and active community member living in San Clemente, CA. When he's not golfing he enjoys Greek food and Greek dancing. This is his first submission to the *Chicken Soup for the Soul* series. E-mail him at nickthgp@gmail.com.

Anna S. Kendall is a Chicago-based writer and editor. In addition to stories in the *Chicken Soup for the Soul* series, Anna has also written a book, *College PaperBuddy*. She earned an MA in Writing Pedagogy from DePaul University in 2007 — a month before her big hang gliding adventure. Follow her on Twitter @annakendall.

Sayzie Koldys is a writer and an editor with a talent for turning your almost-English into English. Whether you're an editor who needs an essay or a scientist whose paper needs polishing, you can find her at www.opercula.net. When she's not working, she's exploring the intersections of food, culture, and the ocean.

Grace Kuikman of Chicago is editor of the Beverly Area Planning Association's Villagers newspaper, and the author of many short stories and poems. She is founder and facilitator of the Longwood Writers Guild, a critique group for adult creative writers, and presents writing workshops.

Angela Lebovic writes fiction (middle grade, YA, and picture books), a food blog, and is a member of the Society of Children's Book Writers and Illustrators. In her spare time, she is active in community theatre, and enjoys drawing and playing the flute. She has a Bachelor's degree and a Master's degree in communications/advertising.

Kate Lemery worked for the National Gallery of Art and Smithsonian Institution for fifteen years before becoming a stay-at-home mom. Her writing has appeared in *The Washington Post*, *Motherwell* magazine, and *Fiction Writers Review*. She's finishing her first novel, which combines her love of art history and literature.

Gretchen Nilsen Lendrum is a freelance writer and retired English teacher who enjoys literature, music, all animals, and long walks by the ocean. Her essays have appeared in several newspapers and magazines. This is her third story published in the *Chicken Soup for the Soul* series.

Elaine Liner is a playwright and solo performer in Dallas, TX. She has performed her one-woman comedy, *Sweater Curse: A Yarn about Love*, twice at the Edinburgh Fringe. Her play *Finishing School* had its world premiere in 2017. Her novel *2084: An American Parable* is available on Amazon. She's still asking "Why not?"

Joyce Lombardi is a writer, mother, and lawyer who lives near the water in Baltimore, MD. She writes about water, race, gender, and dance.

Ruthanna Martin's lifework as publicist, ad copywriter, editor, journalism adviser, and ersatz graphic designer took a U-turn in 2008 when she retired and became a Peace Corps volunteer in Namibia. Since then she has traipsed the world and lived in Uganda and Ecuador. At home in Dallas, TX she is writing a travel memoir.

Mark Mason is a freelance illustrator living in Whittier, CA, who's often heard saying, "A painting is never finished until the check clears." Although not a runner, he does enjoy stepping outside his comfort zone. This is his first attempt at getting published as a writer. E-mail him at got.mark@verizon.net.

Susan G. Mathis is a multi-published author of *The Fabric of Hope: An Irish Family Legacy*, and four other books. Learn more at www.SusanGMathis.com.

Sheryl Maxey is the author of an inspirational blog at Sherylmaxey.com. She homeschooled her seven boys for more than twenty-five years. When she isn't writing she enjoys leading women's Bible studies, quilting, reading, and spending time with her grandchildren. Sheryl lives in Florida.

Carolyn McGovern received her Bachelor of Arts in Criminal Justice from Seton Hall University in South Orange, NJ in 1982, and her Master's degree in Criminal Justice from Rutgers University in Newark, NJ in 1992. She worked as a corrections officer for four years, and as a probation officer for more than twenty years.

Carolyn McLean started her life on a farm in small town Ontario. She is the wife of an Anglican priest and together they have raised three wonderful children. In 2001, a fork in the road took her to Canada's Arctic (Nunavut and Northwest Territories) for twelve years. Carolyn enjoys sharing her stories, travelling and gardening.

Julia Rebecca Miron began writing poetry and song lyrics as a child. She now focuses on memoirs, which she infuses with her passion for personal growth and snappy humor. Julia leads authentic public speaking workshops, and is working on her first book. She loves hip-hop, dinner parties, hiking, good food, and good friends.

Tamara Moran-Smith is a freelance writer and contributor to the *Chicken Soup for the Soul* series. She is the proud mother of an adult son and a furry daughter, a Border Collie named Rosy. Her favorite subjects are God, family, and friends. E-mail her at hotflashofgenius@cox.net.

Ann Morrow is a writer, humorist, and frequent contributor to the *Chicken Soup for the Soul* series. She and her husband enjoy small town life in the Black Hills of South Dakota. Learn more at annmorrow.net.

Annie Nason is pursuing her Master's degree in Education, and thrilled to be published in the *Chicken Soup for the Soul* series! Her work has also appeared in *Chicken Soup for the Soul: Think Possible* and *Chicken Soup for the Soul: The Power of Gratitude*. She is passionate about sharing her story with those who are affected by cerebral palsy.

At eleven, **Sharon Pearson** had a small red journal with a lock and key. Her first entries included, "Piano Lesson," and "Nothing Happened Today." When she was twelve, she read *The Diary of Anne Frank*, which inspired her to pen her deeper feelings. Sharon continues to keep a journal and loves writing about the adventures in life.

Jon Peirce holds a B.A. and a Ph.D. in English and an M.I.R. in industrial relations. A retired English professor and labor relations officer, he acts in community theatre productions and writes plays. Jon enjoys cooking, tennis, and dancing. His publications include an essay collection and an industrial relations textbook.

Kristen Mai Pham loves *Star Wars*, Corgis, and her husband Paul. (Not in that order!) She is delighted to be a contributor to the *Chicken Soup for the Soul* series. Follow her on Instagram @kristenmaipham or e-mail her at kristenmaipham3@gmail.com.

Lori Chidori Phillips writes about everyday life and spirituality. A fourth generation Japanese American, she earned her Bachelor of Science and Master's degree in communications/journalism and education respectively. Her interests include botanical propagation, metaphysics, learning languages, and writing children's books.

Mary C.M. Phillips is a caffeinated wife, working mother, and writer. Her essays and short stories have been published in numerous anthologies including the *Chicken Soup for the Soul* series, *A Cup of Comfort*, and most recently *What Jane Austen Didn't Tell Us!* She blogs at www.CaffeineEpiphanies.com Follow her on twitter @MaryCMPhil.

Sherry Poff teaches, writes, and meanders in and around Chattanooga, TN. She is a member of the Chattanooga Writers' Guild.

Connie Kaseweter Pullen lives in rural Sandy, OR, near her five children and several grandchildren. She earned her Bachelor of Arts degree at the University of Portland in 2006, with a double major in Psychology and Sociology. Connie has been caring for her now ninety-seven-year-old mother for ten years.

Elana Rabinowitz is a writer, a teacher and a world traveler. She was born and raised in Brooklyn, NY where she currently teaches. She is passionate about facing her fears.

Linda Holland Rathkopf is a playwright and fine artist/illustrator. Her plays have been produced in six states, her writings have been published in anthologies, and her artwork has been displayed in galleries around the country. She is the proud grandmother of four boys whom she encourages to color outside the lines.

Linda Sabourin lives in northwest Arkansas, where she spends her time going to auctions, selling vintage goodies on Ebay, and rescuing cats. You can read about her cat adventures on Facebook and Twitter at River Valley Cats. This is her seventh story published in the *Chicken Soup for the Soul* series.

Beverly LaHote Schwind writes a column, "Patches of Life," for her local paper. She teaches at the jail and rehab center. At eighty-three she won a gold medal playing basketball in the National Senior Olympics. She and Jim celebrated sixty-five years of marriage. They have four children and eighteen grandchildren. She was Patches on a children's TV show.

Doug Sletten taught in the public schools for a number of years before going into business for himself. He wrote a humor column in a weekly newspaper for twenty-five years. He has two children, Mitch and Sara, and currently lives in Mesa, AZ with his fiancée Kathi.

David Michael Smith celebrates his tenth published story in the *Chicken Soup for the Soul* series. To date he's been professionally published over thirty times and continues to credit God for all success. He is the father of Rebekah and Matthew, and happy husband to Geri. The Smiths live in Georgetown, DE.

Alvena Stanfield always loved writing and, after she had children, storytelling.

Diane Stark is a wife, mother of five, and freelance writer. She loves to write about the important things in life: her family and her faith. E-mail her at DianeStark19@yahoo.com.

Gary Stein co-founded an NYSE-member investment banking firm. He was a strategy advisor to Lionsgate, Miramax and Seventh Generation and built a thirty-time Emmy-winning kids TV business. Gary is a proud mentor to several outstanding young women, and has been a frequent contributor to the *Chicken Soup for the Soul* series. E-mail him at gm.stein@verizon.net.

Polly Hare Tafrate is an eclectic freelancer who has published articles on many topics — education, parenting, travel, health, volunteering, German Saturday Schools, cooking, grandmotherhood, opinion pieces, Appalachian Trail Angels, and whatever else piques her interest. She welcomes assignments. E-mail her at pollytafrate@hotmail.com.

Lisa Timpf received a Bachelor of Physical Education degree from McMaster University, where she also covered women's sports for the student newspaper. A retired HR and communications professional, Lisa enjoys organic gardening, bicycling, and spending outdoor time with her Border Collie, Emma.

A.L. Tompkins has a Bachelor of Science, with honours, from the University of Trent, and lives in Ontario, Canada. She has several pieces of short fiction published, and enjoys reading and going on long walks with her dog.

Miriam Van Scott is an author and photographer whose credits include children's books, magazine articles, television productions, website content and reference books. Her latest titles include *Song of Old: An Advent Calendar for the Spirit* and the *Shakespeare Goes Pop* series. Learn more at miriamvanscott.com.

Patricia Voyce writes from her home in Pleasant Hill, IA. She enjoys making clothing and teaching garment construction to her students. In addition to writing, she enjoys photography.

John Davis Walker is from Pensacola, FL. He joined the U.S. Merchant Marine in 1980 and worked his way up from a deckhand position to become a ship's Captain in the U.S. and Panama. He traveled worldwide for twenty years before retiring to Hollywood, CA. He now resides there and works as an actor and model.

Roz Warren writes for everyone from the *Funny Times* to *The New York Times* and is the author of *Our Bodies, Our Shelves: A Collection* *of Library Humor* and *Just Another Day at Your Local Public Library: An Insider's Tales of Library Life*, both of which you should buy immediately. E-mail her at roswarren@gmail.com.

Rick Weber won the Casey Medal for Meritorious Journalism for a package on teenage runaways, has been honored twice by the Associated Press Sports Editors, and is the author of an inspirational biography, *Pink Lips and Fingertips*. He has been published in three other *Chicken Soup for the Soul* books. E-mail him at pink@rickweber.org.

Paul Winick M.D. lives in Hollywood, FL, with his wife Dorothy. He practiced pediatrics for thirty years and holds the rank of adjunct full Professor of Pediatrics at the University of Miami, School of Medicine. He has two children and five grandchildren. This is his eleventh story published in the *Chicken Soup for the Soul* series. E-mail pwinick10@gmail.com.

Bill Woolley is a native of New Jersey who earned a Master's degree in counseling psychology from Lesley College Graduate School. He volunteers for an environmental nonprofit, as an English teacher for Afghan students, and helps socialize cats for adoption at an animal shelter. Bill's hobbies include cycling and writing.

Meet Amy Newmark

Amy Newmark is the bestselling author, editor-in-chief, and publisher of the *Chicken Soup for the Soul* book series. Since 2008, she has published more than 150 new books, most of them national bestsellers in the U.S. and Canada, more than doubling the number of Chicken Soup for the Soul titles in print today. She is also the author of *Simply Happy*, a crash course in Chicken Soup for the Soul advice and wisdom that is filled with easy-to-implement, practical tips for enjoying a better life.

Amy is credited with revitalizing the Chicken Soup for the Soul brand, which has been a publishing industry phenomenon since the first book came out in 1993. By compiling inspirational and aspirational true stories curated from ordinary people who have had extraordinary experiences, Amy has kept the twenty-five-year-old Chicken Soup for the Soul brand fresh and relevant.

Amy graduated *magna cum laude* from Harvard University where she majored in Portuguese and minored in French. She then embarked on a three-decade career as a Wall Street analyst, a hedge fund manager, and a corporate executive in the technology field. She is a Chartered Financial Analyst.

Her return to literary pursuits was inevitable, as her honors thesis in college involved traveling throughout Brazil's impoverished northeast region, collecting stories from regular people. She is delighted to have come full circle in her writing career — from collecting stories "from the people" in Brazil as a twenty-year-old to, three decades later, collecting stories "from the people" for Chicken Soup for the Soul.

When Amy and her husband Bill, the CEO of Chicken Soup for the Soul, are not working, they are visiting their four grown children and their first grandchild.

Follow Amy on Twitter @amynewmark. Listen to her free podcast, The Chicken Soup for the Soul Podcast, on Apple Podcasts, Google Play, the Podcasts app on iPhone, or by using your favorite podcast app on other devices.

Thank You

We owe huge thanks to all of our contributors and fans. We were overwhelmed with fabulous stories about the myriad ways that our fans have used the power of yes and stepped outside their comfort zones. There had to be at least 6,000 submissions on this very popular topic, and our editorial team — Elaine Kimbler, Ronelle Frankel, Susan Heim, Barbara LoMonaco, Mary Fisher, and D'ette Corona — read every single one. Then, Amy Newmark chose 202 stories, instead of 101, from a field of 557 finalists. Why? Because we made two books — this one, and its predecessor, *Chicken Soup for the Soul: Step Outside Your Comfort Zone*.

Susan Heim did the first round of editing, D'ette Corona chose the perfect quotations to put at the beginning of each story, and Amy Newmark edited the stories and shaped the final manuscript.

This book was inspirational for all of us — to go even further outside our comfort zones than we already do, and we're a pretty adventurous group. We loved hearing all the different ways that our writers challenged and empowered themselves by trying new things and facing their fears. Our editorial team talks all the time about using the power of yes to expand our lives. We are dedicated to following the examples of our writers!

As we finished our work, Associate Publisher D'ette Corona continued to be Amy's right-hand woman in creating the final manuscript and working with all our wonderful writers. Barbara LoMonaco and Kristiana Pastir, along with Elaine Kimbler, jumped in at the end to proof, proof, proof. And yes, there will always be typos anyway, so feel free to let us know about them at webmaster@chickensoupforthesoul.com and we will correct them in future printings.

The whole publishing team deserves a hand, including our Senior Director of Marketing Maureen Peltier, our Senior Director of Production Victor Cataldo, and our graphic designer Daniel Zaccari, who turned our manuscript into this beautiful book.

Sharing Happiness, Inspiration, and Hope

Real people sharing real stories, every day, all over the world. In 2007, *USA Today* named *Chicken Soup for the Soul* one of the five most memorable books in the last quarter-century. With over 100 million books sold to date in the U.S. and Canada alone, more than 250 titles in print, and translations into nearly fifty languages, "chicken soup for the soul®" is one of the world's best-known phrases.

Today, twenty-five years after we first began sharing happiness, inspiration and hope through our books, we continue to delight our readers with new titles, but have also evolved beyond the bookstore with super premium pet food, television shows, podcasts, positive journalism from aplus.com, movies and TV shows on the Popcornflix app, and licensed products, all revolving around true stories, as we continue "changing the world one story at a time®." Thanks for reading!

Share with Us

We all have had Chicken Soup for the Soul moments in our lives. If you would like to share your story or poem with millions of people around the world, go to chickensoup.com and click on "Submit Your Story." You may be able to help another reader and become a published author at the same time. Some of our past contributors have launched writing and speaking careers from the publication of their stories in our books!

We only accept story submissions via our website. They are no longer accepted via mail or fax. Visit our website, www.chickensoup. com, and click on Submit Your Story for our writing guidelines and a list of topics we are working on.

To contact us regarding other matters, please send us an e-mail through webmaster@chickensoupforthesoul.com, or fax or write us at:

Chicken Soup for the Soul
P.O. Box 700
Cos Cob, CT 06807-0700
Fax: 203-861-7194

One more note from your friends at Chicken Soup for the Soul: Occasionally, we receive an unsolicited book manuscript from one of our readers, and we would like to respectfully inform you that we do not accept unsolicited manuscripts and we must discard the ones that appear.

Changing your life one story at a time®
www.chickensoup.com